Airman Knowledge Testing Supplement for Instrument Rating

2017

U.S. Department of Transportation

FEDERAL AVIATION ADMINISTRATION

Flight Standards Service

Preface

This Airman Knowledge Testing Supplement is designed by the Federal Aviation Administration (FAA) Flight Standards Service. It is intended for use by Airman Knowledge Testing (AKT) Organization Designation Authorization (ODA) Holders and other entities approved and/or authorized to administer airman knowledge tests on behalf of the FAA in the following knowledge areas:

Instrument Rating—Airplane (IRA)
Instrument Rating—Rotorcraft/Helicopter (IRH)
Instrument Rating—Powered Lift (IPL)
Instrument Flight Instructor—Powered Lift (IPI)
Instrument Rating—Foreign Pilot (IFP)
Instrument Flight Instructor—Airplane (FII)
Instrument Flight Instructor—Rotorcraft/Helicopter - (FIH)
Instrument Flight Instructor—Airplane (added rating) (AIF)
Instrument Flight Instructor—Rotorcraft/Helicopter (added rating) (HIF)
Ground Instructor—Instrument (IGI)

FAA-CT-8080-3F supercedes FAA-CT-8080-3E, Computer Testing Supplement for Instrument Rating, dated 2005.

Comments regarding this supplement, or any AFS-630 publication, should be sent in email form to the following address:

AFS630comments@faa.gov

Contents

APPENDIX 1

4

GENERAL INFORMATION

ABBREVIATIONS

The following abbreviations/acronyms are those commonly used within this Directory. Other abbreviations/acronyms may be found in the Legend and are not duplicated below. The abbreviations presented are intended to represent grammatical variations of the basic form. (Example–"req" may mean "request", "requesting", "requested", or "requests").

Abbreviation	Description
A/G	air/ground
AAF	Army Air Field
AAS	Airport Advisory Service
AB	Airbase
abm	abeam
ABn	Aerodrome Beacon
abv	above
ACC	Air Combat Command Area Control Center
acft	aircraft
ACLS	Automatic Carrier Landing System
act	activity
ACWS	Aircraft Control and Warning Squadron
ADA	Advisory Area
ADCC	Air Defense Control Center
ADCUS	Advise Customs
addn	addition
ADF	Automatic Direction Finder
adj	adjacent
admin	administration
ADR	Advisory Route
advs	advise
advsy	advisory
AEIS	Aeronautical Enroute Information Service
AER	approach end rwy
AFA	Army Flight Activity
AFB	Air Force Base
afct	affect
AFFF	Aqueous Film Forming Foam
AFHP	Air Force Heliport
AFIS	Aerodrome Flight Information Service
afld	airfield
AFOD	Army Flight Operations Detachment
AFR	Air Force Regulation
AFRC	Armed Forces Reserve Center/Air Force Reserve Command
AFRS	American Forces Radio Stations
AFS	Air Force Station
AFSS	Automated Flight Service Station
AFTN	Aeronautical Fixed Telecommunication Network
AG	Agriculture
A–G, A–GEAR	Arresting Gear
agcy	Agency
AGL	above ground level
AHP	Army heliport
AID	Airport Information Desk
AIS	Aeronautical Information Services
AL	Approach and Landing Chart
ALF	Auxiliary Landing Field
ALS	Approach Light System
ALSF–1	High Intensity ALS Category I configuration with sequenced Flashers (code)
ALSF–2	High Intensity ALS Category II configuration with sequenced Flashers (code)
alt	altitude
altn	alternate

Abbreviation	Description
AM	Amplitude Modulation, midnight til noon
AMC	Air Mobility Command
amdt	amendment
AMSL	Above Mean Sea Level
ANGS	Air National Guard Station
ant	antenna
AOE	Airport/Aerodrome of Entry
AP	Area Planning
APAPI	Abbreviated Precision Approach Path Indicator
apch	approach
apn	apron
APP	Approach Control
Apr	April
aprx	approximate
APU	Auxiliary Power Unit
apv, apvl	approve, approval
ARB	Air Reserve Base
ARCAL (CANADA)	Aircraft Radio Control of Aerodrome Lighting
ARFF	Aircraft Rescue and Fire Fighting
ARINC	Aeronautical Radio Inc
arng	arrange
arpt	airport
arr	arrive
ARS	Air Reserve Station
ARSA	Airport Radar Service Area
ARSR	Air Route Surveillance Radar
ARTCC	Air Route Traffic Control Center
AS	Air Station
ASAP	as soon as possible
ASDA	Accelerate–Stop Distance Available
ASDE	Airport Surface Detection
ASDE–X	Airport Surface Detection Equipment–Model X
asgn	assign
ASL	Above Sea Level
ASOS	Automated Surface Observing System
ASR	Airport Surveillance Radar
ASSC	Airport Surface Surveillance Capability
ASU	Aircraft Starting Unit
ATA	Actual Time of Arrival
ATC	Air Traffic Control
ATCC	Air Traffic Control Center
ATCT	Airport Traffic Control Tower
ATD	Actual Time of Departure Along Track Distance
ATIS	Automatic Terminal Information Service
ATS	Air Traffic Service
attn	attention
Aug	August
auth	authority
auto	automatic
AUW	All Up Weight (gross weight)
aux	auxiliary
AVASI	abbreviated VASI
avbl	available
AvGas	Aviation gasoline
avn	aviation
AvOil	aviation oil

LEGEND 1.—Abbreviations.

3

GENERAL INFORMATION 5

Abbreviation	Description
AWOS	Automatic Weather Observing System
AWSS	Automated Weather Sensor System
awt	await
awy	airway
az	azimuth
BA	braking action
BASH	Bird Aircraft Strike Hazard
BC	back course
bcn	beacon
bcst	broadcast
bdry	boundary
bldg	building
blkd	blocked
blo, blw	below
BOQ	Bachelor Officers Quarters
brg	bearing
btn	between
bus	business
byd	beyond
C	Commercial Circuit (Telephone)
CAC	Centralized Approach Control
cap	capacity
cat	category
CAT	Clear Air Turbulence
CCW or cntclkws	counterclockwise
ceil	ceiling
CERAP	Center Radar Approach Control
CG	Coast Guard
CGAF	Coast Guard Air Facility
CGAS	Coast Guard Air Station
CH, chan	channel
CHAPI	Chase Helicopter Approach Path Indicator
chg	change
cht	chart
cir	circle, circling
CIV, civ	Civil, civil, civilian
ck	check
CL	Centerline Lighting System
cl	class
clnc	clearance
clsd	closed
CNATRA	Chief of Naval Air Training
cnl	cancel
cntr	center
cntrln	centerline
Co	Company, County
CO	Commanding Officer
com	communication
comd	command
Comdr	Commander
coml	commercial
compul	compulsory
comsn	commission
conc	concrete
cond	condition
const	construction
cont	continue
CONUS	Continental United States
convl	conventional
coord	coordinate
copter	helicopter
corr	correct
CPDLC	Controller Pilot Data Link Communication

Abbreviation	Description
crdr	corridor
cros	cross
CRP	Compulsory Reporting Point
crs	course
CS	call sign
CSTMS	Customs
CTA	Control Area
CTAF	Common Traffic Advisory Frequency
ctc	contact
ctl	control
CTLZ	Control Zone
CVFR	Controlled Visual Flight Rules Areas
CW	Clockwise, Continuous Wave, Carrier Wave
dalgt	daylight
D–ATIS	Digital Automatic Terminal Information Service
daylt	daylight
db	decibel
DCL	Departure Clearance
Dec	December
decom	decommission
deg	degree
del	delivery
dep	depart
DEP	Departure Control
destn	destination
det	detachment
DF	Direction Finder
DH	Decision Height
DIAP	DoD Instrument Approach Procedure
direc	directional
disem	disseminate
displ	displace
dist	district, distance
div	division
DL	Direct Line to FSS
dlt	delete
dly	daily
DME	Distance Measuring Equipment (UHF standard, TACAN compatible)
DNVT	Digital Non–Secure Voice Telephone
DoD	Department of Defense
drct	direct
DSN	Defense Switching Network (Telephone)
DSN	Defense Switching Network
dsplcd	displaced
DT	Daylight Savings Time
dur	during
durn	duration
DV	Distinguished Visitor
E	East
ea	each
EAT	Expected Approach Time
ECN	Enroute Change Notice
EFAS	Enroute Flight Advisory Service
eff	effective, effect
E–HA	Enroute High Altitude
E–LA	Enroute Low Altitude
elev	elevation
ELT	Emergency Locator Transmitter
EMAS	Engineered Material Arresting System
emerg	emergency
eng	engine

LEGEND 1A.—Abbreviations.

6   GENERAL INFORMATION

Abbreviation	Description	Abbreviation	Description
EOR	End of Runway	govt	government
eqpt	equipment	GP	Glide Path
ERDA	Energy Research and Development Administration	Gp	Group
		GPI	Ground Point of Intercept
E–S	Enroute Supplement	grad	gradient
est	estimate	grd	guard
estab	establish	GS	glide slope
ETA	Estimated Time of Arrival	GWT	gross weight
ETD	Estimated Time of Departure		
ETE	Estimated Time Enroute	H	Enroute High Altitude Chart (followed by identification)
ETS	European Telephone System		
EUR	European (ICAO Region)	H+	Hours or hours plus...minutes past the hour
ev	every		
evac	evacuate	H24	continuous operation
exc	except	HAA	Height Above Airport/Aerodrome
excld	exclude	HAL	Height Above Landing Area
exer	exercise	HAR	Height Above Runway
exm	exempt	HAT	Height Above Touchdown
exp	expect	haz	hazard
extd	extend	hdg	heading
extn	extension	HDTA	High Density Traffic Airport/Aerodrome
extv	extensive	HF	High Frequency (3000 to 30,000 KHz)
		hgr	hangar
F/W	Fixed Wing	hgt	height
FAA	Federal Aviation Administration	hi	high
fac	facility	HIRL	High Intensity Runway Lights
FAWS	Flight Advisory Weather Service	HIWAS	Hazardous Inflight Weather Advisory Service
fax	facsimile		
FBO	Fixed Base Operator	HO	Service available to meet operational requirements
FCC	Flight Control Center		
FCG	Foreign Clearance Guide	hol	holiday
FCLP	field carrier landing practice	HOLF	Helicopter Outlying Field
fcst	forecast	hosp	hospital
Feb	February	HQ	Headquarters
FIC	Flight Information Center	hr	hour
FIH	Flight Information Handbook	HS	Service available during hours of scheduled operations
FIR	Flight Information Region		
FIS	Flight Information Service	hsg	housing
FL	flight level	hvy	heavy
fld	field	HW	Heavy Weight
flg	flashing	hwy	highway
FLIP	Flight Information Publication	HX	station having no specific working hours
flt	flight		
flw	follow	Hz	Hertz (cycles per second)
FM	Fan Marker, Frequency Modulation		
FOC	Flight Operations Center	I	Island
FOD	Foreign Object Damage	IAP	Instrument Approach Procedure
fone	telephone	IAS	Indicated Air Speed
FPL	Flight Plan	IAW	in accordance with
fpm	feet per minute	ICAO	International Civil Aviation Organization
fr	from	ident	identification
freq	frequency, frequent	IFF	Identification, Friend or Foe
Fri	Friday	IFR	Instrument Flight Rules
frng	firing	IFR–S	FLIP IFR Supplement
FSC	Flight Service Center	IFSS	International Flight Service Station
FSS	Flight Service Station	ILS	Instrument Landing System
ft	foot	IM	Inner Marker
ftr	fighter	IMC	Instrument Meteorological Conditions
		IMG	Immigration
GA	Glide Angle	immed	immediate
gal	gallon	inbd	inbound
GAT	General Air Traffic (Europe–Asia)	Inc	Incorporated
GCA	Ground Control Approach	incl	include
GCO	Ground Communication Outlet	incr	increase
gldr	glider	indef	indefinite
GND	Ground Control	info	information
gnd	ground	inop	inoperative
		inst	instrument

LEGEND 1B.—Abbreviations.

Appendix 1

Abbreviation	Description
instl	install
instr	instruction
int	intersection
intcntl	intercontinental
intcp	intercept
intl	international
intmt	intermittent
ints	intense, intensity
invof	in the vicinity of
irreg	Irregularly
Jan	January
JASU	Jet Aircraft Starting Unit
JATO	Jet Assisted Take–Off
JOAP	Joint Oil Analysis Program
JOSAC	Joint Operational Support Airlift Center
JRB	Joint Reserve Base
Jul	July
Jun	June
K or Kt	Knots
kHz	kilohertz
KIAS	Knots Indicated Airspeed
KLIZ	Korea Limited Identification Zone
km	Kilometer
kw	kilowatt
L	Compass locator (Component of ILS system) under 25 Watts, 15 NM, Enroute Low Altitude Chart (followed by identification)
L	Local Time
LAA	Local Airport Advisory
LAHSO	Land and Hold–Short Operations
L-AOE	Limited Airport of Entry
LAWRS	Limited Aviation Weather Reporting Station
lb, lbs	pound (weight)
LC	local call
lcl	local
LCP	French Peripheral Classification Line
lctd	located
lctn	location
lctr	locator
LCVASI	Low Cost Visual Approach Slope Indicator
lczr	localizer
LD	long distance
LDA	Landing Distance Available
ldg	landing
LDIN	Lead–in Lights
LDOCF	Long Distance Operations Control Facility
len	length
lgt, lgtd, lgts	light, lighted, lights
LIRL	Low Intensity Runway Lights
LLWAS	Low–Level Wind Shear Alert System
LLZ	Localizer (Instrument Approach Procedures Identification only)
LMM	Compass locator at Middle Marker ILS
lo	low
LoALT or LA	Low Altitude
LOC	Localizer
LOM	Compass locator at Outer Marker ILS
LR	Long Range, Lead Radial
LRA	Landing Rights Airport
LRRS	Long Range RADAR Station

Abbreviation	Description
LSB	lower side band
ltd	limited
M	meters, magnetic (after a bearing), Military Circuit (Telephone)
MACC	Military Area Control Center
mag	magnetic
maint	maintain, maintenance
maj	major
MALS	Medium Intensity Approach Lighting System
MALSF	MALS with Sequenced Flashers
MALSR	MALS with Runway Alignment Indicator Lights
Mar	March
MARA	Military Activity Restricted Area
MATO	Military Air Traffic Operations
MATZ	Military Aerodrome Traffic Zone
max	maximum
mb	millibars
MCAC	Military Common Area Control
MCAF	Marine Corps Air Facility
MCALF	Marine Corps Auxiliary Landing Field
MCAS	Marine Corps Air Station
MCB	Marine Corps Base
MCC	Military Climb Corridor
MCOLF	Marine Corps Outlying Field
MDA	Minimum Descent Altitude
MEA	Minimum Enroute Altitude
med	medium
MEHT	Minimum Eye Height over Threshold
mem	memorial
MET	Meteorological, Meteorology
METAR	Aviation Routine Weather Report (in international MET figure code)
METRO	Pilot–to–Metro voice cell
MF	Medium Frequency (300 to 3000 KHz), Mandatory Frequency (Canada)
MFA	Minimum Flight Altitude
mgmt	Management
mgr	manager
MHz	Megahertz
mi	mile
MID/ASIA	Middle East/Asia (ICAO Region)
MIJI	Meaconing, Intrusion, Jamming, and Interference
Mil, mil	military
min	minimum, minute
MIRL	Medium Intensity Runway Lights
misl	missile
mkr	marker (beacon)
MM	Middle Marker of ILS
mnt	monitor
MOA	Military Operations Area
MOCA	Minimum Obstruction Clearance Altitude
mod	modify
MOG	Maximum (aircraft) on the Ground
Mon	Monday
MP	Maintenance Period
MR	Medium Range
MRA	Minimum Reception Altitude
mrk	mark, marker
MSAW	minimum safe altitude warning
msg	message
MSL	Mean Sea Level
msn	Mission

Legend 1C.—Abbreviations.

8   GENERAL INFORMATION

Abbreviation	Description
mt	mount, mountain
MTAF	Mandatory Traffic Advisory Frequency
MTCA	Military Terminal Control Area
mthly	monthly
MUAC	Military Upper Area Control
muni	municipal
MWARA	Major World Air Route Area
N	North
N/A	not applicable
NA	not authorized (For Instrument Approach Procedure take–off and alternate MINIMA only)
NAAS	Naval Auxiliary Air Station
NADC	Naval Air Development Center
NADEP	Naval Air Depot
NAEC	Naval Air Engineering Center
NAES	Naval Air Engineering Station
NAF	Naval Air Facility
NALCO	Naval Air Logistics Control Office
NALF	Naval Auxiliary Landing Field
NALO	Navy Air Logistics Office
NAS	Naval Air Station
NAT	North Atlantic (ICAO Region)
natl	national
nav	navigation
navaid	navigation aid
NAVMTO	Navy Material Transportation Office
NAWC	Naval Air Warfare Center
NAWS	Naval Air Weapons Station
NCRP	Non–Compulsory Reporting Point
NDB	Non–Directional Radio Beacon
NE	Northeast
nec	necessary
NEW	Net Explosives Weight
ngt	night
NM	nautical miles
nml	normal
NMR	nautical mile radius
No or Nr	number
NOLF	Naval Outlying Field
NORDO	Lost communications or no radio installed/available in aircraft
NOTAM	Notice to Airmen
Nov	November
npi	non precision instrument
Nr or No	number
NS	Naval Station
NS ABTMT	Noise Abatement
NSA	Naval Support Activity
NSF	Naval Support Facility
NSTD, nstd	nonstandard
ntc	notice
NVD	Night Vision Devices
NVG	Night Vision Goggles
NW	Northwest
NWC	Naval Weapons Center
O/A	On or about
O/S	out of service
O/R	On Request
OAT	Operational Air Traffic
obsn	observation
obst	obstruction
OCA	Oceanic Control Area
ocnl	occasional
Oct	October

Abbreviation	Description
ODALS	Omnidirectional Approach Lighting System
ODO	Operations Duty Officer
offl	official
OIC	Officer In Charge
OLF	Outlying Field
OLS	Optical Landing System
OM	Outer Marker, ILS
opr	operate, operator, operational
OPS, ops	operations
orig	original
OROCA	Off Route Obstruction Clearance Altitude
ORTCA	Off Route Terrain Clearance Altitude
OT	other times
OTS	out of service
outbd	outbound
ovft	overflight
ovrn	overrun
OX	oxygen
P/L	plain language
PAC	Pacific (ICAO Region)
PAEW	personnel and equipment working
PALS	Precision Approach and Landing System (NAVY)
PAPI	Precision Approach Path Indicator
PAR	Precision Approach Radar
para	paragraph
parl	parallel
pat	pattern
PAX	Passenger
PCL	pilot controlled lighting
pent	penetrate
perm	permanent
perms	permission
pers	personnel
PFC	Porous Friction Courses
PJE	Parachuting Activities/Exercises
p–line	power line
PM	Post meridian, noon til midnight
PMRF	Pacific Missile Range Facility
PMSV	Pilot–to–Metro Service
PN	prior notice
POB	persons on board
POL	Petrol, Oils and Lubricants
posn	position
PPR	prior permission required
prcht	parachute
pref	prefer
prev	previous
prim	primary
prk	park
PRM	Precision Runway Monitor
pro	procedure
proh	prohibited
pt	point
PTD	Pilot to Dispatcher
pub	publication
publ	publish
PVASI	Pulsating Visual Approach Slope Indicator
pvt	private
pwr	power
QFE	Altimeter Setting above station

LEGEND 1D.—Abbreviations.

GENERAL INFORMATION

Abbreviation	Description
QNE	Altimeter Setting of 29.92 inches which provides height above standard datum plane
QNH	Altimeter Setting which provides height above mean sea level
qtrs	quarters
quad	quadrant
R/T	Radiotelephony
R/W	Rotary/Wing
RACON	Radar Beacon
rad	radius, radial
RAIL	Runway Alignment Indicator Lights
RAMCC	Regional Air Movement Control Center
R–AOE	Regular Airport of Entry
RAPCON	Radar Approach Control (USAF)
RATCF	Radar Air Traffic Control Facility (Navy)
RCAG	Remote Center Air to Ground Facility
RCAGL	Remote Center Air to Ground Facility Long Range
RCL	runway centerline
RCLS	Runway Centerline Light System
RCO	Remote Communications Outlet
rcpt	reception
RCR	Runway Condition Reading
rcv	receive
rcvr	receiver
rdo	radio
reconst	reconstruct
reful	refueling
reg	regulation, regular
REIL	Runway End Identifier Lights
rel	reliable
relctd	relocated
REP	Reporting Point
req	request
RETIL	Rapid Exit Taxiway Indicator Light
Rgn	Region
Rgnl	Regional
rgt	right
rgt tfc	right traffic
rlgd	realigned
RLLS	Runway Lead-in Light System
rmk	remark
rng	range, radio range
RNP	Required Navigation Performance
RON	Remain Overnight
Rot Lt or Bcn	Rotating Light or Beacon
RPI	Runway Point of Intercept
rpt	report
rqr	require
RR	Railroad
RRP	Runway Reference Point
RSC	Runway Surface Condition
RSDU	Radar Storm Detection Unit
RSE	Runway Starter Extension/Starter Strip
RSRS	Reduced Same Runway Separation
rstd	restricted
rte	route
ruf	rough
RVR	Runway Visual Range
RVSM	Reduced Vertical Separation Minima
rwy	runway
S	South
S/D	Seadrome
SALS	Short Approach Lighting System

Abbreviation	Description
SAR	Search and Rescue
Sat	Saturday
SAVASI	Simplified Abbreviated Visual Approach Slope Indicator
SAWRS	Supplement Aviation Weather Reporting Station
sby	standby
Sched	scheduled services
sctr	sector
SDF	Simplified Directional Facility
SE	Southeast
sec	second, section
secd	secondary
SELCAL	Selective Calling System
SELF	Strategic Expeditionary Landing Field
SEng	Single Engine
Sep	September
SFA	Single Frequency Approach
sfc	surface
SFL	Sequence Flashing Lights
SFRA	Special Flight Rules Area
SID	Standard Instrument Departure
SIDA	Secure Identification Display Area
SIF	Selective Identification Feature
sked	schedule
SM	statute miles
SOAP	Spectrometric Oil Analysis Program
SOF	Supervisor of Flying
SPB	Seaplane Base
SR	sunrise
SRE	Surveillance Radar Element of GCA (Instrument Approach Procedures Identification only)
SS	sunset
SSALS/R	Simplified Short Approach Lighting System/with RAIL
SSB	Single Sideband
SSR	Secondary Surveillance Radar
STA	Straight-in Approach
std	standard
stn	station
stor	storage
str–in	Straight–in
stu	student
subj	subject
sum	summer
Sun	Sunday
sur	surround
survl	survival, surveillance
suspd	suspended
svc	service
svcg	servicing
SW	Southwest
sys	system
TA	Transition Altitude
TAC	Tactical Air Command
TAF	Aerodrome (terminal or alternate) forecast in abbreviated form
TALCE	Tanker Aircraft Control Element
TCA	Terminal Control Area
TCH	Threshold Crossing Height
TCTA	Transcontinental Control Area
TD	Touchdown
TDWR	Terminal Doppler Weather Radar
TDZ	Touchdown Zone
TDZL	Touchdown Zone Lights

LEGEND 1E.—Abbreviations.

10 GENERAL INFORMATION

Abbreviation	Description
tfc	traffic
thld	threshold
thou	thousand
thru	through
Thu	Thursday
til	until
tkf, tkof	take-off
TLv	Transition Level
tmpry	temporary
TODA	Take-Off Distance Available
TORA	Take-Off Run Available
TP	Tire Pressure
TPA	Traffic Pattern Altitude
TRACON	Terminal Radar Approach Control (FAA)
tran	transient
trans	transmit
trml	terminal
trng	training
trns	transition
TRSA	Terminal Radar Service Area
Tue	Tuesday
TV	Television
TWEB	Transcribed Weather Broadcast
twr	tower
twy	taxiway
UACC	Upper Area Control Center (used outside US)
UAS	Unmanned Aerial Systems
UC	Under Construction
UCN	Urgent Change Notice
UDA	Upper Advisory Area
UDF	Ultra High Frequency Direction Finder
UFN	until further notice
UHF	Ultra High Frequency (300 to 3000 MHz)
UIR	Upper Flight Information Region
unauthd	unauthorized
unavbl	unavailable
unctl	uncontrolled
unk	unknown
unlgtd	unlighted
unltd	unlimited
unmrk	unmarked
unmto	unmonitored
unrel	unreliable
unrstd	unrestricted
unsatfy	unsatisfactory
unsked	unscheduled
unsvc	unserviceable
unuse, unusbl	unusable
USA	United States Army
USAF	United States Air Force
USB	Upper Side Band
USCG	United States Coast Guard
USMC	United States Marine Corps
USN	United States Navy
UTA	Upper Control Area
UTC	Coordinated Universal Time
V	Defense Switching Network (telephone, formerly AUTOVON)
V/STOL	Vertical and Short Take-off and Landing aircraft
VAL	Visiting Aircraft Line
var	variation (magnetic variation)
VASI	Visual Approach Slope Indicator

Abbreviation	Description
vcnty	vicinity
VDF	Very High Frequency Direction Finder
veh	vehicle
vert	vertical
VFR	Visual Flight Rules
VFR-S	FLIP VFR Supplement
VHF	Very High Frequency (30 to 300 MHz)
VIP	Very Important Person
vis	visibility
VMC	Visual Meteorological Conditions
VOIP	Voice Over Internet Protocol
VOLMET	Meteorological Information for Aircraft in Flight
VOT	VOR Receiver Testing Facility
W	Warning Area (followed by identification), Watts, West, White
WCH	Wheel Crossing Height
Wed	Wednesday
Wg	Wing
WIE	with immediate effect
win	winter
WIP	work in progress
WSO	Weather Service Office
WSFO	Weather Service Forecast Office
wk	week
wkd	weekday
wkly	weekly
wng	warning
wo	without
WSP	Weather System Processor
wt	weight
wx	weather
yd	yard
yr	year
Z	Greenwich Mean Time (time groups only)

LEGEND 1F.—Abbreviations.

Appendix 1

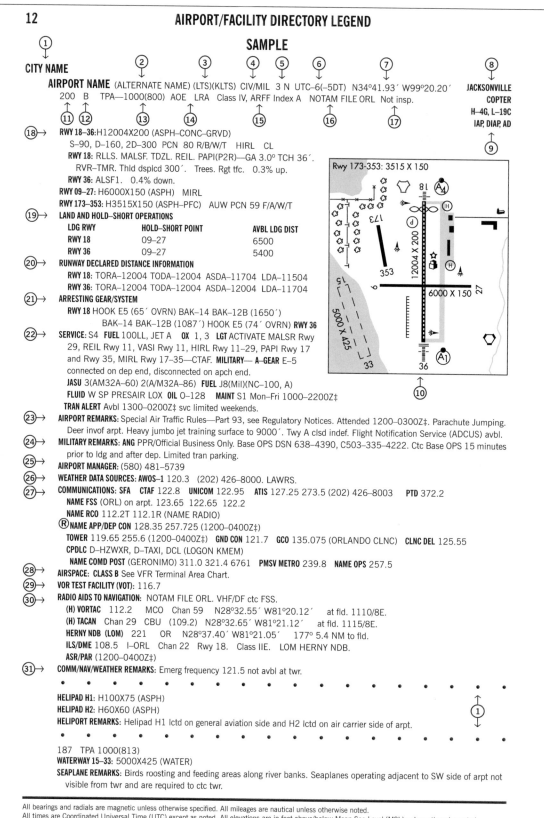

SAMPLE

① CITY NAME

② ③ ④ ⑤ ⑥ ⑦ ⑧
AIRPORT NAME (ALTERNATE NAME) (LTS)(KLTS) CIV/MIL 3 N UTC–6(–5DT) N34°41.93′ W99°20.20′   JACKSONVILLE
200 B TPA—1000(800) AOE LRA Class IV, ARFF Index A NOTAM FILE ORL Not insp.   COPTER
⑪ ⑫ ⑬ ⑭ ⑮ ⑯ ⑰   H–4G, L–19C
IAP, DIAP, AD
⑨

⑱→ **RWY 18–36:** H12004X200 (ASPH–CONC–GRVD)
      S–90, D–160, 2D–300 PCN 80 R/B/W/T   HIRL   CL
      RWY 18: RLLS. MALSF. TDZL. REIL. PAPI(P2R)—GA 3.0° TCH 36′.
        RVR–TMR. Thld dsplcd 300′.   Trees. Rgt tfc.   0.3% up.
      RWY 36: ALSF1.   0.4% down.
    RWY 09–27: H6000X150 (ASPH)   MIRL
    RWY 173–353: H3515X150 (ASPH–PFC)   AUW PCN 59 F/A/W/T

⑲→ **LAND AND HOLD–SHORT OPERATIONS**

LDG RWY	HOLD–SHORT POINT	AVBL LDG DIST
RWY 18	09–27	6500
RWY 36	09–27	5400

⑳→ **RUNWAY DECLARED DISTANCE INFORMATION**
      RWY 18: TORA–12004 TODA–12004 ASDA–11704 LDA–11504
      RWY 36: TORA–12004 TODA–12004 ASDA–12004 LDA–11704

㉑→ **ARRESTING GEAR/SYSTEM**
      RWY 18 HOOK E5 (65′ OVRN) BAK–14 BAK–12B (1650′)
               BAK–14 BAK–12B (1087′) HOOK E5 (74′ OVRN) **RWY 36**

㉒→ **SERVICE:** S4 **FUEL** 100LL, JET A   **OX** 1, 3   **LGT** ACTIVATE MALSR Rwy
      29, REIL Rwy 11, VASI Rwy 11, HIRL Rwy 11–29, PAPI Rwy 17
      and Rwy 35, MIRL Rwy 17–35—CTAF. **MILITARY— A–GEAR** E–5
      connected on dep end, disconnected on apch end.
      JASU 3(AM32A–60) 2(A/M32A–86) **FUEL** J8(Mil)(NC–100, A)
      FLUID W SP PRESAIR LOX **OIL** O–128 **MAINT** S1 Mon–Fri 1000–2200Z‡
      TRAN ALERT Avbl 1300–0200Z‡ svc limited weekends.

㉓→ **AIRPORT REMARKS:** Special Air Traffic Rules—Part 93, see Regulatory Notices. Attended 1200–0300Z‡. Parachute Jumping.
      Deer invof arpt. Heavy jumbo jet training surface to 9000′. Twy A clsd indef. Flight Notification Service (ADCUS) avbl.

㉔→ **MILITARY REMARKS: ANG** PPR/Official Business Only. Base OPS DSN 638–4390, C503–335–4222. Ctc Base OPS 15 minutes
      prior to ldg and after dep. Limited tran parking.

㉕→ **AIRPORT MANAGER:** (580) 481–5739

㉖→ **WEATHER DATA SOURCES: AWOS–1** 120.3   (202) 426–8000. LAWRS.

㉗→ **COMMUNICATIONS: SFA CTAF** 122.8   **UNICOM** 122.95   **ATIS** 127.25 273.5 (202) 426–8003   **PTD** 372.2
      NAME FSS (ORL) on arpt. 123.65 122.65 122.2
      NAME RCO 112.2T 112.1R (NAME RADIO)
    Ⓡ**NAME APP/DEP CON** 128.35 257.725 (1200–0400Z‡)
      TOWER 119.65 255.6 (1200–0400Z‡)   **GND CON** 121.7   **GCO** 135.075 (ORLANDO CLNC)   **CLNC DEL** 125.55
      CPDLC D–HZWXR, D–TAXI, DCL (LOGON KMEM)
      NAME COMD POST (GERONIMO) 311.0 321.4 6761   **PMSV METRO** 239.8   **NAME OPS** 257.5

㉘→ **AIRSPACE: CLASS B** See VFR Terminal Area Chart.

㉙→ **VOR TEST FACILITY (VOT):** 116.7

㉚→ **RADIO AIDS TO NAVIGATION:** NOTAM FILE ORL. VHF/DF ctc FSS.
      (H) VORTAC 112.2   MCO   Chan 59   N28°32.55′ W81°20.12′   at fld. 1110/8E.
      (H) TACAN Chan 29 CBU   (109.2) N28°32.65′ W81°21.12′   at fld. 1115/8E.
      HERNY NDB (LOM) 221   OR   N28°37.40′ W81°21.05′   177° 5.4 NM to fld.
      ILS/DME 108.5 I–ORL   Chan 22 Rwy 18.   Class IIE.   LOM HERNY NDB.
      ASR/PAR (1200–0400Z‡)

㉛→ **COMM/NAV/WEATHER REMARKS:** Emerg frequency 121.5 not avbl at twr.

• • • • • • • • • • • • • •

HELIPAD H1: H100X75 (ASPH)
HELIPAD H2: H60X60 (ASPH)   ①
HELIPORT REMARKS: Helipad H1 lctd on general aviation side and H2 lctd on air carrier side of arpt.

• • • • • • • • • • • • • •

187   TPA 1000(813)
WATERWAY 15–33: 5000X425 (WATER)
SEAPLANE REMARKS: Birds roosting and feeding areas along river banks. Seaplanes operating adjacent to SW side of arpt not
      visible from twr and are required to ctc twr.

All bearings and radials are magnetic unless otherwise specified. All mileages are nautical unless otherwise noted.
All times are Coordinated Universal Time (UTC) except as noted. All elevations are in feet above/below Mean Sea Level (MSL) unless otherwise noted.
The horizontal reference datum of this publication is North American Datum of 1983 (NAD83), which for charting purposes is considered equivalent to World
Geodetic System 1984 (WGS 84).

Legend 2.—Airport/Facility Directory.

⑩ SKETCH LEGEND

RUNWAYS/LANDING AREAS

Hard Surfaced . . . .

Metal Surface . . . .

Sod, Gravel, etc. . . . .

Light Plane, ...
Ski Landing Area or Water

Under Construction . . . . .

Closed . . . .

Helicopter Landings Area . . . . ⓗ

Displaced Threshold . . . .

Taxiway, Apron and Stopways . .

RADIO AIDS TO NAVIGATION

VORTAC . . .   VOR . . . .

VOR/DME . .   NDB . . . .

TACAN . . . .   NDB/DME . . . .

DME . . . .

MISCELLANEOUS AERONAUTICAL FEATURES

Airport Beacon . . . .

Wind Cone . . . .

Landing Tee . . . .

Tetrahedron . . . .

Control Tower . . . .   or TWR

When control tower and rotating beacon are co-located beacon symbol will be used and further identified as TWR.

MISCELLANEOUS BASE AND CULTURAL FEATURES

Buildings . . . .

Power Lines . . . . —T——T—

Fence . . . .

Towers . . . .

Wind Turbine. . . . .

Tanks . . . .

Oil Well . . . .

Smoke Stack . . . .

Obstruction   5812

Controlling Obstruction . . . . +5812

Trees . . . .

Populated Places . . . .

Cuts and Fills . . . . . .   Cut   Fill

Cliffs and Depressions . .

Ditch . . . .

Hill . . . .

APPROACH LIGHTING SYSTEMS

A dot "•" portrayed with approach lighting letter identifier indicates sequenced flashing lights (F) installed with the approach lighting system e.g. Ⓐ Negative symbology, e.g., Ⓐ1
Ⓥ indicates Pilot Controlled Lighting (PCL).

Runway Centerline Lighting . . . . .

Ⓐ Approach Lighting System ALSF-2 . .

Ⓐ1 Approach Lighting System ALSF-1 . .

Ⓐ2 Short Approach Lighting System SALS/SALSF . . . .

Ⓐ3 Simplified Short Approach Lighting System (SSALR) with RAIL . . . . .

Ⓐ4 Medium Intensity Approach Lighting System (MALS and MALSF)/(SSALS and SSALF) . . . .

Ⓐ5 Medium Intensity Approach Lighting System (MALSR) and RAIL . . . . . .

Ⓐ6 Omnidirectional Approach Lighting System (ODALS) . . . .

Ⓓ Navy Parallel Row and Cross Bar . . .

⊕ Air Force Overrun . . . .

Ⓥ Visual Approach Slope Indicator with Standard Threshold Clearance provided

Ⓥ2 Pulsating Visual Approach Slope Indicator (PVASI)

Ⓥ3 Visual Approach Slope Indicator with a threshold crossing height to accomodate long bodied or jumbo aircraft

Ⓥ4 Tri-color Visual Approach Slope Indicator (TRCV)

Ⓥ5 Approach Path Alignment Panel (APAP)

Ⓟ Precision Approach Path Indicator (PAPI)

LEGEND 3.—Airport/Facility Directory.

14 AIRPORT/FACILITY DIRECTORY LEGEND

LEGEND

This directory is a listing of data on record with the FAA on public–use airports, military airports and selected private–use airports specifically requested by the Department of Defense (DoD) for which a DoD Instrument Approach Procedure has been published in the U.S. Terminal Procedures Publication. Additionally this listing contains data for associated terminal control facilities, air route traffic control centers, and radio aids to navigation within the conterminous United States, Puerto Rico and the Virgin Islands. Civil airports and joint Civil/Military airports which are open to the public are listed alphabetically by state, associated city and airport name and cross–referenced by airport name. Military airports and private–use (limited civil access) joint Military/Civil airports are listed alphabetically by state and official airport name and cross–referenced by associated city name. Navaids, flight service stations and remote communication outlets that are associated with an airport, but with a different name, are listed alphabetically under their own name, as well as under the airport with which they are associated.

The listing of an airport as open to the public in this directory merely indicates the airport operator's willingness to accommodate transient aircraft, and does not represent that the airport conforms with any Federal or local standards, or that it has been approved for use on the part of the general public. Military airports, private–use airports, and private–use (limited civil access) joint Military/Civil airports are open to civil pilots only in an emergency or with prior permission. See Special Notice Section, Civil Use of Military Fields.

The information on obstructions is taken from reports submitted to the FAA. Obstruction data has not been verified in all cases. Pilots are cautioned that objects not indicated in this tabulation (or on the airports sketches and/or charts) may exist which can create a hazard to flight operation. Detailed specifics concerning services and facilities tabulated within this directory are contained in the Aeronautical Information Manual, Basic Flight Information and ATC Procedures.

The legend items that follow explain in detail the contents of this Directory and are keyed to the circled numbers on the sample on the preceding pages.

① CITY/AIRPORT NAME

Civil and joint Civil/Military airports which are open to the public are listed alphabetically by state and associated city. Where the city name is different from the airport name the city name will appear on the line above the airport name. Airports with the same associated city name will be listed alphabetically by airport name and will be separated by a dashed rule line. A solid rule line will separate all others. FAA approved helipads and seaplane landing areas associated with a land airport will be separated by a dotted line. Military airports and private–use (limited civil access) joint Military/Civil airports are listed alphabetically by state and official airport name.

② ALTERNATE NAME

Alternate names, if any, will be shown in parentheses.

③ LOCATION IDENTIFIER

The location identifier is a three or four character FAA code followed by a four–character ICAO code, when assigned, to airports. If two different military codes are assigned, both codes will be shown with the primary operating agency's code listed first. These identifiers are used by ATC in lieu of the airport name in flight plans, flight strips and other written records and computer operations. Zeros will appear with a slash to differentiate them from the letter "O".

④ OPERATING AGENCY

Airports within this directory are classified into two categories, Military/Federal Government and Civil airports open to the general public, plus selected private–use airports. The operating agency is shown for military, private–use and joint use airports. The operating agency is shown by an abbreviation as listed below. When an organization is a tenant, the abbreviation is enclosed in parenthesis. No classification indicates the airport is open to the general public with no military tenant.

A	US Army	MC	Marine Corps
AFRC	Air Force Reserve Command	MIL/CIV	Joint Use Military/Civil Limited Civil Access
AF	US Air Force	N	Navy
ANG	Air National Guard	NAF	Naval Air Facility
AR	US Army Reserve	NAS	Naval Air Station
ARNG	US Army National Guard	NASA	National Air and Space Administration
CG	US Coast Guard	P	US Civil Airport Wherein Permit Covers Use by
CIV/MIL	Joint Use Civil/Military Open to the Public		Transient Military Aircraft
DND	Department of National Defense Canada	PVT	Private Use Only (Closed to the Public)

⑤ AIRPORT LOCATION

Airport location is expressed as distance and direction from the center of the associated city in nautical miles and cardinal points, e.g., 4 NE.

⑥ TIME CONVERSION

Hours of operation of all facilities are expressed in Coordinated Universal Time (UTC) and shown as "Z" time. The directory indicates the number of hours to be subtracted from UTC to obtain local standard time and local daylight saving time UTC–5(–4DT). The symbol ‡ indicates that during periods of Daylight Saving Time (DST) effective hours will be one hour earlier than shown. In those areas where daylight saving time is not observed the (–4DT) and ‡ will not be shown. Daylight saving time is in effect from 0200 local time the second Sunday in March to 0200 local time the first Sunday in November. Canada and all U.S. Conterminous States observe daylight saving time except Arizona and Puerto Rico, and the Virgin Islands. If the state observes daylight saving time and the operating times are other than daylight saving times, the operating hours will include the dates, times and no ‡ symbol will be shown, i.e., April 15–Aug 31 0630–1700Z, Sep 1–Apr 14 0600–1700Z.

LEGEND 4.—Airport/Facility Directory.

AIRPORT/FACILITY DIRECTORY LEGEND 15

⑦ GEOGRAPHIC POSITION OF AIRPORT—AIRPORT REFERENCE POINT (ARP)

Positions are shown as hemisphere, degrees, minutes and hundredths of a minute and represent the approximate geometric center of all usable runway surfaces.

⑧ CHARTS

Charts refer to the Sectional Chart and Low and High Altitude Enroute Chart and panel on which the airport or facility is located. Helicopter Chart locations will be indicated as COPTER. IFR Gulf of Mexico West and IFR Gulf of Mexico Central will be depicted as GOMW and GOMC.

⑨ INSTRUMENT APPROACH PROCEDURES, AIRPORT DIAGRAMS

IAP indicates an airport for which a prescribed (Public Use) FAA Instrument Approach Procedure has been published. DIAP indicates an airport for which a prescribed DoD Instrument Approach Procedure has been published in the U.S. Terminal Procedures. See the Special Notice Section of this directory, Civil Use of Military Fields and the Aeronautical Information Manual 5–4–5 Instrument Approach Procedure Charts for additional information. AD indicates an airport for which an airport diagram has been published. Airport diagrams are located in the back of each Chart Supplement volume alphabetically by associated city and airport name.

⑩ AIRPORT SKETCH

The airport sketch, when provided, depicts the airport and related topographical information as seen from the air and should be used in conjunction with the text. It is intended as a guide for pilots in VFR conditions. Symbology that is not self–explanatory will be reflected in the sketch legend. The airport sketch will be oriented with True North at the top. Airport sketches will be added incrementally.

⑪ ELEVATION

The highest point of an airport's usable runways measured in feet from mean sea level. When elevation is sea level it will be indicated as "00". When elevation is below sea level a minus "–" sign will precede the figure.

⑫ ROTATING LIGHT BEACON

B indicates rotating beacon is available. Rotating beacons operate sunset to sunrise unless otherwise indicated in the AIRPORT REMARKS or MILITARY REMARKS segment of the airport entry.

⑬ TRAFFIC PATTERN ALTITUDE

Traffic Pattern Altitude (TPA)—The first figure shown is TPA above mean sea level. The second figure in parentheses is TPA above airport elevation. Multiple TPA shall be shown as "TPA—See Remarks" and detailed information shall be shown in the Airport or Military Remarks Section. Traffic pattern data for USAF bases, USN facilities, and U.S. Army airports (including those on which ACC or U.S. Army is a tenant) that deviate from standard pattern altitudes shall be shown in Military Remarks.

⑭ AIRPORT OF ENTRY, LANDING RIGHTS, AND CUSTOMS USER FEE AIRPORTS

U.S. CUSTOMS USER FEE AIRPORT—Private Aircraft operators are frequently required to pay the costs associated with customs processing.

AOE—Airport of Entry. A customs Airport of Entry where permission from U.S. Customs is not required to land. However, at least one hour advance notice of arrival is required.

LRA—Landing Rights Airport. Application for permission to land must be submitted in advance to U.S. Customs. At least one hour advance notice of arrival is required.

NOTE: Advance notice of arrival at both an AOE and LRA airport may be included in the flight plan when filed in Canada or Mexico. Where Flight Notification Service (ADCUS) is available the airport remark will indicate this service. This notice will also be treated as an application for permission to land in the case of an LRA. Although advance notice of arrival may be relayed to Customs through Mexico, Canada, and U.S. Communications facilities by flight plan, the aircraft operator is solely responsible for ensuring that Customs receives the notification. (See Customs, Immigration and Naturalization, Public Health and Agriculture Department requirements in the International Flight Information Manual for further details.)

U.S. CUSTOMS AIR AND SEA PORTS, INSPECTORS AND AGENTS

Northeast Sector (New England and Atlantic States—ME to MD)	407–975–1740
Southeast Sector (Atlantic States—DC, WV, VA to FL)	407–975–1780
Central Sector (Interior of the US, including Gulf states—MS, AL, LA)	407–975–1760
Southwest East Sector (OK and eastern TX)	407–975–1840
Southwest West Sector (Western TX, NM and AZ)	407–975–1820
Pacific Sector (WA, OR, CA, HI and AK)	407–975–1800

⑮ CERTIFICATED AIRPORT (14 CFR PART 139)

Airports serving Department of Transportation certified carriers and certified under 14 CFR part 139 are indicated by the Class and the ARFF Index; e.g. Class I, ARFF Index A, which relates to the availability of crash, fire, rescue equipment. Class I airports can have an ARFF Index A through E, depending on the aircraft length and scheduled departures. Class II, III, and IV will always carry an Index A.

AIRPORT CLASSIFICATIONS

Type of Air Carrier Operation	Class I	Class II	Class III	Class IV
Scheduled Air Carrier Aircraft with 31 or more passenger seats	X			
Unscheduled Air Carrier Aircraft with 31 or more passengers seats	X	X		X
Scheduled Air Carrier Aircraft with 10 to 30 passenger seats	X	X	X	

LEGEND 5.—Airport/Facility Directory.

16   **AIRPORT/FACILITY DIRECTORY LEGEND**

INDICES AND AIRCRAFT RESCUE AND FIRE FIGHTING EQUIPMENT REQUIREMENTS

Airport Index	Required No. Vehicles	Aircraft Length	Scheduled Departures	Agent + Water for Foam
A	1	<90′	≥1	500#DC or HALON 1211 or 450#DC + 100 gal H$_2$0
B	1 or 2	≥90′, <126′ ——— ——— ≥126′, <159′	≥5 ——— <5	Index A + 1500 gal H$_2$O
C	2 or 3	≥126′, <159′ ——— ≥159′, <200′	≥5 ——— <5	Index A + 3000 gal H$_2$O
D	3	≥159′, <200′ ——— >200′	——— <5	Index A + 4000 gal H$_2$O
E	3	≥200′	≥5	Index A + 6000 gal H$_2$O

> Greater Than; < Less Than; ≥ Equal or Greater Than; ≤ Equal or Less Than;   H$_2$O–Water; DC–Dry Chemical.

NOTE: The listing of ARFF index does not necessarily assure coverage for non–air carrier operations or at other than prescribed times for air carrier. ARFF Index Ltd.—indicates ARFF coverage may or may not be available, for information contact airport manager prior to flight.

⑯ NOTAM SERVICE

All public use landing areas are provided NOTAM service. A NOTAM FILE identifier is shown for individual landing areas, e.g., "NOTAM FILE BNA". See the AIM, Basic Flight Information and ATC Procedures for a detailed description of NOTAMs. Current NOTAMs are available from flight service stations at 1–800–WX–BRIEF (992–7433) or online through the FAA PilotWeb at https://pilotweb.nas.faa.gov. Military NOTAMs are available using the Defense Internet NOTAM Service (DINS) at https://www.notams.faa.gov. Pilots flying to or from airports not available through the FAA PilotWeb or DINS can obtain assistance from Flight Service.

⑰ FAA INSPECTION

All airports not inspected by FAA will be identified by the note: Not insp. This indicates that the airport information has been provided by the owner or operator of the field.

⑱ RUNWAY DATA

Runway information is shown on two lines. That information common to the entire runway is shown on the first line while information concerning the runway ends is shown on the second or following line. Runway direction, surface, length, width, weight bearing capacity, lighting, and slope, when available are shown for each runway. Multiple runways are shown with the longest runway first. Direction, length, width, and lighting are shown for sea–lanes. The full dimensions of helipads are shown, e.g., 50X150. Runway data that requires clarification will be placed in the remarks section.

RUNWAY DESIGNATION

Runways are normally numbered in relation to their magnetic orientation rounded off to the nearest 10 degrees. Parallel runways can be designated L (left)/R (right)/C (center). Runways may be designated as Ultralight or assault strips. Assault strips are shown by magnetic bearing.

RUNWAY DIMENSIONS

Runway length and width are shown in feet. Length shown is runway end to end including displaced thresholds, but excluding those areas designed as overruns.

RUNWAY SURFACE AND SURFACE TREATMENT

Runway lengths prefixed by the letter "H" indicate that the runways are hard surfaced (concrete, asphalt, or part asphalt–concrete). If the runway length is not prefixed, the surface is sod, clay, etc. The runway surface composition is indicated in parentheses after runway length as follows:

(AFSC)—Aggregate friction seal coat	(GRVL)—Gravel, or cinders	(SAND)—Sand
(AM2)—Temporary metal planks coated with nonskid material	(MATS)—Pierced steel planking, landing mats, membranes	(TURF)—Turf
(ASPH)—Asphalt	(PEM)—Part concrete, part asphalt	(TRTD)—Treated
(CONC)—Concrete	(PFC)—Porous friction courses	(WC)—Wire combed
(DIRT)—Dirt	(PSP)—Pierced steel plank	
(GRVD)—Grooved	(RFSC)—Rubberized friction seal coat	

LEGEND 6.—Airport/Facility Directory.

AIRPORT/FACILITY DIRECTORY LEGEND 17

RUNWAY WEIGHT BEARING CAPACITY

Runway strength data shown in this publication is derived from available information and is a realistic estimate of capability at an average level of activity. It is not intended as a maximum allowable weight or as an operating limitation. Many airport pavements are capable of supporting limited operations with gross weights in excess of the published figures. Permissible operating weights, insofar as runway strengths are concerned, are a matter of agreement between the owner and user. When desiring to operate into any airport at weights in excess of those published in the publication, users should contact the airport management for permission. Runway strength figures are shown in thousand of pounds, with the last three figures being omitted. Add 000 to figure following S, D, 2S, 2T, AUW, SWL, etc., for gross weight capacity. A blank space following the letter designator is used to indicate the runway can sustain aircraft with this type landing gear, although definite runway weight bearing capacity figures are not available, e.g., S, D. Applicable codes for typical gear configurations with S=Single, D=Dual, T=Triple and Q=Quadruple:

CURRENT	NEW	NEW DESCRIPTION
S	S	Single wheel type landing gear (DC3), (C47), (F15), etc.
D	D	Dual wheel type landing gear (BE1900), (B737), (A319), etc.
T	D	Dual wheel type landing gear (P3, C9).
ST	2S	Two single wheels in tandem type landing gear (C130).
TRT	2T	Two triple wheels in tandem type landing gear (C17), etc.
DT	2D	Two dual wheels in tandem type landing gear (B707), etc.
TT	2D	Two dual wheels in tandem type landing gear (B757, KC135).
SBTT	2D/D1	Two dual wheels in tandem/dual wheel body gear type landing gear (KC10).
None	2D/2D1	Two dual wheels in tandem/two dual wheels in tandem body gear type landing gear (A340–600).
DDT	2D/2D2	Two dual wheels in tandem/two dual wheels in double tandem body gear type landing gear (B747, E4).
TTT	3D	Three dual wheels in tandem type landing gear (B777), etc.
TT	D2	Dual wheel gear two struts per side main gear type landing gear (B52).
TDT	C5	Complex dual wheel and quadruple wheel combination landing gear (C5).

AUW—All up weight. Maximum weight bearing capacity for any aircraft irrespective of landing gear configuration.

SWL—Single Wheel Loading. (This includes information submitted in terms of Equivalent Single Wheel Loading (ESWL) and Single Isolated Wheel Loading).

PSI—Pounds per square inch. PSI is the actual figure expressing maximum pounds per square inch runway will support, e.g., (SWL 000/PSI 535).

Omission of weight bearing capacity indicates information unknown.

The ACN/PCN System is the ICAO standard method of reporting pavement strength for pavements with bearing strengths greater than 12,500 pounds. The Pavement Classification Number (PCN) is established by an engineering assessment of the runway. The PCN is for use in conjunction with an Aircraft Classification Number (ACN). Consult the Aircraft Flight Manual, Flight Information Handbook, or other appropriate source for ACN tables or charts. Currently, ACN data may not be available for all aircraft. If an ACN table or chart is available, the ACN can be calculated by taking into account the aircraft weight, the pavement type, and the subgrade category. For runways that have been evaluated under the ACN/PCN system, the PCN will be shown as a five–part code (e.g. PCN 80 R/B/W/T). Details of the coded format are as follows:

NOTE: Prior permission from the airport controlling authority is required when the ACN of the aircraft exceeds the published PCN or aircraft tire pressure exceeds the published limits.

(1) The PCN NUMBER—The reported PCN indicates that an aircraft with an ACN equal or less than the reported PCN can operate on the pavement subject to any limitation on the tire pressure.

(2) The type of pavement:
R — Rigid
F — Flexible

(3) The pavement subgrade category:
A — High
B — Medium
C — Low
D — Ultra–low

(4) The maximum tire pressure authorized for the pavement:
W — Unlimited, no pressure limit
X — High, limited to 254 psi (1.75 MPa)
Y — Medium, limited to 181 psi (1.25MPa)
Z — Low, limited to 73 psi (0.50 MPa)

(5) Pavement evaluation method:
T — Technical evaluation
U — By experience of aircraft using the pavement

RUNWAY LIGHTING

Lights are in operation sunset to sunrise. Lighting available by prior arrangement only or operating part of the night and/or pilot controlled lighting with specific operating hours are indicated under airport or military remarks. At USN/USMC facilities lights are available only during airport hours of operation. Since obstructions are usually lighted, obstruction lighting is not included in this code. Unlighted obstructions on or surrounding an airport will be noted in airport or military remarks. Runway lights nonstandard (NSTD) are systems for which the light fixtures are not FAA approved L–800 series: color, intensity, or spacing does not meet FAA standards. Nonstandard runway lights, VASI, or any other system not listed below will be shown in airport remarks or military

LEGEND 7.—Airport/Facility Directory.

18   AIRPORT/FACILITY DIRECTORY LEGEND

service. Temporary, emergency or limited runway edge lighting such as flares, smudge pots, lanterns or portable runway lights will also be shown in airport remarks or military service. Types of lighting are shown with the runway or runway end they serve.

NSTD—Light system fails to meet FAA standards.
LIRL—Low Intensity Runway Lights.
MIRL—Medium Intensity Runway Lights.
HIRL—High Intensity Runway Lights.
RAIL—Runway Alignment Indicator Lights.
REIL—Runway End Identifier Lights.
CL—Centerline Lights.
TDZL—Touchdown Zone Lights.
ODALS—Omni Directional Approach Lighting System.
AF OVRN—Air Force Overrun 1000´ Standard Approach Lighting System.
MALS—Medium Intensity Approach Lighting System.
MALSF—Medium Intensity Approach Lighting System with Sequenced Flashing Lights.
MALSR—Medium Intensity Approach Lighting System with Runway Alignment Indicator Lights.
RLLS—Runway Lead–in Light System

SALS—Short Approach Lighting System.
SALSF—Short Approach Lighting System with Sequenced Flashing Lights.
SSALS—Simplified Short Approach Lighting System.
SSALF—Simplified Short Approach Lighting System with Sequenced Flashing Lights.
SSALR—Simplified Short Approach Lighting System with Runway Alignment Indicator Lights.
ALSAF—High Intensity Approach Lighting System with Sequenced Flashing Lights.
ALSF1—High Intensity Approach Lighting System with Sequenced Flashing Lights, Category I, Configuration.
ALSF2—High Intensity Approach Lighting System with Sequenced Flashing Lights, Category II, Configuration.
SF—Sequenced Flashing Lights.
OLS—Optical Landing System.
WAVE–OFF.

NOTE: Civil ALSF2 may be operated as SSALR during favorable weather conditions. When runway edge lights are positioned more than 10 feet from the edge of the usable runway surface a remark will be added in the "Remarks" portion of the airport entry. This is applicable to Air Force, Air National Guard and Air Force Reserve Bases, and those joint use airfields on which they are tenants.

VISUAL GLIDESLOPE INDICATORS

APAP—A system of panels, which may or may not be lighted, used for alignment of approach path.

| PNIL | APAP on left side of runway | PNIR | APAP on right side of runway |

PAPI—Precision Approach Path Indicator

| P2L | 2–identical light units placed on left side of runway | P4L | 4–identical light units placed on left side of runway |
| P2R | 2–identical light units placed on right side of runway | P4R | 4–identical light units placed on right side of runway |

PVASI—Pulsating/steady burning visual approach slope indicator, normally a single light unit projecting two colors.

| PSIL | PVASI on left side of runway | PSIR | PVASI on right side of runway |

SAVASI—Simplified Abbreviated Visual Approach Slope Indicator

| S2L | 2–box SAVASI on left side of runway | S2R | 2–box SAVASI on right side of runway |

TRCV—Tri–color visual approach slope indicator, normally a single light unit projecting three colors.

| TRIL | TRCV on left side of runway | TRIR | TRCV on right side of runway |

VASI—Visual Approach Slope Indicator

V2L	2–box VASI on left side of runway	V6L	6–box VASI on left side of runway
V2R	2–box VASI on right side of runway	V6R	6–box VASI on right side of runway
V4L	4–box VASI on left side of runway	V12	12–box VASI on both sides of runway
V4R	4–box VASI on right side of runway	V16	16–box VASI on both sides of runway

NOTE: Approach slope angle and threshold crossing height will be shown when available; i.e., –GA 3.5° TCH 37´.

PILOT CONTROL OF AIRPORT LIGHTING

Key Mike	Function
7 times within 5 seconds	Highest intensity available
5 times within 5 seconds	Medium or lower intensity (Lower REIL or REIL–Off)
3 times within 5 seconds	Lowest intensity available (Lower REIL or REIL–Off)

Available systems will be indicated in the Service section, e.g., **LGT** ACTIVATE HIRL Rwy 07–25, MALSR Rwy 07, and VASI Rwy 07—122.8.

Where the airport is not served by an instrument approach procedure and/or has an independent type system of different specification installed by the airport sponsor, descriptions of the type lights, method of control, and operating frequency will be explained in clear text. See AIM, "Basic Flight Information and ATC Procedures," for detailed description of pilot control of airport lighting.

RUNWAY SLOPE

When available, runway slope data will be provided. Runway slope will be shown only when it is 0.3 percent or greater. On runways less than 8000 feet, the direction of the slope up will be indicated, e.g., 0.3% up NW. On runways 8000 feet or greater, the slope will be shown (up or down) on the runway end line, e.g., RWY 13: 0.3% up., RWY 31: Pole. Rgt tfc. 0.4% down.

LEGEND 8.—Airport/Facility Directory.

AIRPORT/FACILITY DIRECTORY LEGEND 19

RUNWAY END DATA

Information pertaining to the runway approach end such as approach lights, touchdown zone lights, runway end identification lights, visual glideslope indicators, displaced thresholds, controlling obstruction, and right hand traffic pattern, will be shown on the specific runway end. "Rgt tfc"—Right traffic indicates right turns should be made on landing and takeoff for specified runway end. Runway Visual Range shall be shown as "RVR" appended with "T" for touchdown, "M" for midpoint, and "R" for rollout; e.g., RVR-TMR.

⑲ LAND AND HOLD–SHORT OPERATIONS (LAHSO)

LAHSO is an acronym for "Land and Hold–Short Operations" These operations include landing and holding short of an intersection runway, an intersecting taxiway, or other predetermined points on the runway other than a runway or taxiway. Measured distance represents the available landing distance on the landing runway, in feet.

Specific questions regarding these distances should be referred to the air traffic manager of the facility concerned. The Aeronautical Information Manual contains specific details on hold–short operations and markings.

⑳ RUNWAY DECLARED DISTANCE INFORMATION

TORA—Take–off Run Available. The length of runway declared available and suitable for the ground run of an aeroplane take–off.
TODA—Take–off Distance Available. The length of the take–off run available plus the length of the clearway, if provided.
ASDA—Accelerate–Stop Distance Available. The length of the take–off run available plus the length of the stopway, if provided.
LDA—Landing Distance Available. The length of runway which is declared available and suitable for the ground run of an aeroplane landing.

㉑ ARRESTING GEAR/SYSTEMS

Arresting gear is shown as it is located on the runway. The a–gear distance from the end of the appropriate runway (or into the overrun) is indicated in parentheses. A–Gear which has a bi–direction capability and can be utilized for emergency approach end engagement is indicated by a (B). Up to 15 minutes advance notice may be required for rigging A–Gear for approach and engagement. Airport listing may show availability of other than US Systems. This information is provided for emergency requirements only. Refer to current aircraft operating manuals for specific engagement weight and speed criteria based on aircraft structural restrictions and arresting system limitations.

Following is a list of current systems referenced in this publication identified by both Air Force and Navy terminology:

BI–DIRECTIONAL CABLE (B)

TYPE	DESCRIPTION
BAK–9	Rotary friction brake.
BAK–12A	Standard BAK–12 with 950 foot run out, 1–inch cable and 40,000 pound weight setting. Rotary friction brake.
BAK–12B	Extended BAK–12 with 1200 foot run, 1¼ inch Cable and 50,000 pounds weight setting. Rotary friction brake.
E28	Rotary Hydraulic (Water Brake).
M21	Rotary Hydraulic (Water Brake) Mobile.

The following device is used in conjunction with some aircraft arresting systems:

TYPE	DESCRIPTION
BAK–14	A device that raises a hook cable out of a slot in the runway surface and is remotely positioned for engagement by the tower on request. (In addition to personnel reaction time, the system requires up to five seconds to fully raise the cable.)
H	A device that raises a hook cable out of a slot in the runway surface and is remotely positioned for engagement by the tower on request. (In addition to personnel reaction time, the system requires up to one and one–half seconds to fully raise the cable.)

UNI–DIRECTIONAL CABLE

TYPE	DESCRIPTION
MB60	Textile brake—an emergency one–time use, modular braking system employing the tearing of specially woven textile straps to absorb the kinetic energy.
E5/E5–1/E5–3	Chain Type. At USN/USMC stations E–5 A–GEAR systems are rated, e.g., E–5 RATING–13R–1100 HW (DRY), 31L/R–1200 STD (WET). This rating is a function of the A–GEAR chain weight and length and is used to determine the maximum aircraft engaging speed. A dry rating applies to a stabilized surface (dry or wet) while a wet rating takes into account the amount (if any) of wet overrun that is not capable of withstanding the aircraft weight. These ratings are published under Service/Military/A–Gear in the entry.

FOREIGN CABLE

TYPE	DESCRIPTION	US EQUIVALENT
44B–3H	Rotary Hydraulic (Water Brake)	
CHAG	Chain	E–5

UNI–DIRECTIONAL BARRIER

TYPE	DESCRIPTION
MA–1A	Web barrier between stanchions attached to a chain energy absorber.
BAK–15	Web barrier between stanchions attached to an energy absorber (water squeezer, rotary friction, chain). Designed for wing engagement.

NOTE: Landing short of the runway threshold on a runway with a BAK–15 in the underrun is a significant hazard. The barrier in the down position still protrudes several inches above the underrun. Aircraft contact with the barrier short of the runway threshold can cause damage to the barrier and substantial damage to the aircraft.

OTHER

TYPE	DESCRIPTION
EMAS	Engineered Material Arresting System, located beyond the departure end of the runway, consisting of high energy absorbing materials which will crush under the weight of an aircraft.

LEGEND 9.—Airport/Facility Directory.

AIRPORT/FACILITY DIRECTORY LEGEND

20

㉒ SERVICE

SERVICING—CIVIL

S1: Minor airframe repairs.
S2: Minor airframe and minor powerplant repairs.
S3: Major airframe and minor powerplant repairs.
S4: Major airframe and major powerplant repairs.

S5: Major airframe repairs.
S6: Minor airframe and major powerplant repairs.
S7: Major powerplant repairs.
S8: Minor powerplant repairs.

FUEL—CIVIL

CODE	FUEL	CODE	FUEL
80	Grade 80 gasoline (Red)	A1+	Jet A–1, Kerosene with FS–II*, FP** minus 47° C.
100	Grade 100 gasoline (Green)	B	Jet B, Wide–cut, turbine fuel without FS–II*, FP** minus 50° C.
100LL	100LL gasoline (low lead) (Blue)		
115	Grade 115 gasoline (115/145 military specification) (Purple)	B+	Jet B, Wide–cut, turbine fuel with FS–II*, FP** minus 50° C
A	Jet A, Kerosene, without FS–II*, FP** minus 40° C.	J4 (JP4)	(JP–4 military specification) FP** minus 58° C.
A+	Jet A, Kerosene, with FS–II*, FP** minus 40°C.	J5 (JP5)	(JP–5 military specification) Kerosene with FS–II, FP** minus 46°C.
A++	Jet A, Kerosene, with FS–II*, CI/LI#, SDA##, FP** minus 40°C.	J8 (JP8)	(JP–8 military specification) Jet A–1, Kerosene with FS–II*, CI/LI#, SDA##, FP** minus 47°C.
A++100	Jet A, Kerosene, with FS–II*, CI/LI#, SDA##, FP** minus 40°C, with +100 fuel additive that improves thermal stability characteristics of kerosene jet fuels.	J8+100	(JP–8 military specification) Jet A–1, Kerosene with FS–II*, CI/LI#, SDA##, FP** minus 47°C, with +100 fuel additive that improves thermal stability characteristics of kerosene jet fuels.
A1	Jet A–1, Kerosene, without FS–II*, FP** minus 47°C.	J	(Jet Fuel Type Unknown)
		MOGAS	Automobile gasoline which is to be used as aircraft fuel.

*(Fuel System Icing Inhibitor)   **(Freeze Point)   # (Corrosion Inhibitors/Lubricity Improvers)   ## (Static Dissipator Additive)

NOTE: Certain automobile gasoline may be used in specific aircraft engines if a FAA supplemental type certificate has been obtained. Automobile gasoline, which is to be used in aircraft engines, will be identified as "MOGAS", however, the grade/type and other octane rating will not be published.

Data shown on fuel availability represents the most recent information the publisher has been able to acquire. Because of a variety of factors, the fuel listed may not always be obtainable by transient civil pilots. Confirmation of availability of fuel should be made directly with fuel suppliers at locations where refueling is planned.

OXYGEN—CIVIL

OX 1   High Pressure
OX 2   Low Pressure

OX 3   High Pressure—Replacement Bottles
OX 4   Low Pressure—Replacement Bottles

SERVICE—MILITARY

Specific military services available at the airport are listed under this general heading. Remarks applicable to any military service are shown in the individual service listing.

JET AIRCRAFT STARTING UNITS (JASU)—MILITARY

The numeral preceding the type of unit indicates the number of units available. The absence of the numeral indicates ten or more units available. If the number of units is unknown, the number one will be shown. Absence of JASU designation indicates non–availability.

The following is a list of current JASU systems referenced in this publication:

USAF JASU (For variations in technical data, refer to T.O. 35–1–7.)
ELECTRICAL STARTING UNITS:

A/M32A–86	AC: 115/200v, 3 phase, 90 kva, 0.8 pf, 4 wire
	DC: 28v, 1500 amp, 72 kw (with TR pack)
MC–1A	AC: 115/208v, 400 cycle, 3 phase, 37.5 kva, 0.8 pf, 108 amp, 4 wire
	DC: 28v, 500 amp, 14 kw
MD–3	AC: 115/208v, 400 cycle, 3 phase, 60 kva, 0.75 pf, 4 wire
	DC: 28v, 1500 amp, 45 kw, split bus
MD–3A	AC: 115/208v, 400 cycle, 3 phase, 60 kva, 0.75 pf, 4 wire
	DC: 28v, 1500 amp, 45 kw, split bus
MD–3M	AC: 115/208v, 400 cycle, 3 phase, 60 kva, 0.75 pf, 4 wire
	DC: 28v, 500 amp, 15 kw
MD–4	AC: 120/208v, 400 cycle, 3 phase, 62.5 kva, 0.8 pf, 175 amp, "WYE" neutral ground, 4 wire, 120v, 400 cycle, 3 phase, 62.5 kva, 0.8 pf, 303 amp, "DELTA" 3 wire, 120v, 400 cycle, 1 phase, 62.5 kva, 0.8 pf, 520 amp, 2 wire

LEGEND 10.—Airport/Facility Directory.

AIRPORT/FACILITY DIRECTORY LEGEND   21

AIR STARTING UNITS

AM32–95	150 +/– 5 lb/min (2055 +/– 68 cfm) at 51 +/– 2 psia
AM32A–95	150 +/– 5 lb/min @ 49 +/– 2 psia (35 +/– 2 psig)
LASS	150 +/– 5 lb/min @ 49 +/– 2 psia
MA–1A	82 lb/min (1123 cfm) at 130° air inlet temp, 45 psia (min) air outlet press
MC–1	15 cfm, 3500 psia
MC–1A	15 cfm, 3500 psia
MC–2A	15 cfm, 200 psia
MC–11	8,000 cu in cap, 4000 psig, 15 cfm

COMBINED AIR AND ELECTRICAL STARTING UNITS:

AGPU	AC: 115/200v, 400 cycle, 3 phase, 30 kw gen
	DC: 28v, 700 amp
	AIR: 60 lb/min @ 40 psig @ sea level
AM32A–60*	AIR: 120 +/– 4 lb/min (1644 +/– 55 cfm) at 49 +/– 2 psia
	AC: 120/208v, 400 cycle, 3 phase, 75 kva, 0.75 pf, 4 wire, 120v, 1 phase, 25 kva
	DC: 28v, 500 amp, 15 kw
AM32A–60A	AIR: 150 +/– 5 lb/min (2055 +/– 68 cfm at 51 +/– psia
	AC: 120/208v, 400 cycle, 3 phase, 75 kva, 0.75 pf, 4 wire
	DC: 28v, 200 amp, 5.6 kw
AM32A–60B*	AIR: 130 lb/min, 50 psia
	AC: 120/208v, 400 cycle, 3 phase, 75 kva, 0.75 pf, 4 wire
	DC: 28v, 200 amp, 5.6 kw

*NOTE: During combined air and electrical loads, the pneumatic circuitry takes preference and will limit the amount of electrical power available.

USN JASU

ELECTRICAL STARTING UNITS:

NC–8A/A1	DC: 500 amp constant, 750 amp intermittent, 28v;
	AC: 60 kva @ .8 pf, 115/200v, 3 phase, 400 Hz.
NC–10A/A1/B/C	DC: 750 amp constant, 1000 amp intermittent, 28v;
	AC: 90 kva, 115/200v, 3 phase, 400 Hz.

AIR STARTING UNITS:

GTC–85/GTE–85	120 lbs/min @ 45 psi.
MSU–200NAV/A/U47A–5	204 lbs/min @ 56 psia.
WELLS AIR START SYSTEM	180 lbs/min @ 75 psi or 120 lbs/min @ 45 psi. Simultaneous multiple start capability.

COMBINED AIR AND ELECTRICAL STARTING UNITS:

NCPP–105/RCPT	180 lbs/min @ 75 psi or 120 lbs/min @ 45 psi. 700 amp, 28v DC. 120/208v, 400 Hz AC, 30 kva.

ARMY JASU

59B2–1B	28v, 7.5 kw, 280 amp.

OTHER JASU

ELECTRICAL STARTING UNITS (DND):

CE12	AC 115/200v, 140 kva, 400 Hz, 3 phase
CE13	AC 115/200v, 60 kva, 400 Hz, 3 phase
CE14	AC/DC 115/200v, 140 kva, 400 Hz, 3 phase, 28vDC, 1500 amp
CE15	DC 22–35v, 500 amp continuous 1100 amp intermittent
CE16	DC 22–35v, 500 amp continuous 1100 amp intermittent soft start

AIR STARTING UNITS (DND):

CA2	ASA 45.5 psig, 116.4 lb/min

COMBINED AIR AND ELECTRICAL STARTING UNITS (DND)

CEA1	AC 120/208v, 60 kva, 400 Hz, 3 phase DC 28v, 75 amp
	AIR 112.5 lb/min, 47 psig

ELECTRICAL STARTING UNITS (OTHER)

C–26	28v 45kw 115–200v 15kw 380–800 Hz 1 phase 2 wire
C–26–B, C–26–C	28v 45kw: Split Bus: 115–200v 15kw 380–800 Hz 1 phase 2 wire
E3	DC 28v/10kw

AIR STARTING UNITS (OTHER):

A4	40 psi/2 lb/sec (LPAS Mk12, Mk12L, Mk12A, Mk1, Mk2B)
MA–1	150 Air HP, 115 lb/min 50 psia
MA–2	250 Air HP, 150 lb/min 75 psia

CARTRIDGE:

MXU–4A	USAF

LEGEND 11.—Airport/Facility Directory.

22 AIRPORT/FACILITY DIRECTORY LEGEND

FUEL—MILITARY

Fuel available through US Military Base supply, DESC Into–Plane Contracts and/or reciprocal agreement is listed first and is followed by (Mil). At commercial airports where Into–Plane contracts are in place, the name of the refueling agent is shown. Military fuel should be used first if it is available. When military fuel cannot be obtained but Into–Plane contract fuel is available, Government aircraft must refuel with the contract fuel and applicable refueling agent to avoid any breach in contract terms and conditions. Fuel not available through the above is shown preceded by NC (no contract). When fuel is obtained from NC sources, local purchase procedures must be followed. The US Military Aircraft Identaplates DD Form 1896 (Jet Fuel), DD Form 1897 (Avgas) and AF Form 1245 (Avgas) are used at military installations only. The US Government Aviation Into–Plane Reimbursement (AIR) Card (currently issued by AVCARD) is the instrument to be used to obtain fuel under a DESC Into–Plane Contract and for NC purchases if the refueling agent at the commercial airport accepts the AVCARD. A current list of contract fuel locations is available online at https://cis.energy.dla.mil/ip_cis/. See legend item 14 for fuel code and description.

SUPPORTING FLUIDS AND SYSTEMS—MILITARY

CODE	
ADI	Anti–Detonation Injection Fluid—Reciprocating Engine Aircraft.
W	Water Thrust Augmentation—Jet Aircraft.
WAI	Water–Alcohol Injection Type, Thrust Augmentation—Jet Aircraft.
SP	Single Point Refueling.
PRESAIR	Air Compressors rated 3,000 PSI or more.
De–Ice	Anti–icing/De–icing/Defrosting Fluid (MIL–A–8243).

OXYGEN:

LPOX	Low pressure oxygen servicing.
HPOX	High pressure oxygen servicing.
LHOX	Low and high pressure oxygen servicing.
LOX	Liquid oxygen servicing.
OXRB	Oxygen replacement bottles. (Maintained primarily at Naval stations for use in acft where oxygen can be replenished only by replacement of cylinders.)
OX	Indicates oxygen servicing when type of servicing is unknown.

NOTE: Combinations of above items is used to indicate complete oxygen servicing available;

LHOXRB	Low and high pressure oxygen servicing and replacement bottles;
LPOXRB	Low pressure oxygen replacement bottles only, etc.

NOTE: Aircraft will be serviced with oxygen procured under military specifications only. Aircraft will not be serviced with medical oxygen.

NITROGEN:

LPNIT — Low pressure nitrogen servicing.

HPNIT — High pressure nitrogen servicing.

LHNIT — Low and high pressure nitrogen servicing.

OIL—MILITARY

US AVIATION OILS (MIL SPECS):

CODE	GRADE, TYPE
O–113	1065, Reciprocating Engine Oil (MIL–L–6082)
O–117	1100, Reciprocating Engine Oil (MIL–L–6082)
O–117+	1100, O–117 plus cyclohexanone (MIL–L–6082)
O–123	1065, (Dispersant), Reciprocating Engine Oil (MIL–L–22851 Type III)
O–128	1100, (Dispersant), Reciprocating Engine Oil (MIL–L–22851 Type II)
O–132	1005, Jet Engine Oil (MIL–L–6081)
O–133	1010, Jet Engine Oil (MIL–L–6081)
O–147	None, MIL–L–6085A Lubricating Oil, Instrument, Synthetic
O–148	None, MIL–L–7808 (Synthetic Base) Turbine Engine Oil
O–149	None, Aircraft Turbine Engine Synthetic, 7.5c St
O–155	None, MIL–L–6086C, Aircraft, Medium Grade
O–156	None, MIL–L–23699 (Synthetic Base), Turboprop and Turboshaft Engines
JOAP/SOAP	Joint Oil Analysis Program. JOAP support is furnished during normal duty hours, other times on request. (JOAP and SOAP programs provide essentially the same service, JOAP is now the standard joint service supported program.)

TRANSIENT ALERT (TRAN ALERT)—MILITARY

Tran Alert service is considered to include all services required for normal aircraft turn–around, e.g., servicing (fuel, oil, oxygen, etc.), debriefing to determine requirements for maintenance, minor maintenance, inspection and parking assistance of transient aircraft. Drag chute repack, specialized maintenance, or extensive repairs will be provided within the capabilities and priorities of the base. Delays can be anticipated after normal duty hours/holidays/weekends regardless of the hours of transient maintenance operation. Pilots should not expect aircraft to be serviced for TURN–AROUNDS during time periods when servicing or maintenance manpower is not available. In the case of airports not operated exclusively by US military, the servicing indicated by the remarks will not always be available for US military aircraft. When transient alert services are not shown, facilities are unknown. NO PRIORITY BASIS—means that transient alert services will be provided only after all the requirements for mission/tactical assigned aircraft have been accomplished.

Legend 12.—Airport/Facility Directory.

㉓ AIRPORT REMARKS

The Attendance Schedule is the months, days and hours the airport is actually attended. Airport attendance does not mean watchman duties or telephone accessibility, but rather an attendant or operator on duty to provide at least minimum services (e.g., repairs, fuel, transportation).

Airport Remarks have been grouped in order of applicability. Airport remarks are limited to those items of information that are determined essential for operational use, i.e., conditions of a permanent or indefinite nature and conditions that will remain in effect for more than 30 days concerning aeronautical facilities, services, maintenance available, procedures or hazards, knowledge of which is essential for safe and efficient operation of aircraft. Information concerning permanent closing of a runway or taxiway will not be shown. A note "See Special Notices" shall be applied within this remarks section when a special notice applicable to the entry is contained in the Special Notices section of this publication.

Parachute Jumping indicates parachute jumping areas associated with the airport. See Parachute Jumping Area section of this publication for additional Information.

Landing Fee indicates landing charges for private or non–revenue producing aircraft. In addition, fees may be charged for planes that remain over a couple of hours and buy no services, or at major airline terminals for all aircraft.

Note: Unless otherwise stated, remarks including runway ends refer to the runway's approach end.

㉔ MILITARY REMARKS

Joint Civil/Military airports contain both Airport Remarks and Military Remarks. Military Remarks published for these airports are applicable only to the military. Military and joint Military/Civil airports contain only Military Remarks. Remarks contained in this section may not be applicable to civil users. When both sets of remarks exist, the first set is applicable to the primary operator of the airport. Remarks applicable to a tenant on the airport are shown preceded by the tenant organization, i.e., (A) (AF) (N) (ANG), etc. Military airports operate 24 hours unless otherwise specified. Airport operating hours are listed first (airport operating hours will only be listed if they are different than the airport attended hours or if the attended hours are unavailable) followed by pertinent remarks in order of applicability. Remarks will include information on restrictions, hazards, traffic pattern, noise abatement, customs/agriculture/immigration, and miscellaneous information applicable to the Military.

Type of restrictions:

CLOSED: When designated closed, the airport is restricted from use by all aircraft unless stated otherwise. Any closure applying to specific type of aircraft or operation will be so stated. USN/USMC/USAF airports are considered closed during non–operating hours. Closed airports may be utilized during an emergency provided there is a safe landing area.

OFFICIAL BUSINESS ONLY: The airfield is closed to all transient military aircraft for obtaining routine services such as fueling, passenger drop off or pickup, practice approaches, parking, etc. The airfield may be used by aircrews and aircraft if official government business (including civilian) must be conducted on or near the airfield and prior permission is received from the airfield manager.

AF OFFICIAL BUSINESS ONLY OR NAVY OFFICIAL BUSINESS ONLY: Indicates that the restriction applies only to service indicated.

PRIOR PERMISSION REQUIRED (PPR): Airport is closed to transient aircraft unless approval for operation is obtained from the appropriate commander through Chief, Airfield Management or Airfield Operations Officer. Official Business or PPR does not preclude the use of US Military airports as an alternate for IFR flights. If a non–US military airport is used as a weather alternate and requires a PPR, the PPR must be requested and confirmed before the flight departs. The purpose of PPR is to control volume and flow of traffic rather than to prohibit it. Prior permission is required for all aircraft requiring transient alert service outside the published transient alert duty hours. All aircraft carrying hazardous materials must obtain prior permission as outlined in AFJI 11–204, AR 95–27, OPNAVINST 3710.7.

Note: OFFICIAL BUSINESS ONLY AND PPR restrictions are not applicable to Special Air Mission (SAM) or Special Air Resource (SPAR) aircraft providing person or persons on aboard are designated Code 6 or higher as explained in AFJMAN 11–213, AR 95–11, OPNAVINST 3722–8J. Official Business Only or PPR do not preclude the use of the airport as an alternate for IFR flights.

㉕ AIRPORT MANAGER

The phone number of the airport manager.

㉖ WEATHER DATA SOURCES

Weather data sources will be listed alphabetically followed by their assigned frequencies and/or telephone number and hours of operation.

ASOS—Automated Surface Observing System. Reports the same as an AWOS–3 plus precipitation identification and intensity, and freezing rain occurrence;

AWOS—Automated Weather Observing System

AWOS–A—reports altimeter setting (all other information is advisory only).

AWOS–AV—reports altimeter and visibility.

AWOS–1—reports altimeter setting, wind data and usually temperature, dew point and density altitude.

AWOS–2—reports the same as AWOS–1 plus visibility.

AWOS–3—reports the same as AWOS–1 plus visibility and cloud/ceiling data.

AWOS–3P reports the same as the AWOS–3 system, plus a precipitation identification sensor.

AWOS–3PT reports the same as the AWOS–3 system, plus precipitation identification sensor and a thunderstorm/lightning reporting capability.

LEGEND 13.—Airport/Facility Directory.

24   AIRPORT/FACILITY DIRECTORY LEGEND

AWOS–3T reports the same as AWOS–3 system and includes a thunderstorm/lightning reporting capability.

   See AIM, Basic Flight Information and ATC Procedures for detailed description of Weather Data Sources.

AWOS–4—reports same as AWOS–3 system, plus precipitation occurrence, type and accumulation, freezing rain, thunderstorm and runway surface sensors.

HIWAS—See RADIO AIDS TO NAVIGATION

LAWRS—Limited Aviation Weather Reporting Station where observers report cloud height, weather, obstructions to vision, temperature and dewpoint (in most cases), surface wind, altimeter and pertinent remarks.

LLWAS—indicates a Low Level Wind Shear Alert System consisting of a center field and several field perimeter anemometers.

SAWRS—identifies airports that have a Supplemental Aviation Weather Reporting Station available to pilots for current weather information.

SWSL—Supplemental Weather Service Location providing current local weather information via radio and telephone.

TDWR—indicates airports that have Terminal Doppler Weather Radar.

WSP—indicates airports that have Weather System Processor.

When the automated weather source is broadcast over an associated airport NAVAID frequency (see NAVAID line), it shall be indicated by a bold ASOS, AWOS, or HIWAS followed by the frequency, identifier and phone number, if available.

㉗ COMMUNICATIONS

Airport terminal control facilities and radio communications associated with the airport shall be shown. When the call sign is not the same as the airport name the call sign will be shown. Frequencies shall normally be shown in descending order with the primary frequency listed first. Frequencies will be listed, together with sectorization indicated by outbound radials, and hours of operation. Communications will be listed in sequence as follows:

Single Frequency Approach (SFA), Common Traffic Advisory Frequency (CTAF), Aeronautical Advisory Stations (UNICOM) or (AUNICOM), and Automatic Terminal Information Service (ATIS) along with their frequency is shown, where available, on the line following the heading "COMMUNICATIONS." When the CTAF and UNICOM frequencies are the same, the frequency will be shown as CTAF/UNICOM 122.8.

The FSS telephone nationwide is toll free 1–800–WX–BRIEF (1–800–992–7433). When the FSS is located on the field it will be indicated as "on arpt". Frequencies available at the FSS will follow in descending order. Remote Communications Outlet (RCO) providing service to the airport followed by the frequency and FSS RADIO name will be shown when available. FSS's provide information on airport conditions, radio aids and other facilities, and process flight plans. Airport Advisory Service (AAS) is provided on the CTAF by FSS's for select non–tower airports or airports where the tower is not in operation.

(See AIM, Para 4–1–9 Traffic Advisory Practices at Airports Without Operating Control Towers or AC 90–42C.)

Aviation weather briefing service is provided by FSS specialists. Flight and weather briefing services are also available by calling the telephone numbers listed.

Remote Communications Outlet (RCO)—An unmanned air/ground communications facility that is remotely controlled and provides UHF or VHF communications capability to extend the service range of an FSS.

Civil Communications Frequencies–Civil communications frequencies used in the FSS air/ground system are operated on 122.0, 122.2, 123.6; emergency 121.5; plus receive–only on 122.1.

    a. 122.0 is assigned as the Enroute Flight Advisory Service frequency at selected FSS RADIO outlets.

    b. 122.2 is assigned as a common enroute frequency.

    c. 123.6 is assigned as the airport advisory frequency at select non–tower locations. At airports with a tower, FSS may provide airport advisories on the tower frequency when tower is closed.

    d. 122.1 is the primary receive–only frequency at VOR's.

    e. Some FSS's are assigned 50 kHz frequencies in the 122–126 MHz band (eg. 122.45). Pilots using the FSS A/G system should refer to this directory or appropriate charts to determine frequencies available at the FSS or remoted facility through which they wish to communicate.

Emergency frequency 121.5 and 243.0 are available at all Flight Service Stations, most Towers, Approach Control and RADAR facilities.

Frequencies published followed by the letter "T" or "R", indicate that the facility will only transmit or receive respectively on that frequency. All radio aids to navigation (NAVAID) frequencies are transmit only.

TERMINAL SERVICES

SFA—Single Frequency Approach.

CTAF—A program designed to get all vehicles and aircraft at airports without an operating control tower on a common frequency.

ATIS—A continuous broadcast of recorded non–control information in selected terminal areas.

D–ATIS—Digital ATIS provides ATIS information in text form outside the standard reception range of conventional ATIS via landline & data link communications and voice message within range of existing transmitters.

AUNICOM—Automated UNICOM is a computerized, command response system that provides automated weather, radio check capability and airport advisory information selected from an automated menu by microphone clicks.

UNICOM—A non–government air/ground radio communications facility which may provide airport information.

PTD—Pilot to Dispatcher.

APP CON—Approach Control. The symbol ® indicates radar approach control.

TOWER—Control tower.

GCA—Ground Control Approach System.

GND CON—Ground Control.

LEGEND 14.—Airport/Facility Directory.

AIRPORT/FACILITY DIRECTORY LEGEND 25

GCO—Ground Communication Outlet—An unstaffed, remotely controlled, ground/ground communications facility. Pilots at uncontrolled airports may contact ATC and FSS via VHF to a telephone connection to obtain an instrument clearance or close a VFR or IFR flight plan. They may also get an updated weather briefing prior to takeoff. Pilots will use four "key clicks" on the VHF radio to contact the appropriate ATC facility or six "key clicks" to contact the FSS. The GCO system is intended to be used only on the ground.

DEP CON—Departure Control. The symbol ® indicates radar departure control.

CLNC DEL—Clearance Delivery.

CPDLC—Controller Pilot Data Link Communication. FANS ATC data communication capability from the aircraft to the ATC Data Link system.

PRE TAXI CLNC—Pre taxi clearance.

VFR ADVSY SVC—VFR Advisory Service. Service provided by Non–Radar Approach Control.
   Advisory Service for VFR aircraft (upon a workload basis) ctc APP CON.

COMD POST—Command Post followed by the operator call sign in parenthesis.

PMSV—Pilot–to–Metro Service call sign, frequency and hours of operation, when full service is other than continuous. PMSV installations at which weather observation service is available shall be indicated, following the frequency and/or hours of operation as "Wx obsn svc 1900–0000Z‡" or "other times" may be used when no specific time is given. PMSV facilities manned by forecasters are considered "Full Service". PMSV facilities manned by weather observers are listed as "Limited Service".

OPS—Operations followed by the operator call sign in parenthesis.

CON

RANGE

FLT FLW—Flight Following

MEDIVAC

NOTE: Communication frequencies followed by the letter "X" indicate frequency available on request.

㉘ AIRSPACE

Information concerning Class B, C, and part–time D and E surface area airspace shall be published with effective times, if available.

CLASS B—Radar Sequencing and Separation Service for all aircraft in CLASS B airspace.

CLASS C—Separation between IFR and VFR aircraft and sequencing of VFR arrivals to the primary airport.

TRSA—Radar Sequencing and Separation Service for participating VFR Aircraft within a Terminal Radar Service Area.

Class C, D, and E airspace described in this publication is that airspace usually consisting of a 5 NM radius core surface area that begins at the surface and extends upward to an altitude above the airport elevation (charted in MSL for Class C and Class D). Class E surface airspace normally extends from the surface up to but not including the overlying controlled airspace.

When part–time Class C or Class D airspace defaults to Class E, the core surface area becomes Class E. This will be formatted as:
AIRSPACE: CLASS C svc "times" ctc **APP CON** other times CLASS E:
or
AIRSPACE: CLASS D svc "times" other times CLASS E.

When a part–time Class C, Class D or Class E surface area defaults to Class G, the core surface area becomes Class G up to, but not including, the overlying controlled airspace. Normally, the overlying controlled airspace is Class E airspace beginning at either 700′ or 1200′ AGL and may be determined by consulting the relevant VFR Sectional or Terminal Area Charts. This will be formatted as:
AIRSPACE: CLASS C svc "times" ctc **APP CON** other times CLASS G, with CLASS E 700′ (or 1200′) AGL & abv:
or
AIRSPACE: CLASS D svc "times" other times CLASS G with CLASS E 700′ (or 1200′) AGL & abv:
or
AIRSPACE: CLASS E svc "times" other times CLASS G with CLASS E 700′ (or 1200′) AGL & abv.

NOTE: AIRSPACE SVC "TIMES" INCLUDE ALL ASSOCIATED ARRIVAL EXTENSIONS. Surface area arrival extensions for instrument approach procedures become part of the primary core surface area. These extensions may be either Class D or Class E airspace and are effective concurrent with the times of the primary core surface area. For example, when a part–time Class C, Class D or Class E surface area defaults to Class G, the associated arrival extensions will default to Class G at the same time. When a part–time Class C or Class D surface area defaults to Class E, the arrival extensions will remain in effect as Class E airspace.

NOTE: CLASS E AIRSPACE EXTENDING UPWARD FROM 700 FEET OR MORE ABOVE THE SURFACE, DESIGNATED IN CONJUNCTION WITH AN AIRPORT WITH AN APPROVED INSTRUMENT PROCEDURE.
Class E 700′ AGL (shown as magenta vignette on sectional charts) and 1200′ AGL (blue vignette) areas are designated when necessary to provide controlled airspace for transitioning to/from the terminal and enroute environments. Unless otherwise specified, these 700′/1200′ AGL Class E airspace areas remain in effect continuously, regardless of airport operating hours or surface area status. These transition areas should not be confused with surface areas or arrival extensions.

(See Chapter 3, AIRSPACE, in the Aeronautical Information Manual for further details)

Legend 15.—Airport/Facility Directory.

26 AIRPORT/FACILITY DIRECTORY LEGEND

㉙ **VOR TEST FACILITY (VOT)**

The VOT transmits a signal which provided users a convenient means to determine the operational status and accuracy of an aircraft VOR receiver while on the ground. Ground based VOTs and the associated frequency shall be shown when available. VOTs are also shown with identifier, frequency and referenced remarks in the VOR Receiver Check section in the back of this publication.

㉚ **RADIO AIDS TO NAVIGATION**

The Airport/Facility Directory section of the Chart Supplement lists, by facility name, all Radio Aids to Navigation that appear on FAA, Aeronautical Information Services Visual or IFR Aeronautical Charts and those upon which the FAA has approved an Instrument Approach Procedure, with exception of selected TACANs. All VOR, VORTAC, TACAN and ILS equipment in the National Airspace System has an automatic monitoring and shutdown feature in the event of malfunction. Unmonitored, as used in this publication, for any navigational aid, means that monitoring personnel cannot observe the malfunction or shutdown signal. The NAVAID NOTAM file identifier will be shown as "NOTAM FILE IAD" and will be listed on the Radio Aids to Navigation line. When two or more NAVAIDS are listed and the NOTAM file identifier is different from that shown on the Radio Aids to Navigation line, it will be shown with the NAVAID listing. NOTAM file identifiers for ILSs and its components (e.g., NDB (LOM) are the same as the associated airports and are not repeated. Automated Surface Observing System (ASOS), Automated Weather Observing System (AWOS), and Hazardous Inflight Weather Advisory Service (HIWAS) will be shown when this service is broadcast over selected NAVAIDs.

NAVAID information is tabulated as indicated in the following sample:

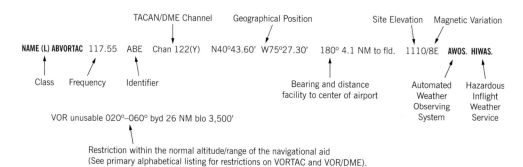

Note: Those DME channel numbers with a (Y) suffix require TACAN to be placed in the "Y" mode to receive distance information.

HIWAS—Hazardous Inflight Weather Advisory Service is a continuous broadcast of inflight weather advisories including summarized SIGMETs, convective SIGMETs, AIRMETs and urgent PIREPs. HIWAS is presently broadcast over selected VOR's throughout the U.S.

ASR/PAR—Indicates that Surveillance (ASR) or Precision (PAR) radar instrument approach minimums are published in the U.S. Terminal Procedures. Only part–time hours of operation will be shown.

LEGEND 16.—Airport/Facility Directory.

AIRPORT/FACILITY DIRECTORY LEGEND

RADIO CLASS DESIGNATIONS

VOR/DME/TACAN Standard Service Volume (SSV) Classifications

SSV Class	Altitudes	Distance (NM)
(T) Terminal	1000′ to 12,000′	25
(L) Low Altitude	1000′ to 18,000′	40
(H) High Altitude	1000′ to 14,500′	40
	14,500′ to 18,000′	100
	18,000′ to 45,000′	130
	45,000′ to 60,000′	100

NOTE: Additionally, (H) facilities provide (L) and (T) service volume and (L) facilities provide (T) service. Altitudes are with respect to the station's site elevation. Coverage is not available in a cone of airspace directly above the facility.

The term VOR is, operationally, a general term covering the VHF omnidirectional bearing type of facility without regard to the fact that the power, the frequency protected service volume, the equipment configuration, and operational requirements may vary between facilities at different locations.

AB	Automatic Weather Broadcast.
DF	Direction Finding Service.
DME	UHF standard (TACAN compatible) distance measuring equipment.
DME(Y)	UHF standard (TACAN compatible) distance measuring equipment that require TACAN to be placed in the "Y" mode to receive DME.
GS	Glide slope.
H	Non–directional radio beacon (homing), power 50 watts to less than 2,000 watts (50 NM at all altitudes).
HH	Non–directional radio beacon (homing), power 2,000 watts or more (75 NM at all altitudes).
H–SAB	Non–directional radio beacons providing automatic transcribed weather service.
ILS	Instrument Landing System (voice, where available, on localizer channel).
IM	Inner marker.
LDA	Localizer Directional Aid.
LMM	Compass locator station when installed at middle marker site (15 NM at all altitudes).
LOM	Compass locator station when installed at outer marker site (15 NM at all altitudes).
MH	Non–directional radio beacon (homing) power less than 50 watts (25 NM at all altitudes).
MM	Middle marker.
OM	Outer marker.
S	Simultaneous range homing signal and/or voice.
SABH	Non–directional radio beacon not authorized for IFR or ATC. Provides automatic weather broadcasts.
SDF	Simplified Direction Facility.
TACAN	UHF navigational facility–omnidirectional course and distance information.
VOR	VHF navigational facility–omnidirectional course only.
VOR/DME	Collocated VOR navigational facility and UHF standard distance measuring equipment.
VORTAC	Collocated VOR and TACAN navigational facilities.
W	Without voice on radio facility frequency.
Z	VHF station location marker at a LF radio facility.

LEGEND 17.—Airport/Facility Directory.

28   **AIRPORT/FACILITY DIRECTORY LEGEND**

ILS FACILITY PEFORMANCE CLASSIFICATION CODES

Codes define the ability of an ILS to support autoland operations. The two portions of the code represent Official Category and farthest point along a Category I, II, or III approach that the Localizer meets Category III structure tolerances.

Official Category: I, II, or III; the lowest minima on published or unpublished procedures supported by the ILS.

Farthest point of satisfactory Category III Localizer performance for Category I, II, or III approaches: A – 4 NM prior to runway threshold, B – 3500 ft prior to runway threshold, C – glide angle dependent but generally 750–1000 ft prior to threshold, T – runway threshold, D – 3000 ft after runway threshold, and E – 2000 ft prior to stop end of runway.

ILS information is tabulated as indicated in the following sample:

      ILS/DME   108.5   I–ORL   Chan 22   Rwy 18.   Class IIE.   LOM HERNY NDB.

                    ILS Facility Performance ↗
                    Classification Code

FREQUENCY PAIRING TABLE

VHF FREQUENCY	TACAN CHANNEL	VHF FREQUENCY	TACAN CHANNEL	VHF FREQUENCY	TACAN CHANNEL	VHF FREQUENCY	TACAN CHANNEL
108.10	18X	108.55	22Y	111.05	47Y	114.85	95Y
108.30	20X	108.65	23Y	111.15	48Y	114.95	96Y
108.50	22X	108.75	24Y	111.25	49Y	115.05	97Y
108.70	24X	108.85	25Y	111.35	50Y	115.15	98Y
108.90	26X	108.95	26Y	111.45	51Y	115.25	99Y
109.10	28X	109.05	27Y	111.55	52Y	115.35	100Y
109.30	30X	109.15	28Y	111.65	53Y	115.45	101Y
109.50	32X	109.25	29Y	111.75	54Y	115.55	102Y
109.70	34X	109.35	30Y	111.85	55Y	115.65	103Y
109.90	36X	109.45	31Y	111.95	56Y	115.75	104Y
110.10	38X	109.55	32Y	113.35	80Y	115.85	105Y
110.30	40X	109.65	33Y	113.45	81Y	115.95	106Y
110.50	42X	109.75	34Y	113.55	82Y	116.05	107Y
110.70	44X	109.85	35Y	113.65	83Y	116.15	108Y
110.90	46X	109.95	36Y	113.75	84Y	116.25	109Y
111.10	48X	110.05	37Y	113.85	85Y	116.35	110Y
111.30	50X	110.15	38Y	113.95	86Y	116.45	111Y
111.50	52X	110.25	39Y	114.05	87Y	116.55	112Y
111.70	54X	110.35	40Y	114.15	88Y	116.65	113Y
111.90	56X	110.45	41Y	114.25	89Y	116.75	114Y
108.05	17Y	110.55	42Y	114.35	90Y	116.85	115Y
108.15	18Y	110.65	43Y	114.45	91Y	116.95	116Y
108.25	19Y	110.75	44Y	114.55	92Y	117.05	117Y
108.35	20Y	110.85	45Y	114.65	93Y	117.15	118Y
108.45	21Y	110.95	46Y	114.75	94Y	117.25	119Y

FREQUENCY PAIRING TABLE

The following is a list of paired VOR/ILS VHF frequencies with TACAN channels.

TACAN CHANNEL	VHF FREQUENCY	TACAN CHANNEL	VHF FREQUENCY	TACAN CHANNEL	VHF FREQUENCY	TACAN CHANNEL	VHF FREQUENCY
2X	134.5	25X	108.80	36X	109.90	47X	111.00
2Y	134.55	25Y	108.85	36Y	109.95	47Y	111.05
11X	135.4	26X	108.90	37X	110.00	48X	111.10
11Y	135.45	26Y	108.95	37Y	110.05	48Y	111.15
12X	135.5	27X	109.00	38X	110.10	49X	111.20
12Y	135.55	27Y	109.05	38Y	110.15	49Y	111.25
17X	108.00	28X	109.10	39X	110.20	50X	111.30
17Y	108.05	28Y	109.15	39Y	110.25	50Y	111.35
18X	108.10	29X	109.20	40X	110.30	51X	111.40
18Y	108.15	29Y	109.25	40Y	110.35	51Y	111.45
19X	108.20	30X	109.30	41X	110.40	52X	111.50
19Y	108.25	30Y	109.35	41Y	110.45	52Y	111.55
20X	108.30	31X	109.40	42X	110.50	53X	111.60
20Y	108.35	31Y	109.45	42Y	110.55	53Y	111.65
21X	108.40	32X	109.50	43X	110.60	54X	111.70
21Y	108.45	32Y	109.55	43Y	110.65	54Y	111.75
22X	108.50	33X	109.60	44X	110.70	55X	111.80
22Y	108.55	33Y	109.65	44Y	110.75	55Y	111.85
23X	108.60	34X	109.70	45X	110.80	56X	111.90
23Y	108.65	34Y	109.75	45Y	110.85	56Y	111.95
24X	108.70	35X	109.80	46X	110.90	57X	112.00
24Y	108.75	35Y	109.85	46Y	110.95	57Y	112.05

LEGEND 18.—Airport/Facility Directory.

AIRPORT/FACILITY DIRECTORY LEGEND 29

TACAN CHANNEL	VHF FREQUENCY	TACAN CHANNEL	VHF FREQUENCY	TACAN CHANNEL	VHF FREQUENCY	TACAN CHANNEL	VHF FREQUENCY
58X	112.10	77X	113.00	96X	114.90	115X	116.80
58Y	112.15	77Y	113.05	96Y	114.95	115Y	116.85
59X	112.20	78X	113.10	97X	115.00	116X	116.90
59Y	112.25	78Y	113.15	97Y	115.05	116Y	116.95
60X	133.30	79X	113.20	98X	115.10	117X	117.00
60Y	133.35	79Y	113.25	98Y	115.15	117Y	117.05
61X	133.40	80X	113.30	99X	115.20	118X	117.10
61Y	133.45	80Y	113.35	99Y	115.25	118Y	117.15
62X	133.50	81X	113.40	100X	115.30	119X	117.20
62Y	133.55	81Y	113.45	100Y	115.35	119Y	117.25
63X	133.60	82X	113.50	101X	115.40	120X	117.30
63Y	133.65	82Y	113.55	101Y	115.45	120Y	117.35
64X	133.70	83X	113.60	102X	115.50	121X	117.40
64Y	133.75	83Y	113.65	102Y	115.55	121Y	117.45
65X	133.80	84X	113.70	103X	115.60	122X	117.50
65Y	133.85	84Y	113.75	103Y	115.65	122Y	117.55
66X	133.90	85X	113.80	104X	115.70	123X	117.60
66Y	133.95	85Y	113.85	104Y	115.75	123Y	117.65
67X	134.00	86X	113.90	105X	115.80	124X	117.70
67Y	134.05	86Y	113.95	105Y	115.85	124Y	117.75
68X	134.10	87X	114.00	106X	115.90	125X	117.80
68Y	134.15	87Y	114.05	106Y	115.95	125Y	117.85
69X	134.20	88X	114.10	107X	116.00	126X	117.90
69Y	134.25	88Y	114.15	107Y	116.05	126Y	117.95
70X	112.30	89X	114.20	108X	116.10		
70Y	112.35	89Y	114.25	108Y	116.15		
71X	112.40	90X	114.30	109X	116.20		
71Y	112.45	90Y	114.35	109Y	116.25		
72X	112.50	91X	114.40	110X	116.30		
72Y	112.55	91Y	114.45	110Y	116.35		
73X	112.60	92X	114.50	111X	116.40		
73Y	112.65	92Y	114.55	111Y	116.45		
74X	112.70	93X	114.60	112X	116.50		
74Y	112.75	93Y	114.65	112Y	116.55		
75X	112.80	94X	114.70	113X	116.60		
75Y	112.85	94Y	114.75	113Y	116.65		
76X	112.90	95X	114.80	114X	116.70		
76Y	112.95	95Y	114.85	114Y	116.75		

(31) **COMM/NAV/WEATHER REMARKS:** These remarks consist of pertinent information affecting the current status of communications, NAVAIDs and weather.

LEGEND 19.—Airport/Facility Directory.

12320
TERMS/LANDING MINIMA DATA

IFR LANDING MINIMA

The United States Standard for Terminal Instrument Procedures (TERPS) is the approved criteria for formulating instrument approach procedures. Landing minima are established for six aircraft approach categories (ABCDE and COPTER). In the absence of COPTER MINIMA, helicopters may use the CAT A minimums of other procedures.

LANDING MINIMA FORMAT

In this example airport elevation is 1179, and runway touchdown zone elevation is 1152.

DA — Visibility (RVR 100's of feet) — Aircraft Approach Category — HAT/HATh

Straight-in ILS to Runway 27

Straight-in with Glide Slope Inoperative or not used to Runway 27

MDA   HAA   Visibility in Statute Miles

All **weather** minimums in parentheses not applicable to Civil Pilots. Military Pilots refer to appropriate regulations.

CATEGORY	A	B	C	D
S-ILS 27	1352/24		200 (200-½)	
S-LOC 27	1440/24	288 (300-½)		1440/50 288 (300-1)
CIRCLING	1540-1 361 (400-1)	1640-1 461 (500-1)	1640-1½ 461 (500-1½)	1740-2 561 (600-2)

COPTER MINIMA ONLY

CATEGORY	COPTER
H-176°	680-½ 363 (400-½)

Copter Approach Direction

Height of MDA/DA Above Landing Area (HAL)

No circling minimums are provided

RNAV (GPS) MINIMA EXAMPLE

CATEGORY	A	B	C	D
LPV DA	1540/24 258 (300-½)			
LNAV/VNAV DA	1600/24 318 (400-½)			1600/40 318 (400-¾)
LNAV MDA	1840/24 558 (600-½)		1840/50 558 (600-1)	1840/60 558 (600-1¼)
CIRCLING	1840-1 545 (600-1)		1840-1½ 545 (600-1½)	1860-2 565 (600-2)

NOTE: The **W** symbol indicates outages of the WAAS vertical guidance may occur daily at this location due to initial system limitations. WAAS NOTAMS for vertical outages are not provided for this approach. Use LNAV minima for flight planning at these locations, whether as a destination or alternate. For flight operations at these locations, when the WAAS avionics indicate that LNAV/VNAV or LPV service is available, then vertical guidance may be used to complete the approach using the displayed level of service. Should an outage occur during the procedure, reversion to LNAV minima may be required. As the WAAS coverage is expanded, the **W** will be removed.

RNAV minimums are dependent on navigation equipment capability, as stated in the applicable AFM, AFMS, or other FAA approved document. See AIM paragraph 5-4-5, AC 90-105 and AC 90-107 for detailed requirements for each line of minima.

AIRCRAFT APPROACH CATEGORIES

Aircraft approach category indicates a grouping of aircraft based on a speed of VREF, if specified, or if VREF not specified, 1.3 VSO at the maximum certificated landing weight. VREF, VSO, and the maximum certificated landing weight are those values as established for the aircraft by the certification authority of the country of registry. Helicopters are Category A aircraft. An aircraft shall fit in only one category. However, if it is necessary to operate at a speed in excess of the upper limit of the speed range for an aircraft's category, the minimums for the category for that speed shall be used. For example, an airplane which fits into Category B, but is circling to land at a speed of 145 knots, shall use the approach Category D minimums. As an additional example, a Category A airplane (or helicopter) which is operating at 130 knots on a straight-in approach shall use the approach Category C minimums. See following category limits:

MANEUVERING TABLE

Approach Category	A	B	C	D	E
Speed (Knots)	0-90	91-120	121-140	141-165	Abv 165

TERMS/LANDING MINIMA DATA

LEGEND 20.—Instrument Approach Procedures Explanation of Terms.

13122

TERMS/LANDING MINIMA DATA

CIRCLING APPROACH OBSTACLE PROTECTED AIRSPACE

The circling MDA provides vertical clearance from obstacles when conducting a circle-to-land maneuver within the obstacle protected area. Circling approach obstacle protected areas extend laterally and longitudinally from the centerlines and ends of all runways at an airport by the distances shown in the following tables. The areas are technically defined by the tangential connection of arcs drawn at the radius distance shown from each runway end.

STANDARD CIRCLING APPROACH MANEUVERING RADIUS

Circling approach protected areas developed prior to late 2012 used the radius distances shown in the following table, expressed in nautical miles (NM), dependent on aircraft approach category. The approaches using standard circling approach areas can be identified by the absence of the C symbol on the circling line of minima.

Circling MDA in feet MSL	Approach Category and Circling Radius (NM)				
	CAT A	CAT B	CAT C	CAT D	CAT E
All Altitudes	1.3	1.5	1.7	2.3	4.5

C EXPANDED CIRCLING APPROACH MANEUVERING AIRSPACE RADIUS

Circling approach protected areas developed after late 2012 use the radius distance shown in the following table, expressed in nautical miles (NM), dependent on aircraft approach category, and the altitude of the circling MDA, which accounts for true airspeed increase with altitude. The approaches using expanded circling approach areas can be identified by the presence of the C symbol on the circling line of minima.

Circling MDA in feet MSL	Approach Category and Circling Radius (NM)				
	CAT A	CAT B	CAT C	CAT D	CAT E
1000 or less	1.3	1.7	2.7	3.6	4.5
1001-3000	1.3	1.8	2.8	3.7	4.6
3001-5000	1.3	1.8	2.9	3.8	4.8
5001-7000	1.3	1.9	3.0	4.0	5.0
7001-9000	1.4	2.0	3.2	4.2	5.3
9001 and above	1.4	2.1	3.3	4.4	5.5

Comparable Values of RVR and Visibility

The following table shall be used for converting RVR to ground or flight visibility. For converting RVR values that fall between listed values, use the next higher RVR value; do not interpolate. For example, when converting 1800 RVR, use 2400 RVR with the resultant visibility of ½ mile.

RVR (feet)	Visibility (statute miles)	RVR (feet)	Visibility (statute miles)
1600	¼	4500	⅞
2400	½	5000	1
3200	⅝	6000	1¼
4000	¾		

RADAR MINIMA

	RWY	GS/TCH/RPI	CAT	DA/ MDA-VIS	HAT/ HATh/ HAA	CEIL-VIS	CAT	DA/ MDA-VIS	HAT/ HATh/ HAA	CEIL-VIS
PAR	10	2.5°/42/1000	ABCDE	**195**/16	100	(100-¼)				
	28	2.5°/48/1068	ABCDE	**187**/16	100	(100-¼)				
ASR	10		ABC	**560**/40	463	(500-¾)	DE	**560**/50	463	(500-1)
	28		AB	**600**/50	513	(600-1)	CDE	**600**/60	513	(600-1¼)
CIR	10		AB	**560**-1¼	463	(500-1¼)	CDE	**560**-1½	463	(500-1½)
	28		AB	**600**-1¼	503	(600-1¼)	CDE	**600**-1½	503	(600-1½)

Visibility (RVR 100's of feet)

Visibility in Statute Miles

All minimums in parentheses not applicable to Civil Pilots. Military Pilots refer to appropriate regulations.

Radar Minima:

1. Minima shown are the lowest permitted by established criteria. Pilots should consult applicable directives for their category of aircraft.
2. The circling MDA and weather minima to be used are those for the runway to which the final approach is flown- not the landing runway. In the above RADAR MINIMA example, a category C aircraft flying a radar approach to runway 10, circling to land on runway 28, must use an MDA of 560 feet with weather minima of 500-1½.

NOTE: Military RADAR MINIMA may be shown with communications symbology that indicates emergency frequency monitoring capability by the radar facility as follows:

(E) VHF and UHF emergency frequencies monitored
(V) VHF emergency frequency (121.5) monitored
(U) UHF emergency frequency (243.0) monitored

Additionally, unmonitored frequencies which are available on request from the controlling agency may be annotated with an "x".

A Alternate Minimums not standard. Civil users refer to tabulation. USA/USN/USAF pilots refer to appropriate regulations.

A NA Alternate minimums are Not Authorized due to unmonitored facility or absence of weather reporting service.

T Takeoff Minimums not standard and/or Departure Procedures are published. Refer to tabulation.

TERMS/LANDING MINIMA DATA

LEGEND 21.—Instrument Approach Procedures Explanation of Terms.

13290
GENERAL INFO

GENERAL INFORMATION

This publication is issued every 56 days and includes Standard Instrument Approach Procedures (SIAPS), Standard Instrument Departures (SIDs), Standard Terminal Arrivals (STARs), IFR Takeoff Minimums and (Obstacle) Departure Procedures (ODPs), IFR Alternate Minimums, and Radar Instrument Approach Minimums for use by civil and military aviation. The organization responsible for SIAPs, Radar Minimums, SIDs, STARs and graphic ODPs is identified in parentheses in the top margin of the procedure; e.g., (FAA), (FAA-O), (USA), (USAF), (USN). SIAPS with the (FAA) and (FAA-O) designation are regulated under 14 CFR, Part 97. SIAPs with the (FAA-O) designation have been developed under Other Transaction Agreement (OTA) by private providers and have been certified by the FAA. See 14 CFR, Part 91.175 (a) and the AIM for further details. 14 CFR, Part 91.175 (g) and the Special Notices section of the Airport/Facility Directory contains information on civil operations at military airports.

STANDARD TERMINAL ARRIVALS AND DEPARTURE PROCEDURES

The use of the associated codified STAR/DP and transition identifiers are requested of users when filing flight plans via teletype and are required for users filing flight plans via computer interface. It must be noted that when filing a STAR/DP with a transition, the first three coded characters of the STAR and the last three coded characters of the DP are replaced by the transition code. Examples: ACTON SIX ARRIVAL, file (AQN.AQN6); ACTON SIX ARRIVAL, EDNAS TRANSITION, file (EDNAS.AQN6). FREEHOLD THREE DEPARTURE, file (FREH3.RBV), FREEHOLD THREE DEPARTURE, ELWOOD CITY TRANSITION, file (FREH3.EWC).

RNAV DP and STAR. Effective March 15,2007, these procedures, formerly identified as Type-A and Type-B, will be designated as RNAV 1 in accordance with amended Advisory Circular (AC) and ICAO terminology.

Refer to AC 90-100A U.S. TERMINAL AND EN ROUTE AREA NAVIGATION (RNAV) OPERATIONS and the Aeronautical Information Manual for additional guidance regarding these procedures.

Standard RNAV 1 Procedure Chart Notes

NOTE: RNAV 1
NOTE: DME/DME/IRU or GPS required

Some procedures may require use of GPS and will be identified by a "GPS required" note.

RNAV 1 Procedure Characteristics and Operations

1. Require use of an RNAV system with DME/DME/IRU, and/or GPS inputs.
2. Require use of a CDI, flight director, and/or autopilot, in lateral navigation mode, for flight guidance while operating on RNAV paths (track, course, or direct leg). Other methods providing an equivalent level of performance may be acceptable.
3. RNAV paths may start as low as 500 feet above airport elevation.

GENERAL INFO
13290

LEGEND 22.—General Information.

AAUP	Attention All Users Page
ADF	Automatic Direction Finder
AFIS	Automatic Flight Information Service
ALS	Approach Light System
ALSF	Approach Light System with Sequenced Flashing Lights
AP	Autopilot System
APCH	Approach
APP CON	Approach Control
ARR	Arrival
ASOS	Automated Surface Observing System
ASR/PAR	Published Radar Minimums at this Airport
ATIS	Automatic Terminal Information Service
AUNICOM	Automated UNICOM
AWOS	Automated Weather Observing System
AZ	Azimuth
BC	Back Course
BND	Bound
C	Circling
CAT	Category
CCW	Counter Clockwise
CDI	Course Deviation Indicator
Chan	Channel
CIR	Circling
CLNC DEL	Clearance Delivery
CNF	Computer Navigation Fix
CTAF	Common Traffic Advisory Frequency
CW	Clockwise
DA	Decision Altitude
DER	Departure End of Runway
DH	Decision Height
DME	Distance Measuring Equipment
DTHR	Displaced Threshold
ELEV	Elevation
EMAS	Engineered Material Arresting System
FAF	Final Approach Fix
FD	Flight Director System
FM	Fan Marker
FMS	Flight Management System
GCO	Ground Communications Outlet
GLS	Ground Based Augmentation System Landing System
GPI	Ground Point of Interception
GPS	Global Positioning System
GS	Glide Slope

HAA	Height above Airport
HAL	Height above Landing
HAT	Height above Touchdown
HATh	Height Above Threshold
HGS	Head-up Guidance System
HIRL	High Intensity Runway Lights
HUD	Head-up Display
IAF	Initial Approach Fix
ICAO	International Civil Aviation Organization
IF	Intermediate Fix
IM	Inner Marker
INT	Intersection
LAAS	Local Area Augmentation System
LDA	Localizer Type Directional Aid
Ldg	Landing
LIRL	Low Intensity Runway Lights
LNAV	Lateral Navigation
LOC	Localizer
LP	Localizer Performance
LPV	Localizer Performance with Vertical Guidance
LR	Lead Radial. Provides at least 2 NM (Copter 1 NM) of lead to assist in turning onto the intermediate/final course.
MAA	Maximum Authorized Altitude
MALS	Medium Intensity Approach Light System
MALSR	Medium Intensity Approach Light System with RAIL
MAP	Missed Approach Point
MDA	Minimum Descent Altitude
MIRL	Medium Intensity Runway Lights
MLS	Microwave Landing System
MM	Middle Marker
MRA	Minimum Reception Altitude
N/A	Not Applicable
NA	Not Authorized
NDB	Non-directional Radio Beacon
NFD	National Flight Database
NM	Nautical Mile
NoPT	No Procedure Turn Required (Procedure Turn shall not be executed without ATC clearance)
ODALS	Omnidirectional Approach Light System
ODP	Obstacle Departure Procedure
OM	Outer Marker
PRM	Precision Runway Monitor

LEGEND 23.—Abbreviations.

14149

GENERAL INFO ABBREVIATIONS

R.	Radial
RA.	Radio Altimeter setting height
RAIL.	Runway Alignment Indicator Lights
RCLS.	Runway Centerline Light System
REIL.	Runway End Identifier Lights
RF.	Radius-to-Fix
RLLS.	Runway Lead-in Light System
RNAV.	Area Navigation
RNP.	Required Navigation Performance
RPI.	Runway Point of Intercept(ion)
RRL.	Runway Remaining Lights
Rwy.	Runway
RVR.	Runway Visual Range
S.	Straight-in
SALS.	Short Approach Light System
SSALR.	Simplified Short Approach Light System with RAIL
SDF.	Simplified Directional Facility
SM.	Statute Mile
SOIA.	Simultaneous Offset Instrument Approach
TAA.	Terminal Arrival Area
TAC.	TACAN
TCH.	Threshold Crossing Height (height in feet Above Ground level)
TDZ.	Touchdown Zone
TDZE.	Touchdown Zone Elevation
TDZ/CL.	Touchdown Zone and Runway Centerline Lighting
TDZL.	Touchdown Zone Lights
THR.	Threshold
THRE.	Threshold Elevation
TODA.	Takeoff Distance Available
TORA.	Takeoff Run Available
TR.	Track
VASI.	Visual Approach Slope Indicator
VCOA.	Visual Climb Over Airport
VDP.	Visual Descent Point
VGSI.	Visual Glide Slope Indicator
VNAV.	Vertical Navigation
WAAS.	Wide Area Augmentation System
WP/WPT.	Waypoint (RNAV)

GENERAL INFO
14149

LEGEND 23A.—Abbreviations.

11349

LEGEND
INSTRUMENT APPROACH PROCEDURES (CHARTS)

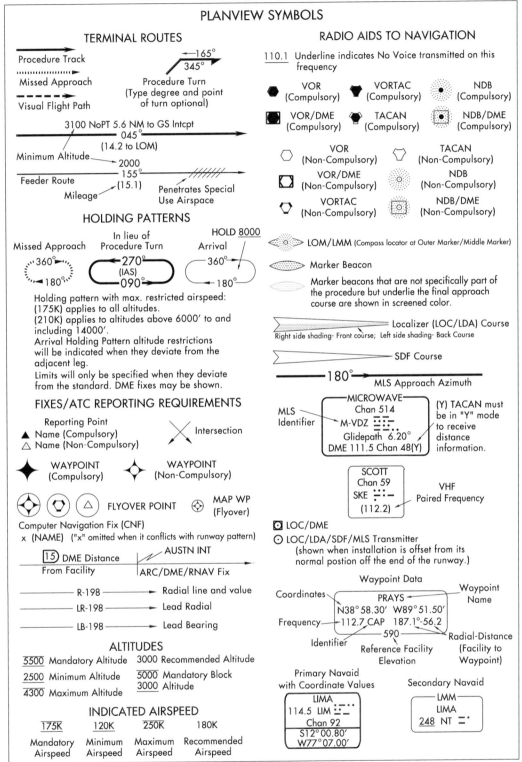

PLANVIEW SYMBOLS

TERMINAL ROUTES

Procedure Track

Missed Approach

Visual Flight Path

Procedure Turn
(Type degree and point
of turn optional)
—165°
345°

3100 NoPT 5.6 NM to GS Intcpt
045°
(14.2 to LOM)
Minimum Altitude
2000
155°
Feeder Route
(15.1)
Mileage
Penetrates Special
Use Airspace

HOLDING PATTERNS

Missed Approach
360°
180°

In lieu of
Procedure Turn
270°
(IAS)
090°

HOLD 8000
Arrival
360°
180°

Holding pattern with max. restricted airspeed:
(175K) applies to all altitudes.
(210K) applies to altitudes above 6000' to and
including 14000'.
Arrival Holding Pattern altitude restrictions
will be indicated when they deviate from the
adjacent leg.
Limits will only be specified when they deviate
from the standard. DME fixes may be shown.

FIXES/ATC REPORTING REQUIREMENTS

Reporting Point
▲ Name (Compulsory)
△ Name (Non-Compulsory)

Intersection

◆ WAYPOINT
(Compulsory)

◇ WAYPOINT
(Non-Compulsory)

FLYOVER POINT

MAP WP
(Flyover)

Computer Navigation Fix (CNF)
x (NAME) ("x" omitted when it conflicts with runway pattern)

15 DME Distance
From Facility

AUSTN INT
ARC/DME/RNAV Fix

R-198 → Radial line and value

LR-198 → Lead Radial

LB-198 → Lead Bearing

ALTITUDES

5500 Mandatory Altitude

2500 Minimum Altitude

4300 Maximum Altitude

3000 Recommended Altitude

5000 Mandatory Block
3000 Altitude

INDICATED AIRSPEED

175K
Mandatory
Airspeed

120K
Minimum
Airspeed

250K
Maximum
Airspeed

180K
Recommended
Airspeed

RADIO AIDS TO NAVIGATION

110.1 Underline indicates No Voice transmitted on this
frequency

VOR
(Compulsory)

VORTAC
(Compulsory)

NDB
(Compulsory)

VOR/DME
(Compulsory)

TACAN
(Compulsory)

NDB/DME
(Compulsory)

VOR
(Non-Compulsory)

TACAN
(Non-Compulsory)

VOR/DME
(Non-Compulsory)

NDB
(Non-Compulsory)

VORTAC
(Non-Compulsory)

NDB/DME
(Non-Compulsory)

LOM/LMM (Compass locator at Outer Marker/Middle Marker)

Marker Beacon

Marker beacons that are not specifically part of
the procedure but underlie the final approach
course are shown in screened color.

Localizer (LOC/LDA) Course
Right side shading- Front course; Left side shading- Back Course

SDF Course

—180°→
MLS Approach Azimuth

MLS
Identifier

MICROWAVE
Chan 514
M-VDZ
Glidepath 6.20°
DME 111.5 Chan 48(Y)

(Y) TACAN must
be in "Y" mode
to receive
distance
information.

SCOTT
Chan 59
SKE
(112.2)

VHF
Paired Frequency

LOC/DME

LOC/LDA/SDF/MLS Transmitter
(shown when installation is offset from its
normal postion off the end of the runway.)

Waypoint Data

Coordinates
Frequency
Identifier

PRAYS
N38°58.30′ W89°51.50′
112.7 CAP 187.1°-56.2
590

Waypoint
Name
Reference Facility
Elevation

Radial-Distance
(Facility to
Waypoint)

Primary Navaid
with Coordinate Values

LIMA
114.5 LIM
Chan 92
S12°00.80′
W77°07.00′

Secondary Navaid

LMM
LIMA
248 NT

LEGEND

LEGEND 24.—Instrument Approach Procedures (Symbols).

10266
LEGEND

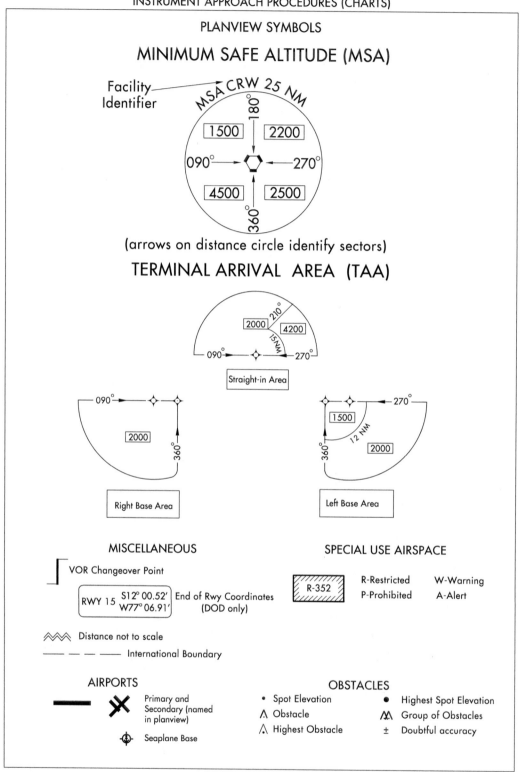

PLANVIEW SYMBOLS

MINIMUM SAFE ALTITUDE (MSA)

(arrows on distance circle identify sectors)

TERMINAL ARRIVAL AREA (TAA)

LEGEND

LEGEND 25.—Instrument Approach Procedures (Symbols).

13346
LEGEND
INSTRUMENT APPROACH PROCEDURES (CHARTS)

PROFILE VIEW

Two different methods are used for vertical guidance:

a. "GS" indicates an electronic glide slope or barometric vertical guidance is present. In the case of an Instrument Landing System (ILS) and Wide Area Augmentation System (WAAS) LPV approach procedures, an electronic signal provides vertical guidance. Barometric vertical guidance is provided for RNP and LNAV/VNAV instrument approach procedures. All ILS, LPV, RNP, and LNAV/VNAV will be in this format $\frac{GS\ 3.00°}{TCH\ 55}$, located in the lower left or right corner.

b. Other charts without electronic or barometric vertical guidance will be in this format $\frac{∠3.00°}{TCH\ 55}$, indicating a non-precision vertical descent angle to assist in preventing controlled flight into terrain. On Civil (FAA) procedures, this information is placed above or below the procedure track following the fix it is based on.

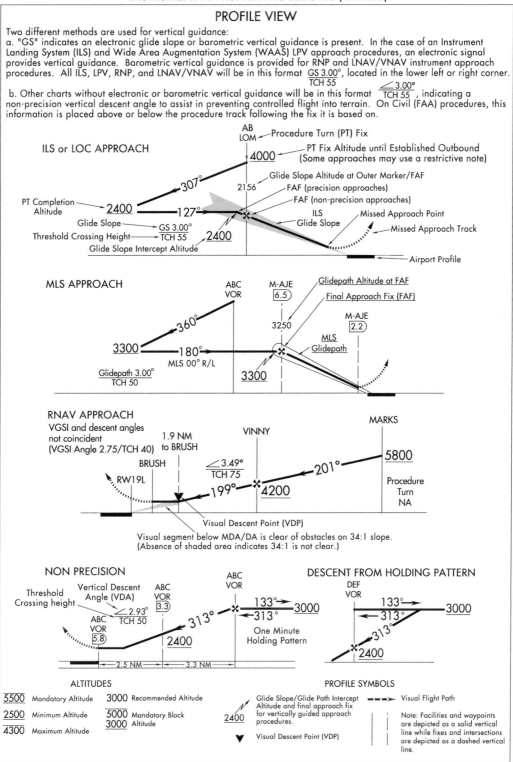

LEGEND
13346

LEGEND 26.—Instrument Approach Procedures (Profile).

CLIMB/DESCENT TABLE 10042

INSTRUMENT TAKEOFF OR APPROACH PROCEDURE CHARTS RATE OF CLIMB/DESCENT TABLE

(ft. per min)

A rate of climb/descent table is provided for use in planning and executing climbs or descents under known or approximate ground speed conditions. It will be especially useful for approaches when the localizer only is used for course guidance. A best speed, power, altitude combination can be programmed which will result in a stable glide rate and altitude favorable for executing a landing if minimums exist upon breakout. Care should always be exercised so that minimum descent altitude and missed approach point are not exceeded.

	CLIMB/ DESCENT ANGLE (degrees and tenths)	ft/NM	GROUND SPEED (knots)										
			60	90	120	150	180	210	240	270	300	330	360
	2.0	210	210	320	425	530	635	743	850	955	1060	1165	1275
	2.5	265	265	400	530	665	795	930	1060	1195	1325	1460	1590
VERTICAL PATH ANGLE	2.7	287	287	430	574	717	860	1003	1147	1290	1433	1576	1720
	2.8	297	297	446	595	743	892	1041	1189	1338	1486	1635	1783
	2.9	308	308	462	616	770	924	1078	1232	1386	1539	1693	1847
	3.0	318	318	478	637	797	956	1115	1274	1433	1593	1752	1911
	3.1	329	329	494	659	823	988	1152	1317	1481	1646	1810	1975
	3.2	340	340	510	680	850	1020	1189	1359	1529	1699	1869	2039
	3.3	350	350	526	701	876	1052	1227	1402	1577	1752	1927	2103
	3.4	361	361	542	722	903	1083	1264	1444	1625	1805	1986	2166
	3.5	370	370	555	745	930	1115	1300	1485	1670	1860	2045	2230
	4.0	425	425	640	850	1065	1275	1490	1700	1915	2125	2340	2550
	4.5	480	480	715	955	1195	1435	1675	1915	2150	2390	2630	2870
	5.0	530	530	795	1065	1330	1595	1860	2125	2390	2660	2925	3190
	5.5	585	585	880	1170	1465	1755	2050	2340	2635	2925	3220	3510
	6.0	640	640	960	1275	1595	1915	2235	2555	2875	3195	3510	3830
	6.5	690	690	1040	1385	1730	2075	2425	2770	3115	3460	3805	4155
	7.0	745	745	1120	1490	1865	2240	2610	2985	3355	3730	4105	4475
	7.5	800	800	1200	1600	2000	2400	2800	3200	3600	4000	4400	4800
	8.0	855	855	1280	1710	2135	2560	2990	3415	3845	4270	4695	5125
	8.5	910	910	1360	1815	2270	2725	3180	3630	4085	4540	4995	5450
	9.0	960	960	1445	1925	2405	2885	3370	3850	4330	4810	5295	5775
	9.5	1015	1015	1525	2035	2540	3050	3560	4065	4575	5085	5590	6100
	10.0	1070	1070	1605	2145	2680	3215	3750	4285	4820	5355	5890	6430

CLIMB/DESCENT TABLE 10042

LEGEND 27.—Instrument Takeoff or Approach Procedure Charts, Rate-of-Climb/Descent Table.

12320
LEGEND

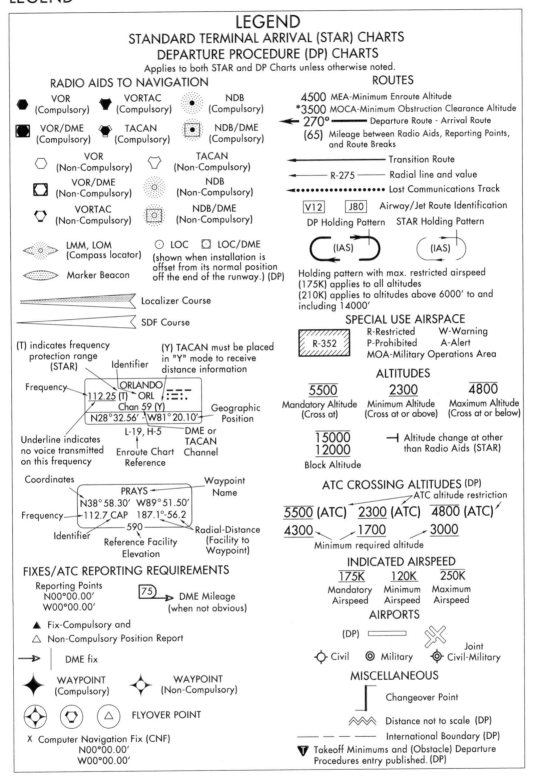

LEGEND
STANDARD TERMINAL ARRIVAL (STAR) CHARTS
DEPARTURE PROCEDURE (DP) CHARTS
Applies to both STAR and DP Charts unless otherwise noted.

RADIO AIDS TO NAVIGATION

VOR (Compulsory) VORTAC (Compulsory) NDB (Compulsory)

VOR/DME (Compulsory) TACAN (Compulsory) NDB/DME (Compulsory)

VOR (Non-Compulsory) TACAN (Non-Compulsory)

VOR/DME (Non-Compulsory) NDB (Non-Compulsory)

VORTAC (Non-Compulsory) NDB/DME (Non-Compulsory)

LMM, LOM (Compass locator) LOC LOC/DME
(shown when installation is offset from its normal position off the end of the runway.) (DP)

Marker Beacon

Localizer Course

SDF Course

(T) indicates frequency protection range (STAR)

(Y) TACAN must be placed in "Y" mode to receive distance information

Identifier

Frequency

ORLANDO ORL
112.25 (T) Chan 59 (Y)
N28°32.56' W81°20.10'
L-19, H-5

Geographic Position

Underline indicates no voice transmitted on this frequency

Enroute Chart Reference

DME or TACAN Channel

Coordinates

Waypoint Name

PRAYS
N38°58.30' W89°51.50'
112.7 CAP 187.1°-56.2
590

Frequency

Identifier

Reference Facility Elevation

Radial-Distance (Facility to Waypoint)

FIXES/ATC REPORTING REQUIREMENTS

Reporting Points
N00°00.00'
W00°00.00'

75 DME Mileage (when not obvious)

▲ Fix-Compulsory and
△ Non-Compulsory Position Report

→ DME fix

WAYPOINT (Compulsory) WAYPOINT (Non-Compulsory)

FLYOVER POINT

X Computer Navigation Fix (CNF)
N00°00.00'
W00°00.00'

ROUTES

4500 MEA-Minimum Enroute Altitude
*3500 MOCA-Minimum Obstruction Clearance Altitude
270° Departure Route - Arrival Route
(65) Mileage between Radio Aids, Reporting Points, and Route Breaks

Transition Route

R-275 Radial line and value

Lost Communications Track

V12 J80 Airway/Jet Route Identification

DP Holding Pattern STAR Holding Pattern

(IAS) (IAS)

Holding pattern with max. restricted airspeed
(175K) applies to all altitudes
(210K) applies to altitudes above 6000' to and including 14000'

SPECIAL USE AIRSPACE

R-352 R-Restricted W-Warning
P-Prohibited A-Alert
MOA-Military Operations Area

ALTITUDES

5500 2300 4800
Mandatory Altitude (Cross at) Minimum Altitude (Cross at or above) Maximum Altitude (Cross at or below)

15000
12000 Altitude change at other than Radio Aids (STAR)

Block Altitude

ATC CROSSING ALTITUDES (DP)

ATC altitude restriction

5500 (ATC) 2300 (ATC) 4800 (ATC)
4300 1700 3000

Minimum required altitude

INDICATED AIRSPEED

175K 120K 250K
Mandatory Airspeed Minimum Airspeed Maximum Airspeed

AIRPORTS

(DP)

Joint

Civil Military Civil-Military

MISCELLANEOUS

Changeover Point

Distance not to scale (DP)

International Boundary (DP)

▼ Takeoff Minimums and (Obstacle) Departure Procedures entry published. (DP)

LEGEND

LEGEND 28.—Standard Arrival/Departure Charts.

13010
LEGEND

AIRPORT DIAGRAM/AIRPORT SKETCH

Runways

| Hard Surface | Other Than Hard Surface | Stopways,Taxiways, Parking Areas, Water Runways | Displaced Threshold |

| Closed Runway | Closed Taxiway | Under Construction | Metal Surface |

ARRESTING GEAR: Specific arresting gear systems; e.g., BAK12, MA-1A etc., shown on airport diagrams, not applicable to Civil Pilots. Military Pilots refer to appropriate DOD publications.

⌐ uni-directional   ⌐ bi-directional   ⟩ Jet Barrier

ARRESTING SYSTEM [   ]

REFERENCE FEATURES

Buildings.. ■

24-Hour Self-Serve Fuel ##.............................. ⛽

Tanks.. ●

Obstructions... ∧

Airport Beacon #.. ☆

Runway
Radar Reflectors.. ⊼

Hot Spot .... ◯

Control Tower #.......................................TWR ■

When Control Tower and Rotating Beacon are co-located, Beacon symbol will be used and further identified as TWR.

A fuel symbol is shown to indicate 24-hour self-serve fuel available, see appropriate A/FD, Alaska or Pacific Supplement for information.

Runway length depicted is the physical length of the runway (end-to-end, including displaced thresholds if any) but excluding areas designated as stopways.

A **D** symbol is shown to indicate runway declared distance information available, see appropriate A/FD, Alaska or Pacific Supplement for distance information.

Runway Weight Bearing Capacity/or PCN Pavement Classification Number is shown as a codified expression. Refer to the appropriate Supplement/Directory for applicable codes e.g., RWY 14-32 PCN 80 F/D/X/U S-75, D-185, 2S-175, 2D-325

Helicopter Alighting Areas   Ⓗ ⊞ Ⓗ ⚠ ⊞

Negative Symbols used to identify Copter Procedures landing point..................... ● ⊞ ◼ ⚠ ✚

Runway Threshold elevation............THRE 123
Runway TDZ elevation....................TDZE 123
←─0.3% DOWN
Runway Slope................................0.8% UP ─→
   (shown when runway slope is greater than or equal to 0.3%)
NOTE:
Runway Slope measured to midpoint on runways 8000 feet or longer.

▣ U.S. Navy Optical Landing System (OLS) "OLS" location is shown because of its height of approximately 7 feet and proximity to edge of runway may create an obstruction for some types of aircraft.

Approach light symbols are shown in the Flight Information Handbook.

Airport diagram scales are variable.

True/magnetic North orientation may vary from diagram to diagram

Coordinate values are shown in 1 or ½ minute increments. They are further broken down into 6 second ticks, within each 1 minute increments.

Positional accuracy within ±600 feet unless otherwise noted on the chart.

NOTE:
All new and revised airport diagrams are shown referenced to the World Geodetic System (WGS) (noted on appropriate diagram), and may not be compatible with local coordinates published in FLIP. (Foreign Only)

SCOPE

Airport diagrams are specifically designed to assist in the movement of ground traffic at locations with complex runway/taxiway configurations. Airport diagrams are not intended to be used for approach and landing or departure operations. For revisions to Airport Diagrams: Consult FAA Order 7910.4.

LEGEND

LEGEND 29.—Airport Diagram.

09239
LEGEND

INSTRUMENT APPROACH PROCEDURES (CHARTS)
APPROACH LIGHTING SYSTEM - UNITED STATES

Approach lighting and visual glide slope systems are indicated on the airport sketch by an identifier, e.g., (A2), (V), etc.

A dot "●" portrayed with approach lighting letter identifier indicates sequenced flashing lights (F) installed with the approach lighting system e.g., (A1). Negative symbology, e.g., (A1), (V) indicates Pilot Controlled Lighting (PCL).

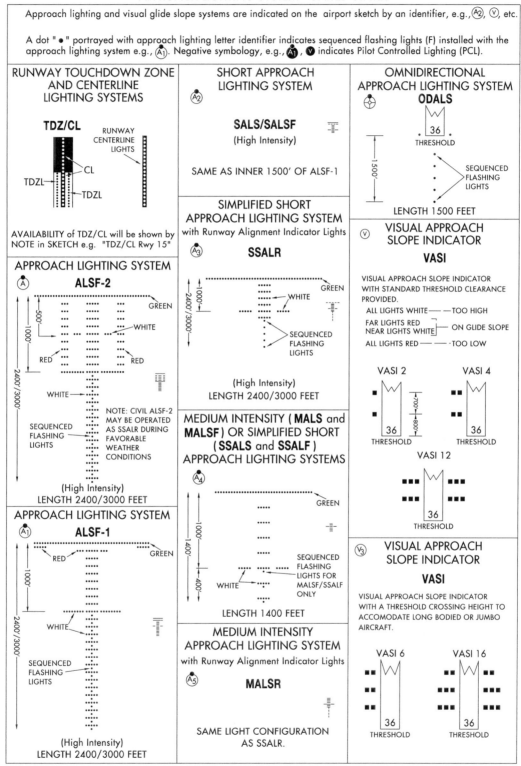

LEGEND

LEGEND

Approach lighting and visual glide slope systems are indicated on the airport sketch by an identifier, Ⓐ₂, Ⓥ etc.

A dot "●" portrayed with approach lighting letter identifier indicates sequenced flashing lights (F) installed with the approach lighting system e.g., Ⓐ₁. Negative symbology, e.g., ⬤₁, ⬤ indicates Pilot Controlled Lighting (PCL).

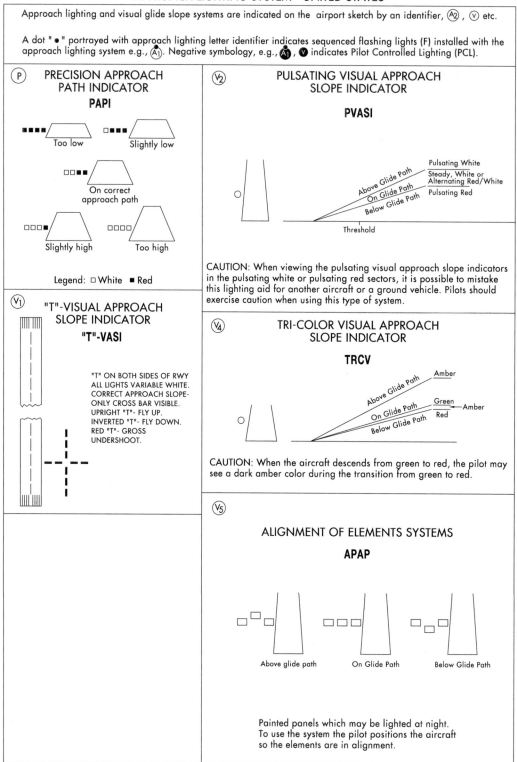

Ⓟ **PRECISION APPROACH PATH INDICATOR**

PAPI

Too low · Slightly low · On correct approach path · Slightly high · Too high

Legend: □ White ■ Red

Ⓥ₁ **"T"-VISUAL APPROACH SLOPE INDICATOR**

"T"-VASI

"T" ON BOTH SIDES OF RWY ALL LIGHTS VARIABLE WHITE. CORRECT APPROACH SLOPE-ONLY CROSS BAR VISIBLE. UPRIGHT "T"- FLY UP. INVERTED "T"- FLY DOWN. RED "T"- GROSS UNDERSHOOT.

Ⓥ₂ **PULSATING VISUAL APPROACH SLOPE INDICATOR**

PVASI

Above Glide Path — Pulsating White
On Glide Path — Steady, White or Alternating Red/White
Below Glide Path — Pulsating Red

Threshold

CAUTION: When viewing the pulsating visual approach slope indicators in the pulsating white or pulsating red sectors, it is possible to mistake this lighting aid for another aircraft or a ground vehicle. Pilots should exercise caution when using this type of system.

Ⓥ₄ **TRI-COLOR VISUAL APPROACH SLOPE INDICATOR**

TRCV

Above Glide Path — Amber
On Glide Path — Green
Below Glide Path — Red — Amber

CAUTION: When the aircraft descends from green to red, the pilot may see a dark amber color during the transition from green to red.

Ⓥ₅

ALIGNMENT OF ELEMENTS SYSTEMS

APAP

Above glide path · On Glide Path · Below Glide Path

Painted panels which may be lighted at night. To use the system the pilot positions the aircraft so the elements are in alignment.

LEGEND

LEGEND 31.—Approach Lighting System.

INOPERATIVE COMPONENTS OR VISUAL AIDS TABLE

Landing minimums published on instrument approach procedure charts are based upon full operation of all components and visual aids associated with the particular instrument approach chart being used. Higher minimums are required with inoperative components or visual aids as indicated below. If more than one component is inoperative, each minimum is raised to the highest minimum required by any single component that is inoperative. ILS glide slope inoperative minimums are published on the instrument approach charts as localizer minimums. This table may be amended by notes on the approach chart. Such notes apply only to the particular approach category(ies) as stated. See legend page for description of components indicated below.

(1) ILS, MLS, PAR and RNAV (LPV line of minima)

Inoperative Component or Aid	Approach Category	Increase Visibility
ALSF 1 & 2, MALSR, & SSALR	ABCD	¼ mile

(2) ILS with visibility minimum of 1,800 RVR

ALSF 1 & 2, MALSR, & SSALR	ABCD	To 4000 RVR
TDZL RCLS	ABCD	To 2400 RVR*
RVR	ABCD	To ½ mile

*1800 RVR authorized with the use of FD or AP or HUD to DA.

(3) VOR, VOR/DME, TACAN, LOC, LOC/DME, LDA, LDA/DME, SDF, SDF/DME, GPS, ASR and RNAV (LNAV/VNAV, LP, LNAV lines of minima)

Inoperative Visual Aid	Approach Category	Increase Visibility
ALSF 1 & 2, MALSR, & SSALR	ABCD	½ mile
SSALS, MALS, & ODALS	ABC	¼ mile

(4) NDB

ALSF 1 & 2, MALSR, & SSALR	C	½ mile
	ABD	¼ mile
MALS, SSALS, ODALS	ABC	¼ mile

INOP COMPONENTS

LEGEND 32.—Inoperative Components or Visual Aids Table.

UNITED STATES GOVERNMENT
FLIGHT INFORMATION PUBLICATION

IFR ENROUTE LOW ALTITUDE - U.S.

For use up to but not including 18,000' MSL
HORIZONTAL DATUM: NORTH AMERICAN DATUM OF 1983

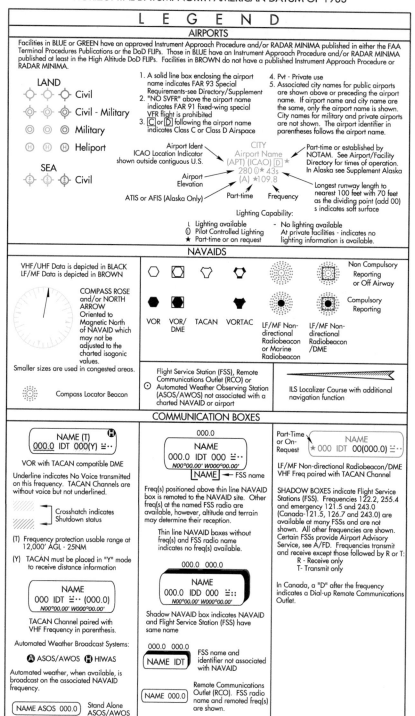

LEGEND 33.—IFR En Route Low Altitude (U.S.)

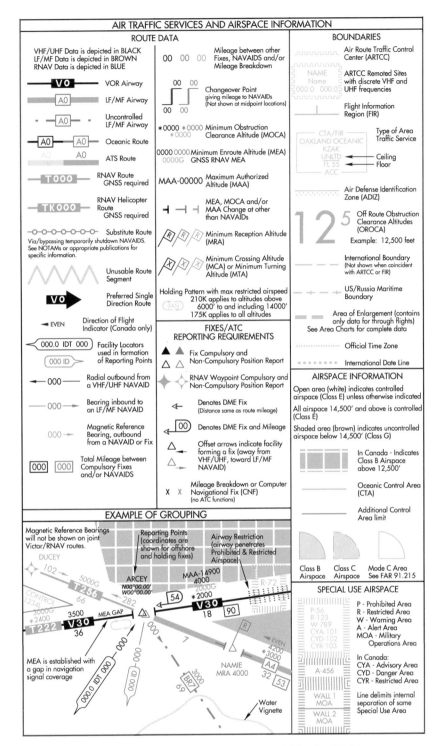

LEGEND 34.—IFR En Route Low Altitude (U.S.)

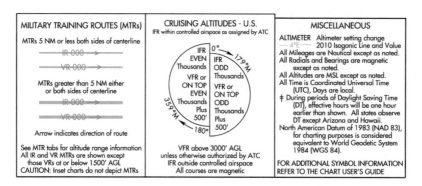

LEGEND 35.—IFR En Route Low Altitude (U.S.)

SUFFIX	Aircraft Equipment Suffixes
AIRCRAFT EQUIPMENT SUFFIXES	
	NO DME
/X	No transponder
/T	Transponder with no Mode C
/U	Transponder with Mode C
	DME
/D	No transponder
/B	Transponder with no Mode C
/A	Transponder with Mode C
	TACAN ONLY
/M	No transponder
/N	Transponder with no Mode C
/P	Transponder with Mode C
	AREA NAVIGATION (RNAV)
/Y	LORAN, VOR/DME, or INS with no transponder
/C	LORAN, VOR/DME, or INS, transponder with no Mode C
/I	LORAN, VOR/DME, or INS, transponder with Mode C
	ADVANCED RNAV WITH TRANSPONDER AND MODE C (if an aircraft is unable to operate with a transponder and/or Mode C, it will revert to the appropriate code listed above under Area Navigation.)
/E	Flight Management System (FMS) with en route, terminal, and approach capability. Equipment requirements are: (a) Dual FMS which meets the specifications of AC 25-15, Approval of Flight Management Systems in Transport Category Airplanes; AC 20-129, Airworthiness Approval of Vertical Navigation (VNAV) Systems for use in the U.S. NAS and Alaska; AC 20-130, Airworthiness Approval of Navigation or Flight Management Systems Integrating Multiple Navigation Sensors; or equivalent criteria as approved by Flight Standards. (b) A flight director and autopilot control system capable of following the lateral and vertical FMS flight path. (c) At least dual inertial reference units (IRU's). (d) A database containing the waypoints and speed/altitude constraints for the route and/or procedure to be flown that is automatically loaded into the FMS flight plan. (e) An electronic map. (U.S. and U.S. territories only unless otherwise authorized.)
/F	A single FMS with en route, terminal, and approach capability that meets the equipment requirements of /E, (a) through (d), above. (U.S. and U.S. territories only unless otherwise authorized.)
/G	Global Positioning System (GPS)/Global Navigation Satellite System (GNSS) equipped aircraft with en route and terminal capability.
/R	Required Navigational Performance (Denotes capability to operate in RNP designated airspace and routes)
/W	Reduced Vertical Separation Minima (RVSM)

LEGEND 36.—Aircraft Equipment Suffixes.

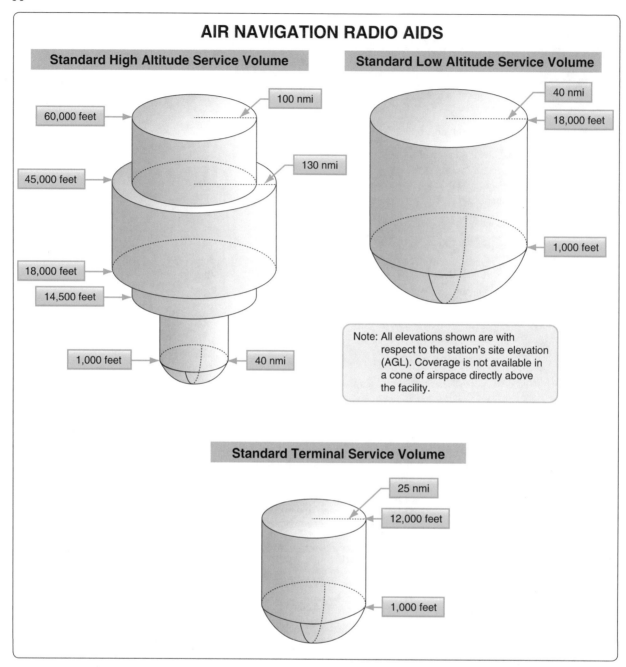

LEGEND 37.—Air Navigation Radio Aids.

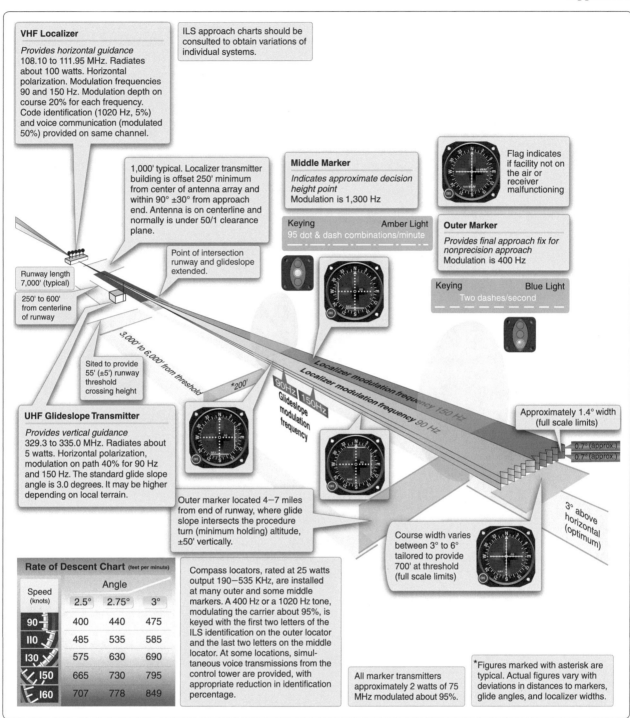

VHF Localizer

Provides horizontal guidance 108.10 to 111.95 MHz. Radiates about 100 watts. Horizontal polarization. Modulation frequencies 90 and 150 Hz. Modulation depth on course 20% for each frequency. Code identification (1020 Hz, 5%) and voice communication (modulated 50%) provided on same channel.

ILS approach charts should be consulted to obtain variations of individual systems.

1,000' typical. Localizer transmitter building is offset 250' minimum from center of antenna array and within 90° ±30° from approach end. Antenna is on centerline and normally is under 50/1 clearance plane.

Middle Marker

Indicates approximate decision height point Modulation is 1,300 Hz

Keying	Amber Light
95 dot & dash combinations/minute	

Flag indicates if facility not on the air or receiver malfunctioning

Outer Marker

Provides final approach fix for nonprecision approach Modulation is 400 Hz

Keying	Blue Light
Two dashes/second	

Point of intersection runway and glideslope extended.

Runway length 7,000' (typical)

250' to 600' from centerline of runway

3,000' to 6,000' from threshold

Sited to provide 55' (±5') runway threshold crossing height

*200'

90Hz 150Hz
Glideslope modulation frequency

Localizer modulation frequency 150 Hz
Localizer modulation frequency 90 Hz

UHF Glideslope Transmitter

Provides vertical guidance 329.3 to 335.0 MHz. Radiates about 5 watts. Horizontal polarization, modulation on path 40% for 90 Hz and 150 Hz. The standard glide slope angle is 3.0 degrees. It may be higher depending on local terrain.

Outer marker located 4–7 miles from end of runway, where glide slope intersects the procedure turn (minimum holding) altitude, ±50' vertically.

Course width varies between 3° to 6° tailored to provide 700' at threshold (full scale limits)

Approximately 1.4° width (full scale limits)

0.7° (approx.)
0.7° (approx.)

3° above horizontal (optimum)

Rate of Descent Chart (feet per minute)

Speed (knots)	Angle		
	2.5°	2.75°	3°
90	400	440	475
110	485	535	585
130	575	630	690
150	665	730	795
160	707	778	849

Compass locators, rated at 25 watts output 190–535 KHz, are installed at many outer and some middle markers. A 400 Hz or a 1020 Hz tone, modulating the carrier about 95%, is keyed with the first two letters of the ILS identification on the outer locator and the last two letters on the middle locator. At some locations, simultaneous voice transmissions from the control tower are provided, with appropriate reduction in identification percentage.

All marker transmitters approximately 2 watts of 75 MHz modulated about 95%.

*Figures marked with asterisk are typical. Actual figures vary with deviations in distances to markers, glide angles, and localizer widths.

LEGEND 38.—ILS Standard Characteristics and Terminology.

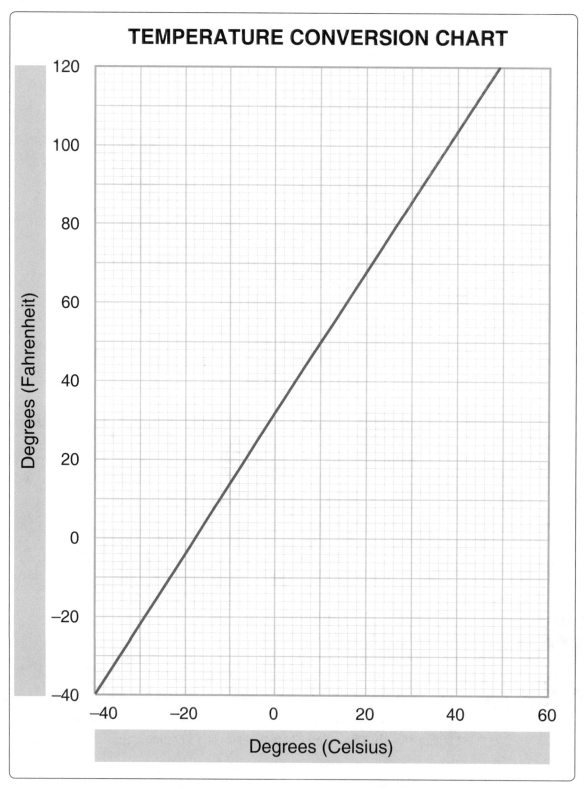

LEGEND 39.—Temperature Conversion Chart.

APPENDIX 2

VALID 1600Z FOR USE 0900-1500Z. TEMPS NEG ABV 24000									
FT	3000	6000	9000	12000	18000	24000	30000	34000	39000
EMI	2807	2715-07	2728-10	2842-13	2867-21	2891-30	751041	771150	780855
ALB	0210	9900-07	2714-09	2728-12	2656-19	2777-28	781842	760150	269658
PSB		1509+04	2119+01	2233-04	2262-14	2368-26	781939	760850	780456
STL	2308	2613+02	2422-03	2431-08	2446-19	2461-30	760142	782650	760559

FIGURE 2.—Wind and Temperatures Aloft Forecast.

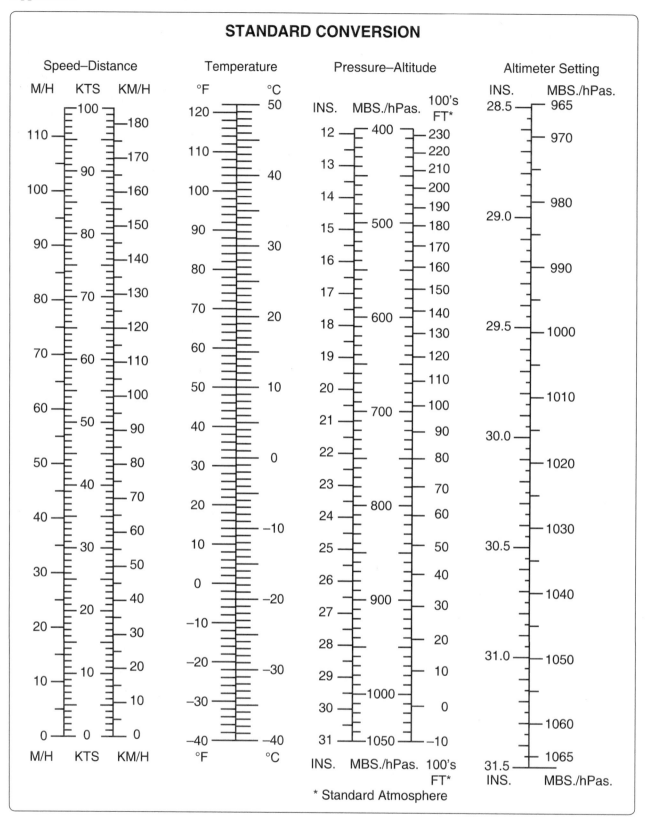

Figure 3.—Standard Conversion Chart.

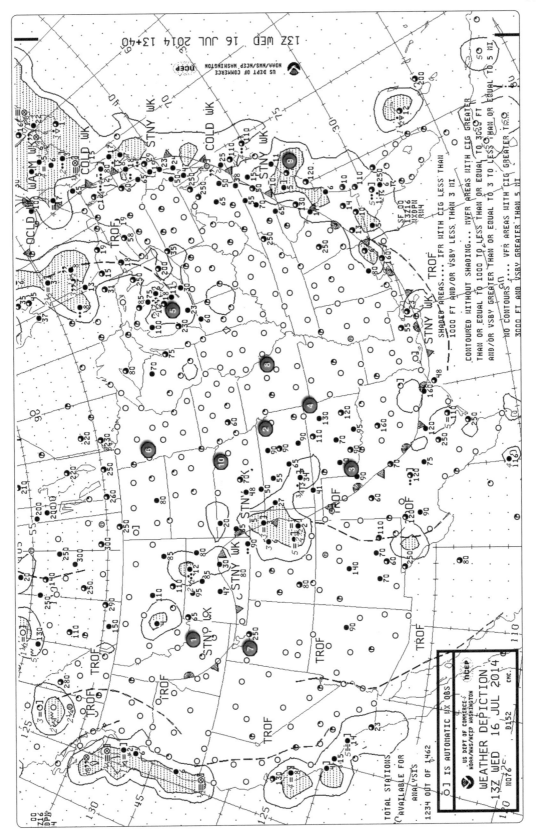

FIGURE 4.—Weather Depiction Chart.

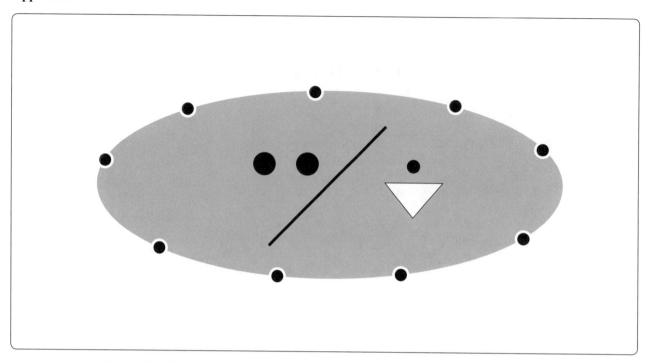

FIGURE 5.—Symbol Used on Low-Level Significant Weather Prognostic Chart.

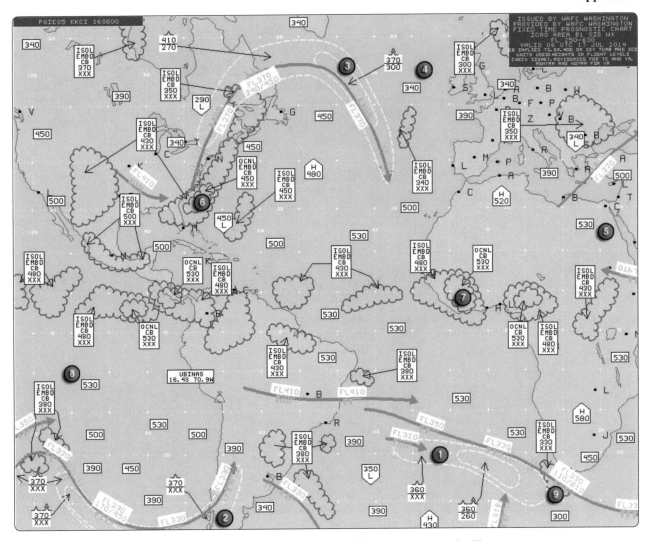

FIGURE 7.—High-Level Significant Weather Prognostic Chart.

Appendix 2

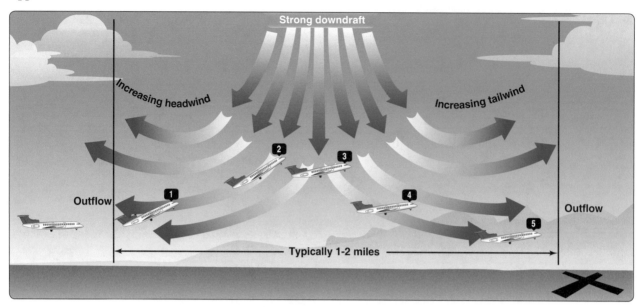

FIGURE 13.—Microburst Section Chart.

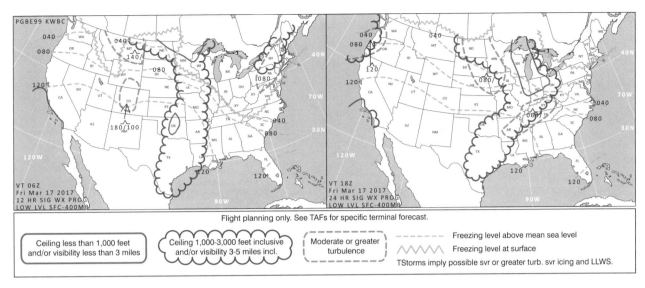

FIGURE 18.—U.S. Low-Level Significant Weather Prognostic Charts.

Appendix 2

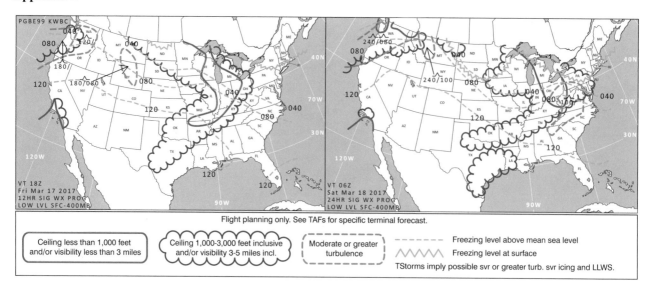

FIGURE 19.—U.S. Low-Level Significant Weather Prognostic Charts.

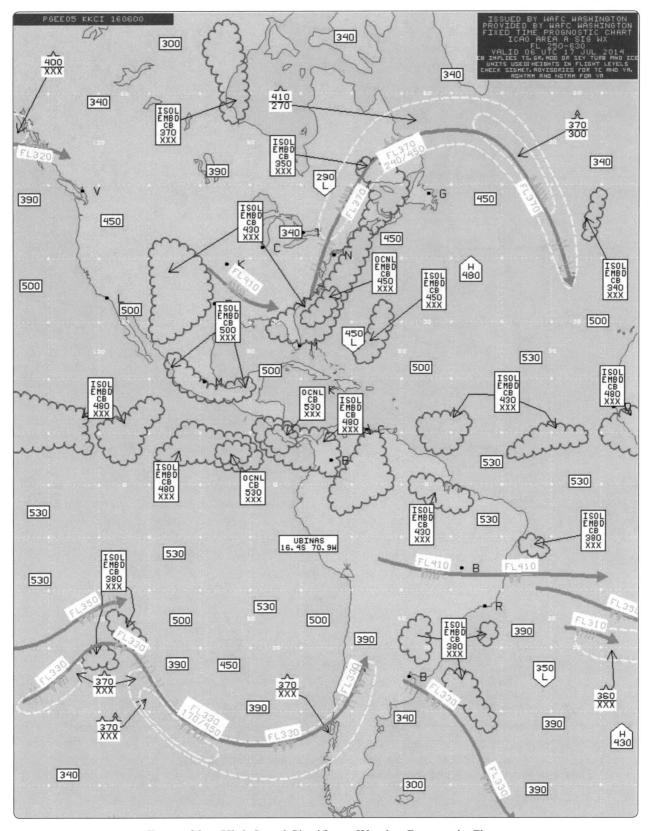

FIGURE 20.—High-Level Significant Weather Prognostic Chart.

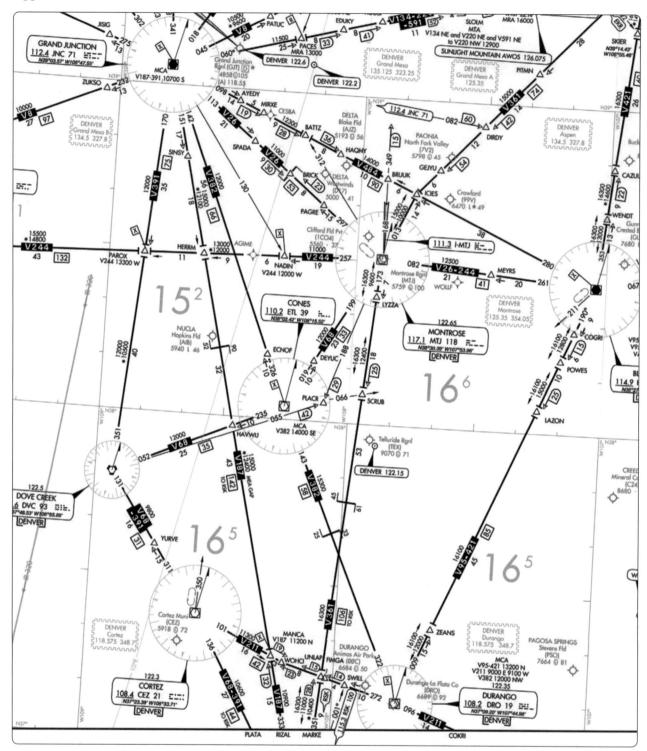

FIGURE 24.—En Route Low-Altitude Chart Segment.
NOTE: Chart is not to scale and should not be used for navigation. Chart is for testing purposes only.

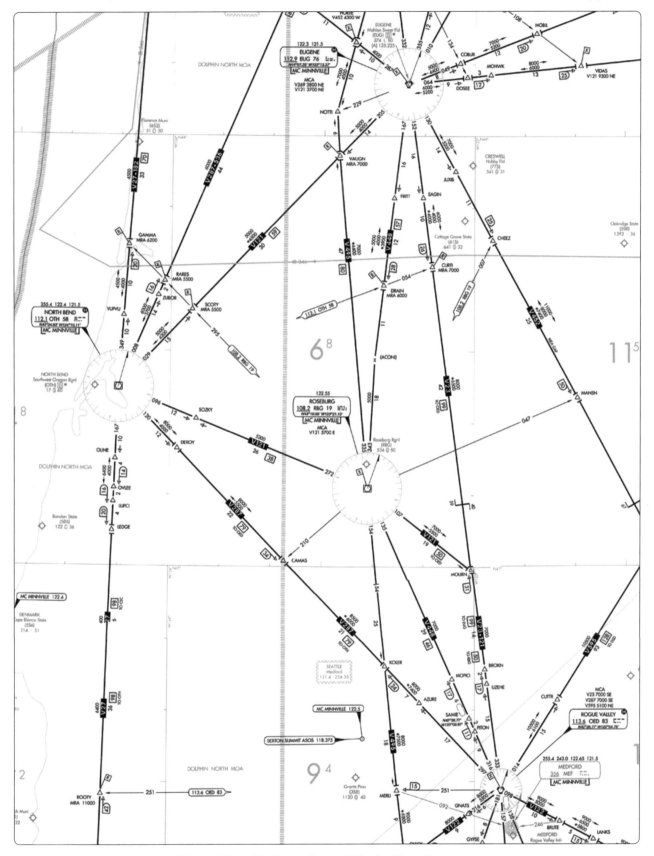

Figure 31.—En Route Low-Altitude Chart Segment.
NOTE: Chart is not to scale and should not be used for navigation. Chart is for testing purposes only.

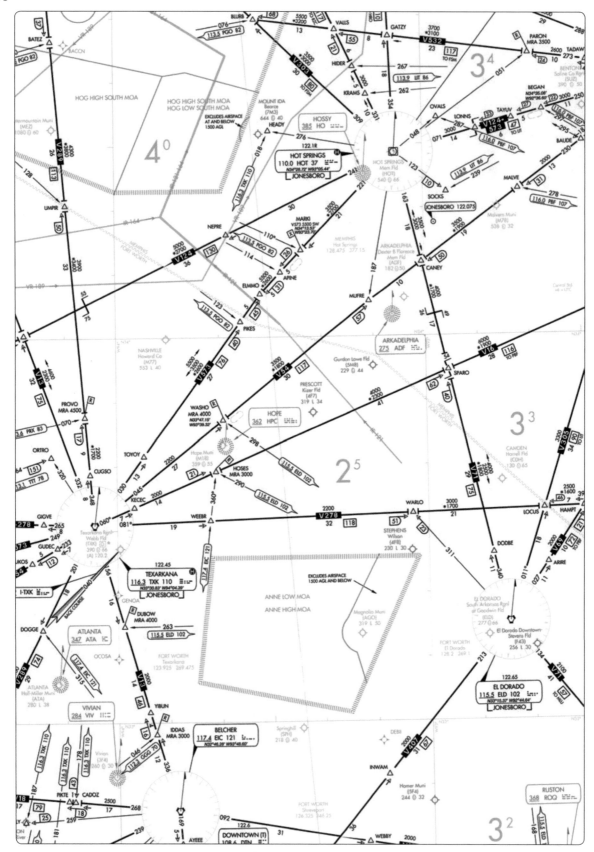

FIGURE 34.—En Route Low-Altitude Chart Segment.
NOTE: Chart is not to scale and should not be used for navigation. Chart is for testing purposes only.

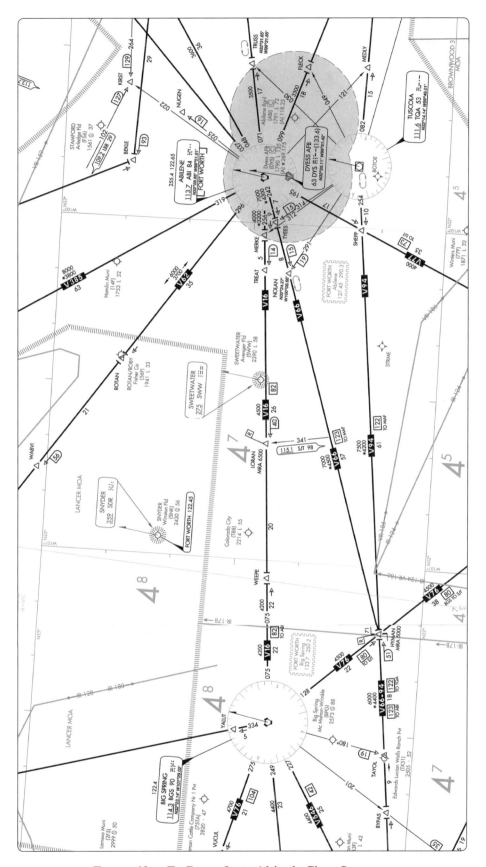

FIGURE 40.—En Route Low-Altitude Chart Segment.
NOTE: Chart is not to scale and should not be used for navigation. Chart is for testing purposes only.

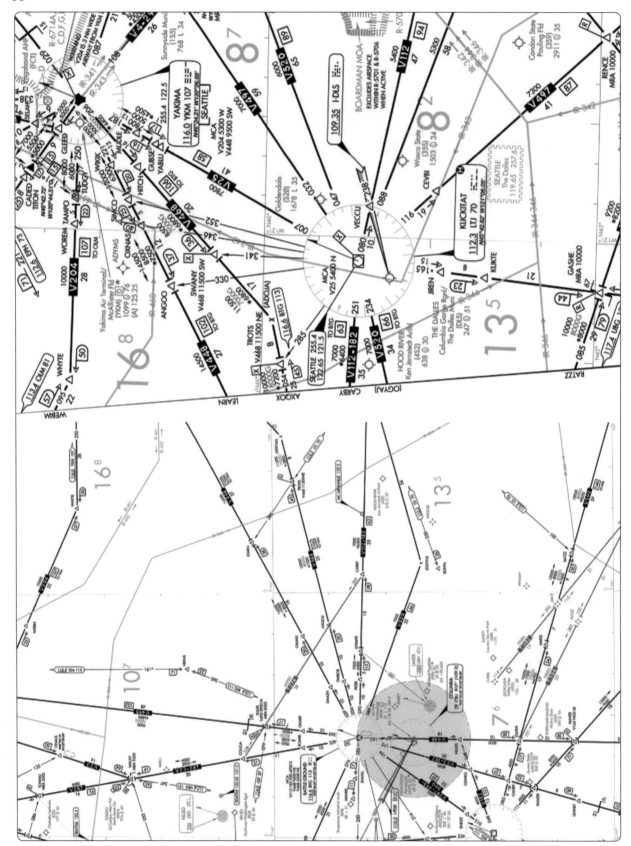

FIGURE 47.—En Route Low-Altitude Chart Segment.
NOTE: Chart is not to scale and should not be used for navigation. Chart is for testing purposes only.

NAV - 1			
FREQ	N.M.	KNOTS	MIN
116.0	9.0	7	////

FIGURE 48.—CDI—NAV 1.

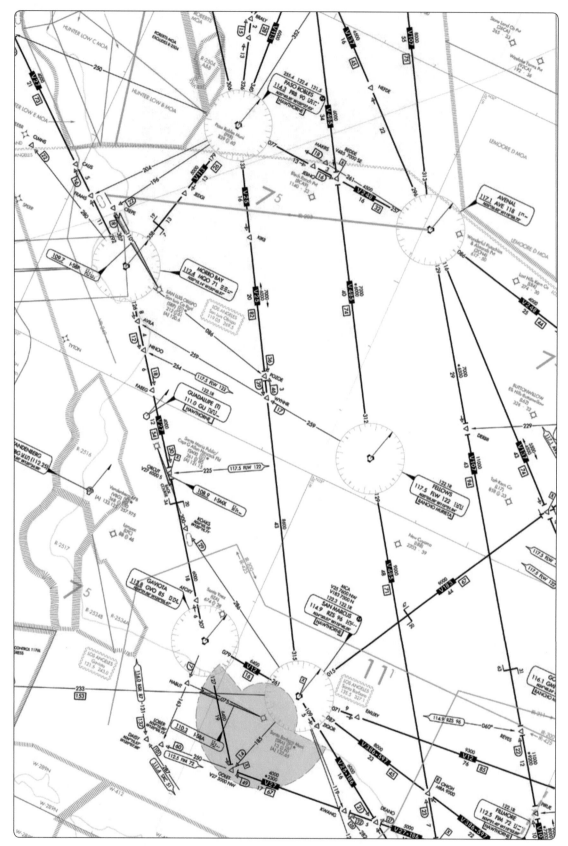

FIGURE 53.—En Route Low-Altitude Chart Segment.
NOTE: Chart is not to scale and should not be used for navigation. Chart is for testing purposes only.

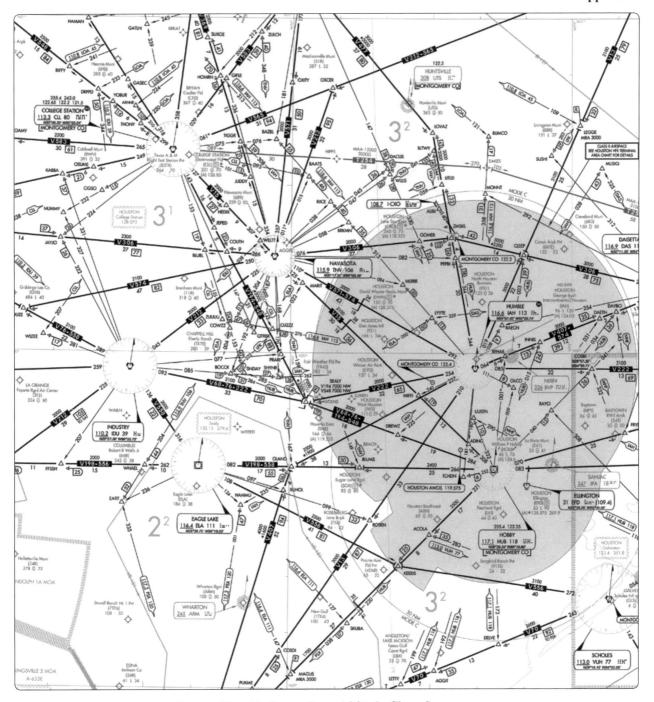

FIGURE 59.—En Route Low-Altitude Chart Segment.
NOTE: Chart is not to scale and should not be used for navigation. Chart is for testing purposes only.

FREQ	OBS	
109.9	038	//////

FIGURE 61.—CDI Indicator.

LOUISIANA
VOR RECEIVER CHECKPOINTS

Facility Name (Arpt Name)	Freq/Ident	Type Check Pt. Gnd. AB/ALT	Azimuth from Fac. Mag	Dist. from Fac. N.M.	Checkpoint Description
Alexandria (Alexandria Intl)	116.1/AEX	G	328	4.3	On runup Rwy 32.
Baton Rouge (Baton Rouge Metro, Ryan).	116.5/BTR	A/1500	063	7.2	Over water tank W side of arpt.
Lafayette (Lafayette Rgnl/Paul Fournet Fld)	109.8/LFT	A/1000	343	22.1	Over rotating beacon at St. Landry Parish–Ahart Fld. arpt.
	109.8/LFT	G	355	0.5	On Twy F run up area Rwy 04L.
	109.8/LFT	G	341	0.9	On Twy B run up area Rwy 11.
	109.8/LFT	G	025	1.4	On Twy J run up area Rwy 22L.
	109.8/LFT	G	039	0.8	On Twy B run up area Rwy 29.
Lake Charles (Lake Charles Rgnl)	113.4/LCH	A/1000	253	6.2	Over rotg bcn on twr.
Monroe (Monroe Rgnl)	117.2/MLU	G	212	0.7	On Twy G South of twr.
Natchez (Concordia Parish)	110.0/HEZ	A/1000	247	10.5	Over hangar NW end of fld.
Reserve (St John The Baptist Parish).......	110.8 RQR	A/1500	270	16.8	Over center of bridge.
Tibby (Houma–Terrebonne)	112.0/TBD	A/1000	121	10.7	Over intersection of Rwys 18–36 and 12–30.
Tibby (Thibodaux Muni)	112.0/TBD	A/1000	356	5.0	Over microwave twr near arpt.

---

84   **LOUISIANA**

LAFAYETTE RGNL (LFT)   2 SE   UTC–6(–5DT)   N30°12.30´ W91°59.27´   HOUSTON
42   B   S4   **FUEL** 100LL, JET A   OX 1, 4   Class I, ARFF Index B   NOTAM FILE LFT   H–7D, L–21B, 22E, GOMC
    RWY 04R–22L: H8001X150 (ASPH–GRVD)   S–140, D–170, 2S–175,   IAP, AD
       2D–290 HIRL
        RWY 04R: REIL. PAPI(P4L)—GA 3.0° TCH 53´. Pole. Rgt tfc.
        RWY 22L: MALSR. PAPI(P4L)—GA 3.0° TCH 52´. Thld dsplcd 342´.
       Trees.
    RWY 11–29: H5401X148 (ASPH–GRVD)   S–85, D–110, 2S–140,
       2D–175 MIRL
        RWY 11: REIL. PAPI(P4L)—GA 3.0° TCH 35´. Trees. Rgt tfc.
        RWY 29: REIL. PAPI(P4L)—GA 3.0° TCH 35´. Tree.
    RWY 04L–22R: H4099X75 (ASPH)   S–25, D–32 MIRL
        RWY 04L: REIL. PAPI(P2L)—GA 3.0° TCH 26´. Tree.
        RWY 22R: REIL. PAPI(P2L)—GA 3.0° TCH 27´. Tree. Rgt tfc.
    RUNWAY DECLARED DISTANCE INFORMATION
        RWY 04L:TORA–4099 TODA–4099   ASDA–4099   LDA–4099
        RWY 04R:TORA–8001 TODA–8001   ASDA–8001   LDA–8001
        RWY 11: TORA–5401 TODA–5401   ASDA–5401   LDA–5401
        RWY 22L:TORA–8001 TODA–8001   ASDA–8001   LDA–7659
        RWY 22R:TORA–4099 TODA–4099   ASDA–4099   LDA–4099
        RWY 29: TORA–5401 TODA–5401   ASDA–5401   LDA–5401
    ARRESTING GEAR/SYSTEM
        RWY 04R: EMAS
        RWY 22L: EMAS
    AIRPORT REMARKS: Attended continuously. Numerous birds on and invof arpt. PPR for unscheduled air carrier ops with more
       than 30 passenger seats call arpt manager 337–266–4400. Rwy 04L–22R not avbl for air carrier ops with more than 30
       passenger seats. Ctc ground control prior to push back from terminal. 155´ oil rig 1 NM southeast of arpt. Rwy 22L
       runway visual range touchdown avbl. Twy B between Twy C and Twy D clsd to acft with wingspan over 80´. Twy F south
       of Twy B clsd to single wheel acft over 25,000 lbs and dual wheel acft over 32,000 lbs. Twy F south of Twy B reduces
       to 40´ wide. When twr clsd ACTIVATE MALSR Rwy 22L—CTAF, MIRL Rwy 04L–22R not avbl.
    WEATHER DATA SOURCES: ASOS (337) 237–8153 HIWAS 109.8 LFT.
    COMMUNICATIONS: CTAF 118.5 ATIS 134.05 UNICOM 122.95
        RCO 122.35 (DE RIDDER RADIO)
   Ⓡ APP/DEP CON 121.1 (020°–210°) 128.7 (211°–019°) (1130–0430Z‡)
   Ⓡ HOUSTON CENTER APP/DEP CON 126.35 (0430–1130Z‡)
        TOWER 118.5 (1130–0430Z‡) GND CON 121.8 CLNC DEL 125.55
    AIRSPACE: CLASS C svc ctc APP CON svc 1130–0430Z‡ other times CLASS E.
    RADIO AIDS TO NAVIGATION: NOTAM FILE LFT.
        (L) VORTACW 109.8   LFT   Chan 35   N30°11.63´ W91°59.55´   at fld. 36/3E.   HIWAS.
        LAFFS NDB (LOM) 375   LF   N30°17.36´ W91°54.48´ 216° 6.5 NM to fld. Unmonitored when ATCT clsd.
        ILS/DME 110.9 I–TYN   Chan 46   Rwy 04R.   Class IE.
        ILS/DME 109.5 I–LFT   Chan 32   Rwy 22L.   Class IE. LOM LAFFS NDB. ILS and LOM unmonitored when ATCT clsd.
        ASR (1130–0430Z‡)

FIGURE 64.—Excerpt from Chart Supplement (LFT).

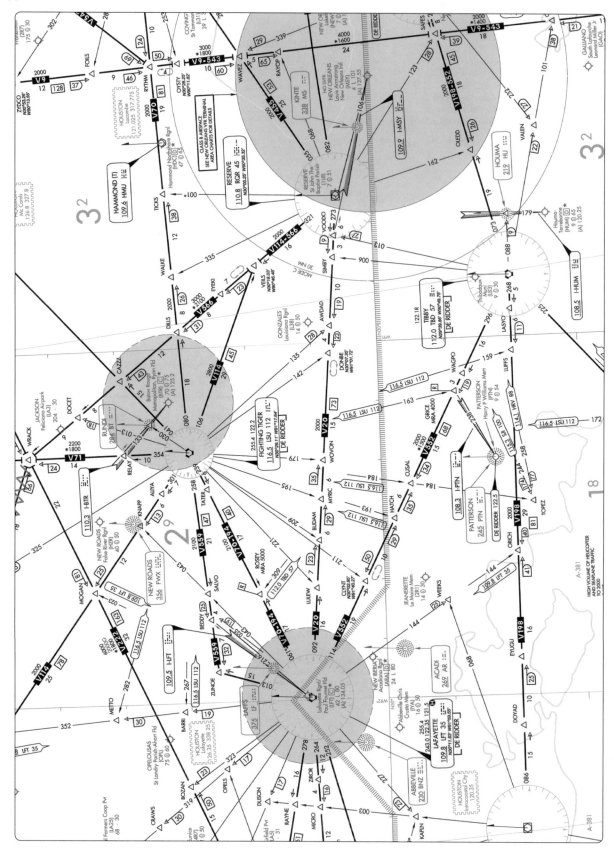

FIGURE 65.—En Route Low-Altitude Chart Segment.
NOTE: Chart is not to scale and should not be used for navigation. Chart is for testing purposes only.

FREQ	OBS	
112.0	116	TO

FREQ	OBS	
108.3	236	//////

FIGURE 66.—CDI and OBS Indicators.

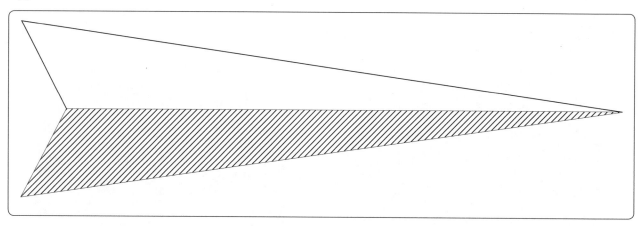

FIGURE 67.—Localizer Symbol.

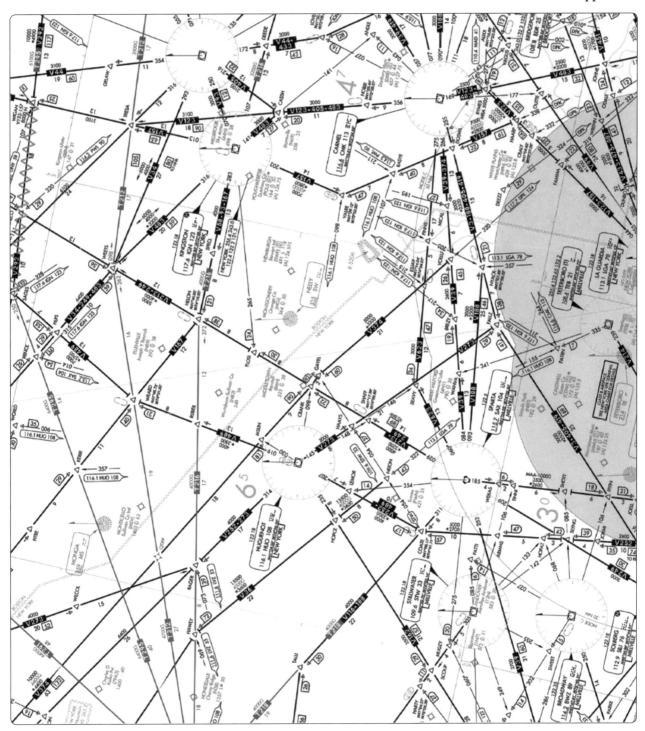

FIGURE 71.—En Route Low-Altitude Chart Segment.
NOTE: Chart is not to scale and should not be used for navigation. Chart is for testing purposes only.

FREQ	OBS	
117.6	265	FROM

FREQ	OBS	
115.7	029	FROM

FIGURE 71A.—CDI and OBS Indicators.

A   **B**   **C**   **D**

HELENA RGNL (HLN)(KHLN) P (ARNG)   2 NE   UTC–7(–6DT)   N46°36.41′ W111°58.97′   **GREAT FALLS**
3877   B   S4   **FUEL** 80, 100, 100LL, JET A   OX 1, 3   LRA   Class I, ARFF Index B   NOTAM FILE HLN   **H–1D, L–13C**
RWY 09–27: H9000X150 (ASPH–PFC)   S–100, D–160, 2S–175,   **IAP, DIAP, AD**
  2D–250   HIRL
  RWY 09: REIL. VASI(V4L)—GA 3.0° TCH 45′. Ground. 0.3% down.
  RWY 27: MALSR. VASI(V4L)—GA 3.0° TCH 47′. Rgt tfc.
RWY 05–23: H4644X75 (ASPH–PFC)   S–21, D–30   MIRL   1.2% up SW
  RWY 05: Road.
  RWY 23: PAPI(P2L)—GA 3.0° TCH 49′. Fence. Rgt tfc.
RWY 16–34: H2989X75 (ASPH–PFC)   S–21, D–30   MIRL   1.7% up SE
  RWY 34: Ground. Rgt tfc.
MILITARY SERVICE: FUEL A+, J8 (C406–442–2190. Opr 1200–0600Z‡, OT
  $150 fee, 90 min PPR.) (NC–80, 100, 100LL)
AIRPORT REMARKS: Attended 1200–0800Z‡. ARFF coverage provided for
  scheduled Part 121 air carriers only exc with prior approval—call
  406–442–2821. Landing rights customs available call
  406–449–5506. Rwy 16–34 and Rwy 05–23 (except between Twy F
  and Rwy 09–27) not available for air carrier use by acft with greater
  than 30 passenger seats. Twys A, B, and C between Twy A and Rwy 34
  not available for air carrier use by acft with greater than 30 passenger
  seats. When tower closed ACTIVATE HIRL Rwy 09–27, MIRL Rwy
  05–23 and Rwy 16–34, REIL Rwy 09. MALSR Rwy 27—CTAF. Ldg fee
  for all commercial acft and all acft over 10,000 pounds. Flight Notification Service (ADCUS) avbl. NOTE: See SPECIAL
  NOTICE.
MILITARY REMARKS: ARNG Opr Mon–Fri 1400–0030Z‡, except holidays. Exercise caution while taxiing, AASF ramp not
  stressed for large acft. Ctc flight ops for ramp advisory 126.2, DSN 324–3055/56, C406–324–3055/56. No trans svc
  Sat, Sun, holidays or after 2300Z‡ Mon–Fri.
WEATHER DATA SOURCES: ASOS (406) 443–4317
COMMUNICATIONS: CTAF 118.3 **ATIS** 120.4 **UNICOM** 122.95
  RCO 122.55 255.4 (GREAT FALLS RADIO)
  APP/DEP CON 119.5 229.4 (1300–0500Z‡)
  SALT LAKE CENTER APP/DEP CON 133.4 285.4 (0500–1300Z‡)
  TOWER 118.3 257.8 (1300–0500Z‡) **GND CON** 121.9
  ARNG OPS 40.65 126.2 321.45
AIRSPACE: CLASS D svc 1300–0500Z‡ other times CLASS E.
RADIO AIDS TO NAVIGATION: NOTAM FILE HLN.
  (H) VORTACW 117.7   HLN   Chan 124   N46°36.41′ W111°57.21′   254° 1.2 NM to fld. 3823/16E.
  VOR portion unusable: TACAN DME unusable: TACAN AZIMUTH unusable:
    035°–050° byd 35 NM blo 12,000′   035°–070° byd 35 NM blo 13,000′   105°–150° byd 15 NM
    105°–165° byd 25 NM blo 17,000′   105°–150° byd 25 NM   150°–165° byd 15 NM blo 17,000′
    165°–185° byd 25 NM blo 13,500′   105°–210° byd 15 NM blo 11,100′   185°–210° byd 15 NM
    185°–230° byd 25 NM blo 17,500′   105°–210° byd 20 NM blo 12,000′   210°–250° byd 15 NM blo 17,500′
    203°–213° byd 22 NM blo 13,000′   150°–165° byd 25 NM blo 17,000′
    230°–270° byd 25 NM blo 12,500′   165°–185° byd 25 NM blo 13,500′
  TACAN AZIMUTH and DME unusable: 185°–210° byd 25 NM
    035°–070° byd 35 NM blo 13,000′   203°–213° byd 22 NM blo 13,000′
    165°–185° byd 25 NM blo 13,500′   210°–250° byd 15 NM blo 12,000′
    250°–300° byd 25 NM blo 14,000′   210°–250° byd 25 NM blo 17,500′
    320°–035° byd 25 NM blo 13,000′   250°–300° byd 25 NM blo 14,000′
                    320°–035° byd 25 NM blo 13,000′

  CAPITOL NDB (HW) 335   CVP   N46°36.40′ W111°56.23′   258° 1.9 NM to fld. NDB unmonitored when ATCT clsd.
  HAUSER NDB (MHW) 386   HAU   N46°34.13′ W111°45.48′   268° 9.6 NM to fld. NDB unmonitored when HLN
    ATCT clsd.
  ILS 110.1   I–HLN   Rwy 27.   Unmonitored when ATCT closed. Localizer backcourse unusable byd 22° rgt of course,
    unusable within 2.7 DME.

Rwy 16-34: 2989 X 75

9000 X 150

4644 X 75

34

27

A5

VOR RECEIVER CHECKPOINTS

Facility Name (Arpt Name)	Freq/Ident	Type Check Pt. Gnd. AB/ALT	Azimuth from Fac. Mag	Dist. from Fac. N.M.	Checkpoint Description
Helena (Helena Rgnl)	117.7/HLN	G	238	0.7	On Twy E on South side of Rwy 27.
Kalispell (Glacier Park Intl)	113.2/FCA	A/4000	316	6.4	Over apch end Rwy 30.
Lewistown (Lewistown Muni)	112.0/LWT	A/5200	075	5.6	Over apch end Rwy 07.
Livingston	116.1/LVM	A/6500	237	5.5	Over northern most radio twr NE of city.
Miles City (Frank Wiley Field)	112.1/MLS	G	036	4.2	On twy leading to Rwy 30.
Missoula (Missoula Intl)	112.8/MSO	G	344	0.6	Terminal ramp east of Twy D.

FIGURE 76.—VOR Indications and Excerpts from Chart Supplement (HLN).

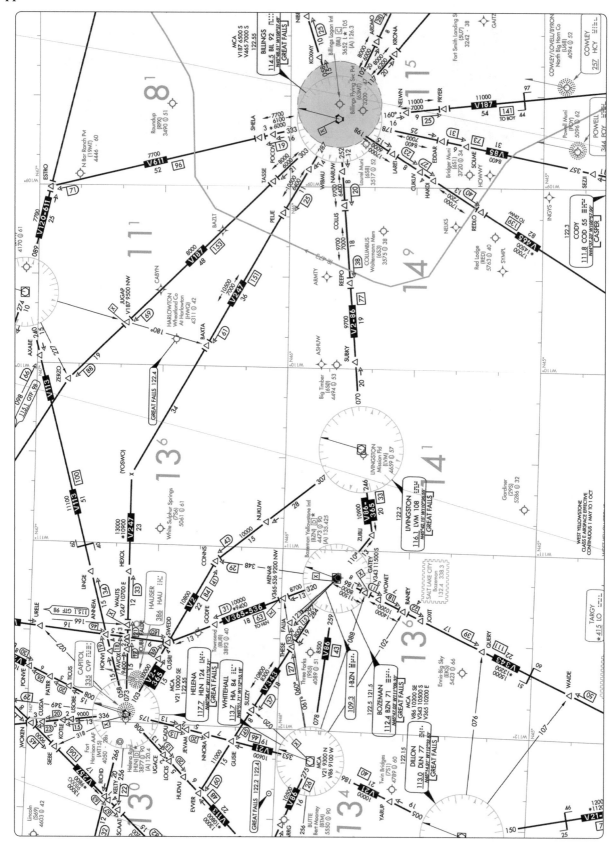

FIGURE 78.—En Route Low-Altitude Chart Segment.
NOTE: Chart is not to scale and should not be used for navigation. Chart is for testing purposes only.

FIGURE 81.—Dual VOR System, VOT Check.

FIGURE 82.—Dual VOR System, Accuracy Check.

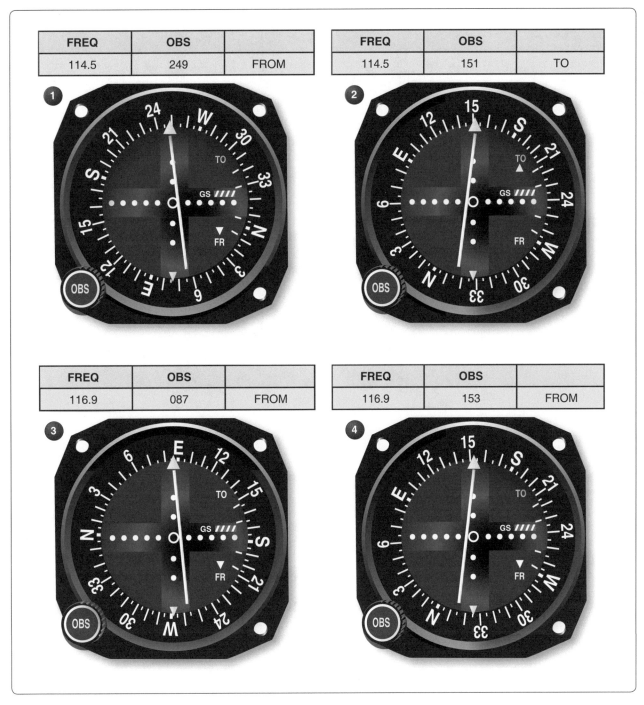

FREQ	OBS	
114.5	249	FROM

FREQ	OBS	
114.5	151	TO

FREQ	OBS	
116.9	087	FROM

FREQ	OBS	
116.9	153	FROM

FIGURE 86.—CDI and OBS Indicators.

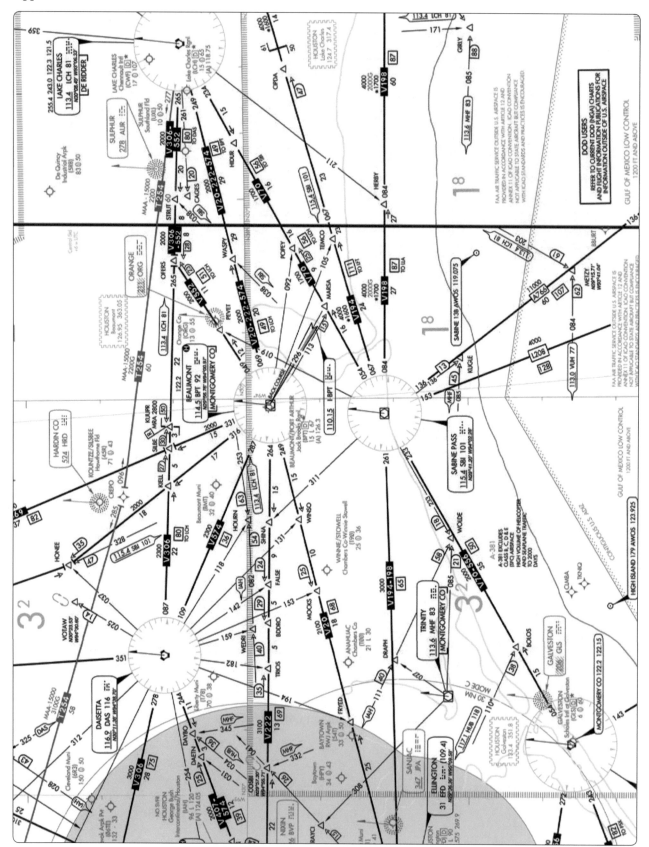

FIGURE 87.—En Route Low-Altitude Chart Segment.
NOTE: Chart is not to scale and should not be used for navigation. Chart is for testing purposes only.

FREQ	OBS	
114.5	264	FROM

FREQ	OBS	
116.9	139	FROM

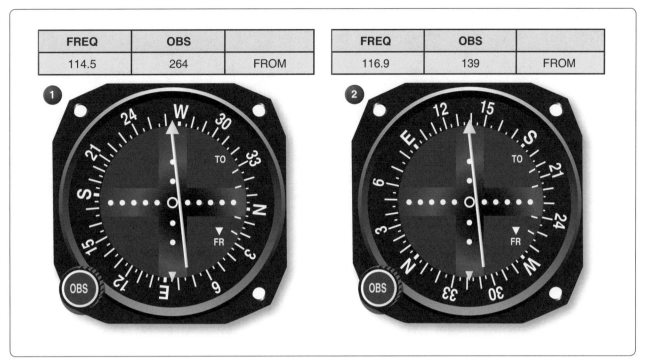

FIGURE 88.—CDI and OBS Indicators.

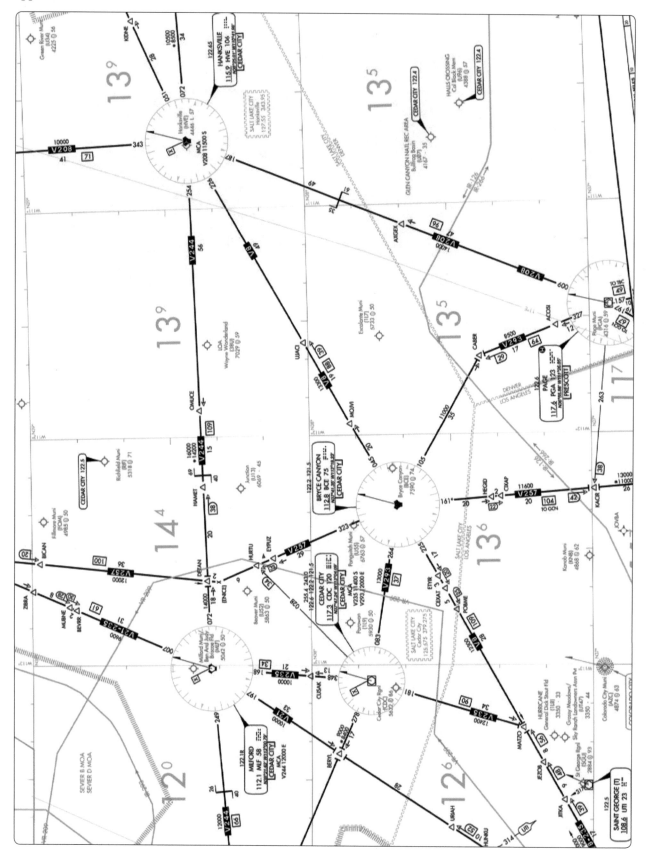

FIGURE 89.—En Route Low-Altitude Chart Segment.
NOTE: Chart is not to scale and should not be used for navigation. Chart is for testing purposes only.

FREQ	OBS	
112.8	033	FROM

FREQ	OBS	
115.9	046	TO

FIGURE 90.—CDI/OBS Indicators.

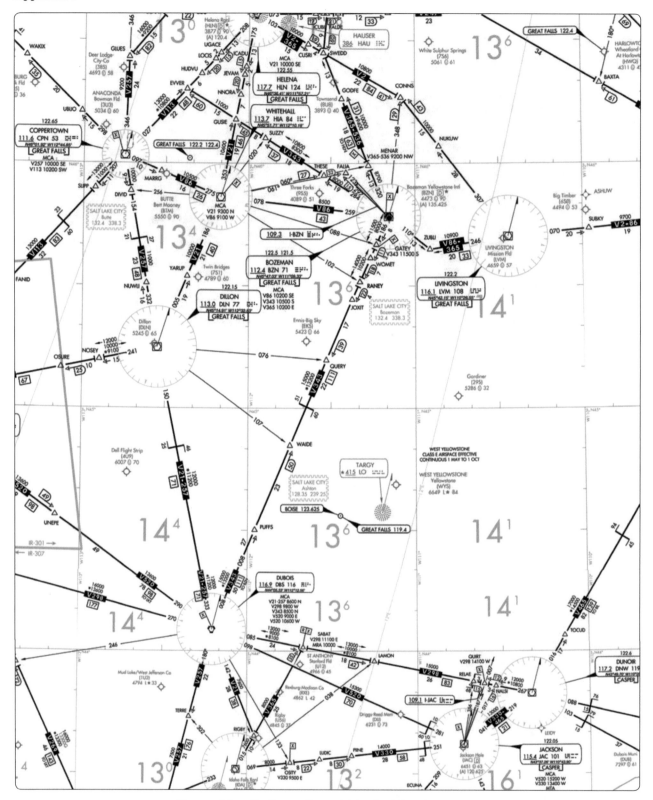

FIGURE 91.—En Route Low-Altitude Chart Segment.
NOTE: Chart is not to scale and should not be used for navigation. Chart is for testing purposes only.

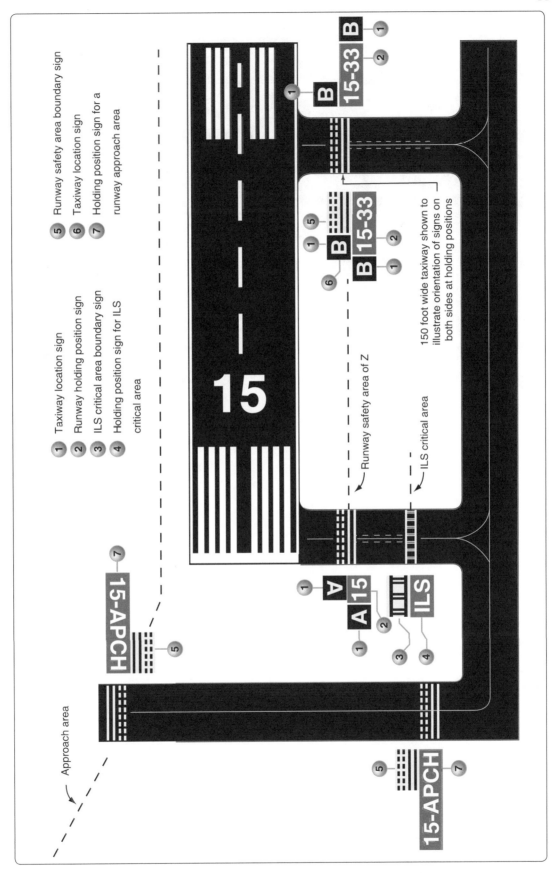

FIGURE 94.—Application Examples for Holding Positions.

Appendix 2

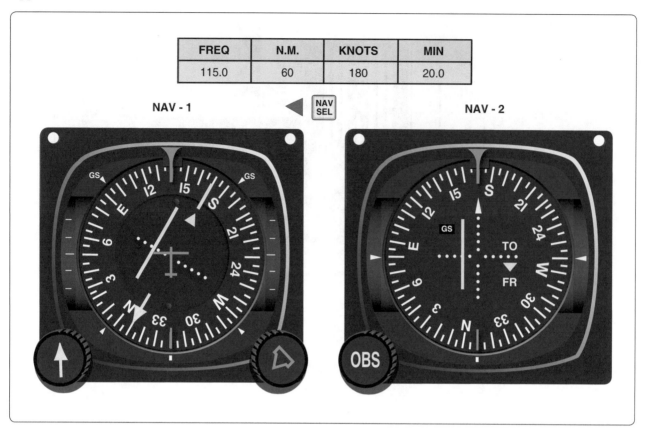

FREQ	N.M.	KNOTS	MIN
115.0	60	180	20.0

FIGURE 95.—No. 1 and No. 2 NAV Presentation.

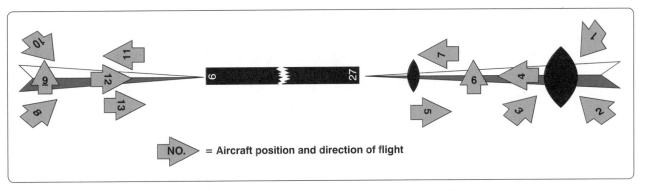

FIGURE 96.—Aircraft Position and Direction of Flight.

FIGURE 97.—HSI Presentation.

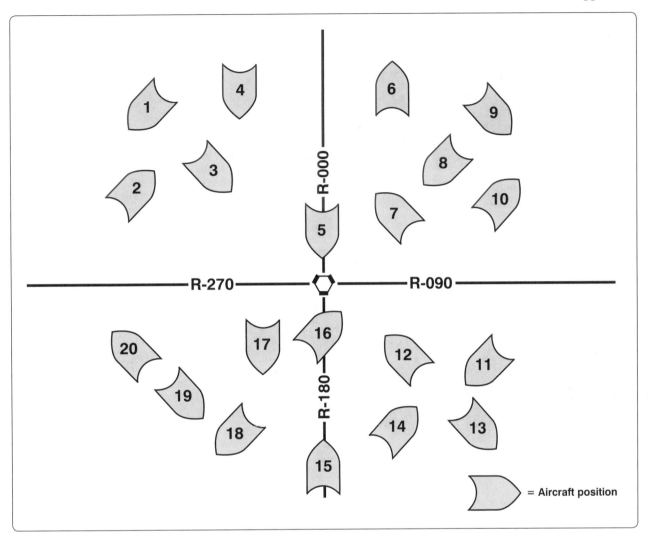

FIGURE 98.—Aircraft Position.

FIGURE 99.—HSI Presentation.

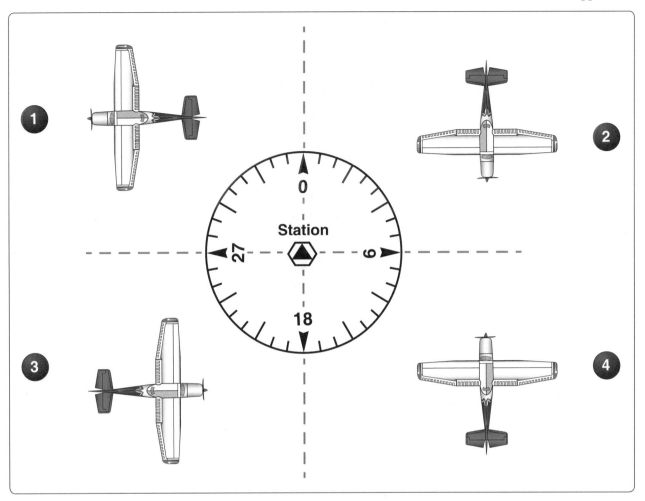

FIGURE 106.—Aircraft Location Relative to VOR.

FIGURE 109.—CDI Direction from VORTAC.

FIGURE 110.—CDI Direction from VORTAC.

FIGURE 111.—CDI Direction from VORTAC.

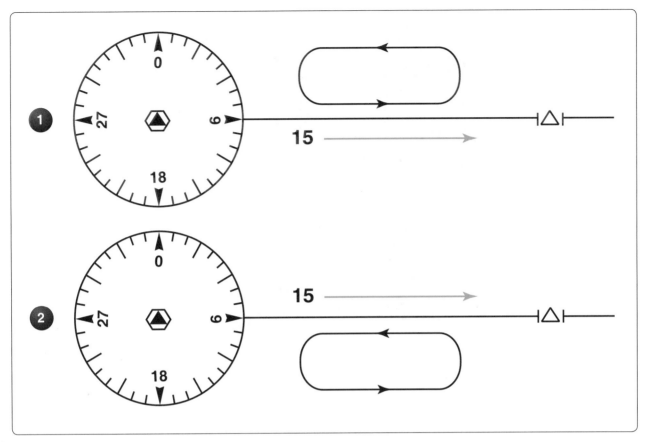

FIGURE 112.—Holding Entry Procedure.

FIGURE 113.—Aircraft Course and DME Indicator.

FIGURE 114.—Aircraft Course and DME Indicator.

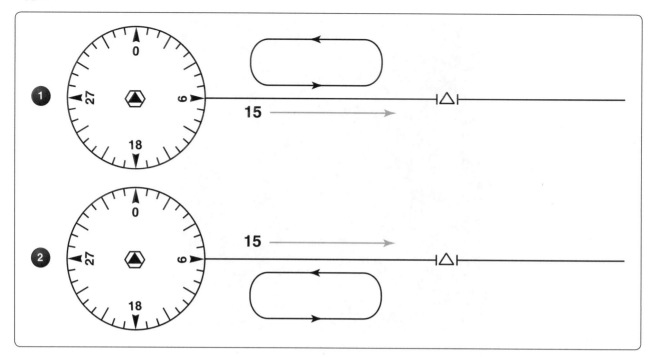

FIGURE 115.—DME Fix with Holding Pattern.

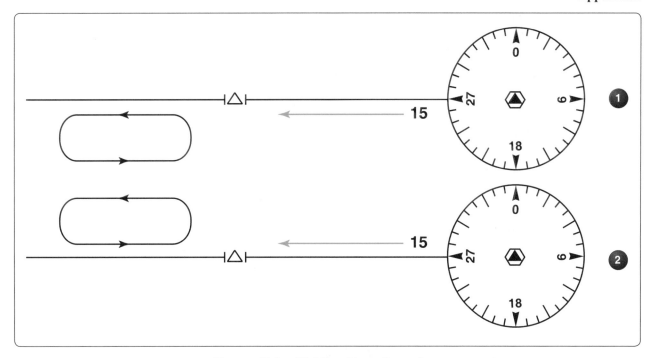

FIGURE 116.—Holding Entry Procedure.

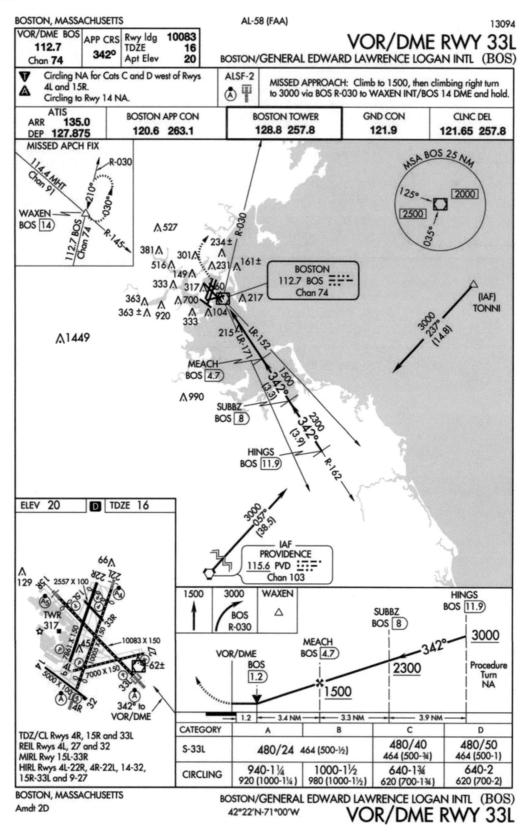

FIGURE 131.—VOR/DME RWY 33L.

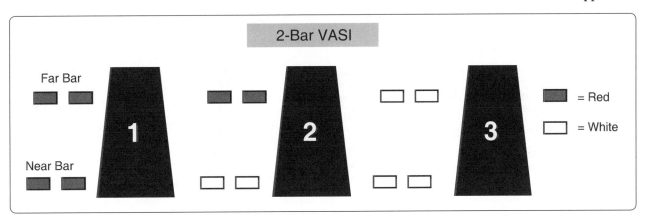

FIGURE 134.—2-BAR VASI.

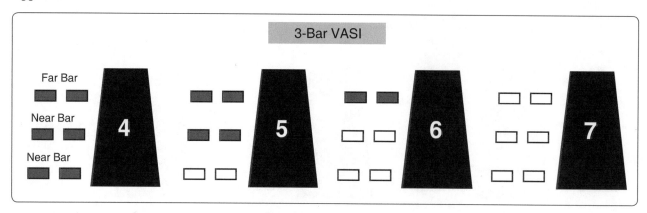

FIGURE 135.—3-BAR VASI.

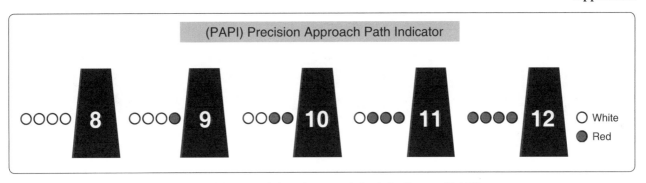

F<small>IGURE</small> 136.—Precision Approach Path Indicator (PAPI).

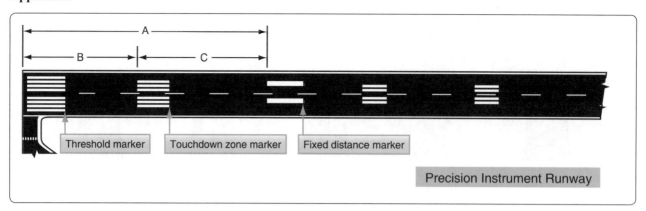

FIGURE 137.—Precision Instrument Runway.

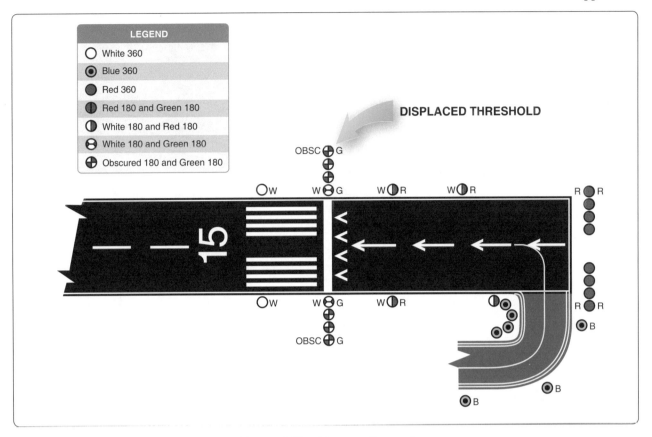

FIGURE 138.—Runway Legend.

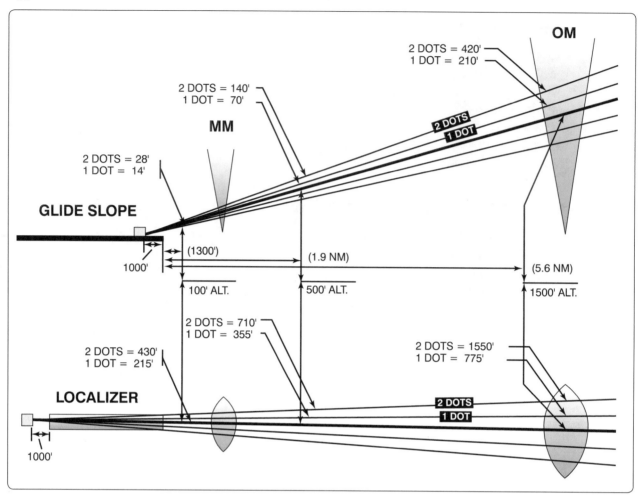

FIGURE 139.—Glide Slope and Localizer Illustration.

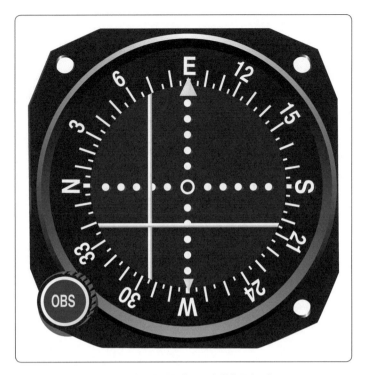

FIGURE 140.—OBS, ILS, and GS Displacement.

FIGURE 141.—OBS, ILS, and GS Displacement.

FIGURE 142.—OBS, ILS, and GS Displacement.

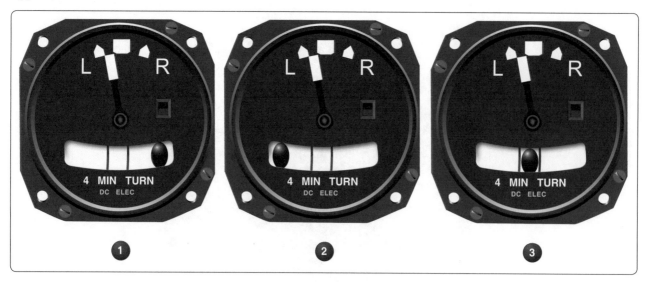

FIGURE 144.—Turn-and-Slip indicator.

FIGURE 145.—Instrument Sequence (Unusual Attitude).

FIGURE 146.—Instrument Sequence (System Failed).

FIGURE 147.—Instrument Sequence (Unusual Attitude).

FIGURE 148.—Instrument Interpretation (System Malfunction).

FIGURE 149.—Instrument Interpretation (System Malfunction).

FIGURE 150.—Instrument Interpretation (Instrument Malfunction).

FIGURE 151.—Instrument Interpretation (Instrument Malfunction).

(JNC6.JNC) 12320   SL-634 (FAA)   GRAND JUNCTION RGNL (GJT)
GRAND JUNCTION SIX DEPARTURE
GRAND JUNCTION, COLORADO

ATIS 118.55
GND CON 121.7 257.8
GRAND JUNCTION TOWER ★
118.1 257.8
DENVER DEP CON ★
119.7 317.4
UNICOM 122.95

NOTE: Chart not to scale.

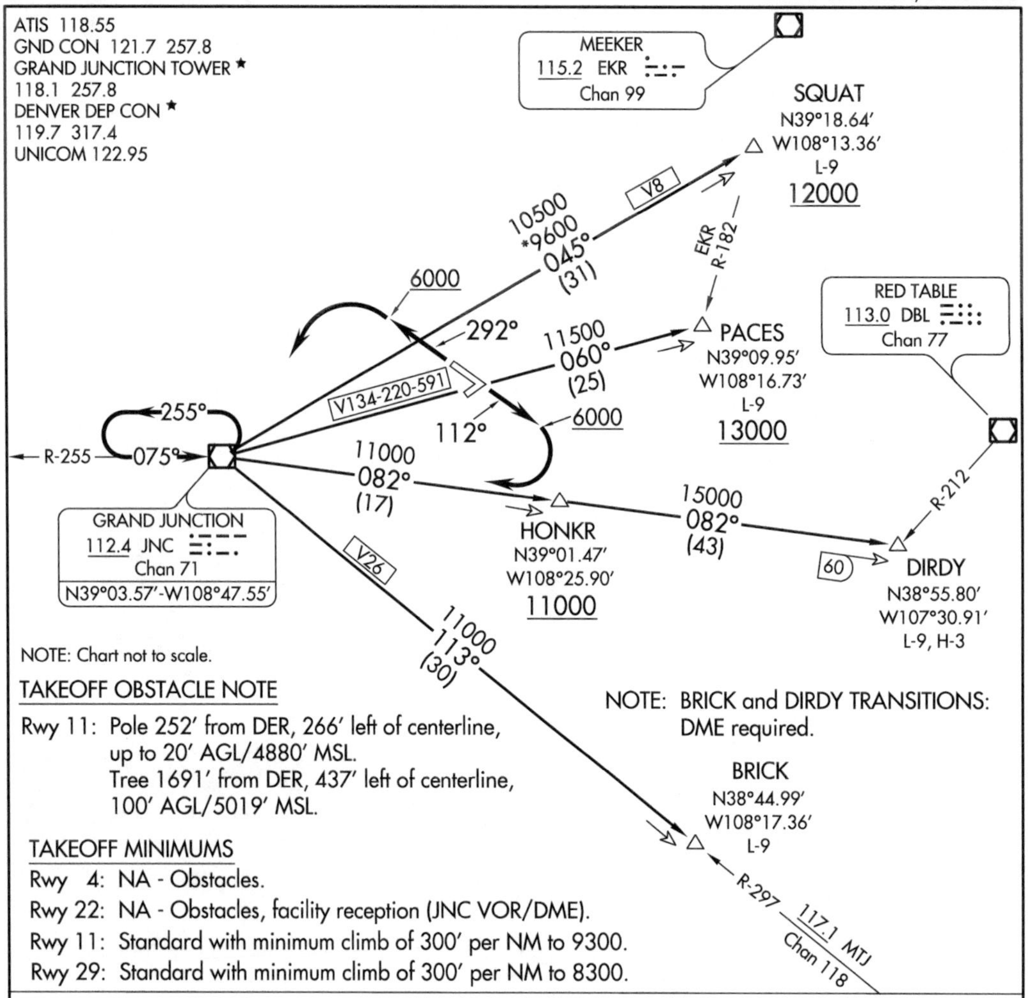

TAKEOFF OBSTACLE NOTE

Rwy 11: Pole 252' from DER, 266' left of centerline,
up to 20' AGL/4880' MSL.
Tree 1691' from DER, 437' left of centerline,
100' AGL/5019' MSL.

TAKEOFF MINIMUMS

Rwy 4: NA - Obstacles.
Rwy 22: NA - Obstacles, facility reception (JNC VOR/DME).
Rwy 11: Standard with minimum climb of 300' per NM to 9300.
Rwy 29: Standard with minimum climb of 300' per NM to 8300.

NOTE: BRICK and DIRDY TRANSITIONS:
DME required.

DEPARTURE ROUTE DESCRIPTION

TAKEOFF RUNWAY 11: Climb heading 112° to 6000, then climbing right turn
direct JNC VOR/DME, thence. . . .

TAKEOFF RUNWAY 29: Climb heading 292° to 6000, then climbing left turn
direct JNC VOR/DME, thence. . . .

. . . .on transition/route.

BRICK TRANSITION (JNC6.BRICK): From over JNC VOR/DME via JNC R-113 to
BRICK/JNC 30 DME.

DIRDY TRANSITION (JNC6.DIRDY): From over JNC VOR/DME via JNC R-082 to
DIRDY INT/JNC 60 DME.

PACES TRANSITION (JNC6.PACES): From over JNC VOR/DME via JNC R-060 to
PACES INT/JNC 25 DME.

SQUAT TRANSITION (JNC6.SQUAT): From over JNC VOR/DME via JNC R-045 to
SQUAT INT/JNC 31 DME.

GRAND JUNCTION SIX DEPARTURE
(JNC6.JNC) 12320

GRAND JUNCTION, COLORADO
GRAND JUNCTION RGNL (GJT)

FIGURE 155.—Grand Junction Six Departure (JNC6.JNC).

HOT SPOTS

An "airport surface hot spot" is a location on an aerodrome movement area with a history or potential risk of collision or runway incursion, and where heightened attention by pilots/drivers is necessary.

A "hot spot" is a runway safety related problem area on an airport that presents increased risk during surface operations. Typically it is a complex or confusing taxiway/taxiway or taxiway/runway intersection. The area of increased risk has either a history of or potential for runway incursions or surface incidents, due to a variety of causes, such as but not limited to: airport layout, traffic flow, airport marking, signage and lighting, situational awareness, and training. Hot spots are depicted on airport diagrams as open circles or polygons designated as "HS 1", "HS 2", etc. and tabulated in the list below with a brief description of each hot spot. Hot spots will remain charted on airport diagrams until such time the increased risk has been reduced or eliminated.

CITY/AIRPORT	HOT SPOT	DESCRIPTION*
ALAMOGORDO, NM		
HOLLOMAN AFB (HMN)	HS1	Twy R, Twy G, and Twy L have multiple hold lines for Rwy 07-25 and Rwy 04-22. Contact tower if confused or lost.
	HS2	Hold line on Twy /EOR A and Twy/EOR H have multiple POV access roads, possibility of high vehicle traffic.
	HS3	Hold line on Twy /EOR B and Twy C for Rwy 07-25 have multiple POV access roads, possibility of high vehicle traffic.
	HS4	Multiple hold lines at intersecting rwys. Landing/departing aircraft disregard hold lines, taxiing aircraft contact tower prior to crossing hold lines.
	HS5	Multiple hold lines where rwys intersect. Hold line also at Twy D. Contact tower if confused or lost.
	HS6	POV crossing controlled by tower. Hold line located on each side of Rwy 07-25. Possibility of high vehicular traffic.
ALBUQUERQUE, NM		
ALBUQUERQUE INTL		
SUNPORT (ABQ)	HS 1	Hold Position Marking on Twy E1 for Rwy 08 and Rwy 12.
	HS 2	Twy G1 from Cutter Aviation ramp and Rwy 12-30.
	HS 3	Complex int at Twy F, Twy C, Twy G. Twy G and Rwy 03-21
ASPEN, CO		
ASPEN-PITKIN COUNTY /		
SARDY FIELD (ASE)	HS 1	Twy A2. Short taxi distance from ramp to rwy.
	HS 2	Twy A3. Short taxi distance from ramp to rwy.
	HS 3	Twy A4. Short taxi distance from ramp to rwy.
COLORADO SPRINGS, CO		
CITY OF COLORADO		
SPRINGS (COS)	HS 1	The apch ends of Rwy 13 and Rwy 17R; and Twy A1.
	HS 2	Twy A4 and Twy G at Rwy 17R-35L.
	HS 3	Int of Twy E4, Twy G, Twy H and Twy E.
	HS 4	Apch ends of Rwy 35R and Rwy 35L.
DENVER, CO		
CENTENNIAL (APA)	HS 1	Rwy 17L at Twy A1.
	HS 2	Twy A, Twy A8, Twy A9 and Twy C1 congested INT.
	HS 3	Twy C1 and Twy D1 close proximity to Rwy 10.
DENVER, CO		
DENVER INTL (DEN)	HS 1	Rwy 35L hold signs may not be visible from Twy SC or Twy A until entering Twy M, pilots sometimes enter Rwy 35L without authorization.
	HS 2	Rwy 17R Apch Hold Position.
DENVER, CO		
ROCKY MOUNTAIN		
METROPOLITAN (BJC)	HS 1	Frequent helicopter operations.
	HS 2	Multiple hold lines in close proximity. Hold line on Twy B south of Rwy 11R-29L is prior to Twy D.
EAGLE, CO		
EAGLE COUNTY RGNL (EGE)	HS 1	High density parking area.
GRAND JUNCTION, CO		
GRAND JUNCTION RGNL (GJT)	HS 1	Rwy 22 and Rwy 29 close proximity, wrong rwy departure risk.

FIGURE 156.—Grand Junction Hot Spots.

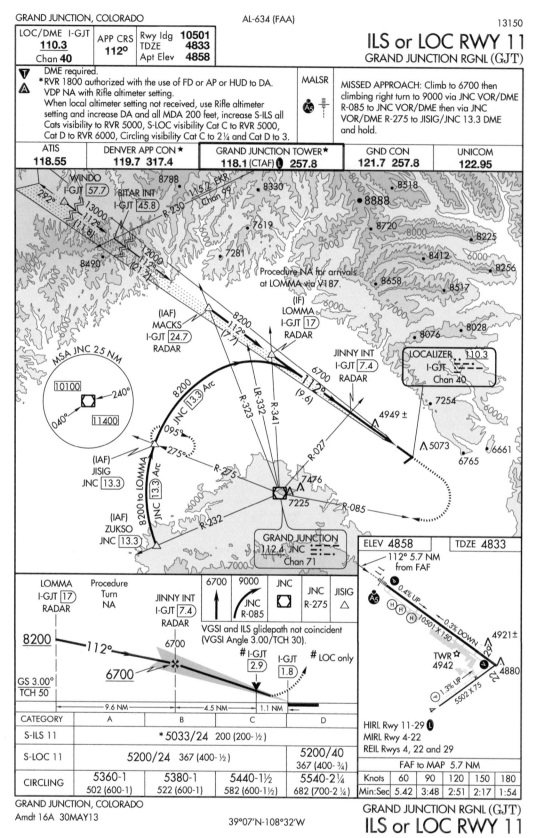

FIGURE 157.—ILS RWY 11 (GJT).

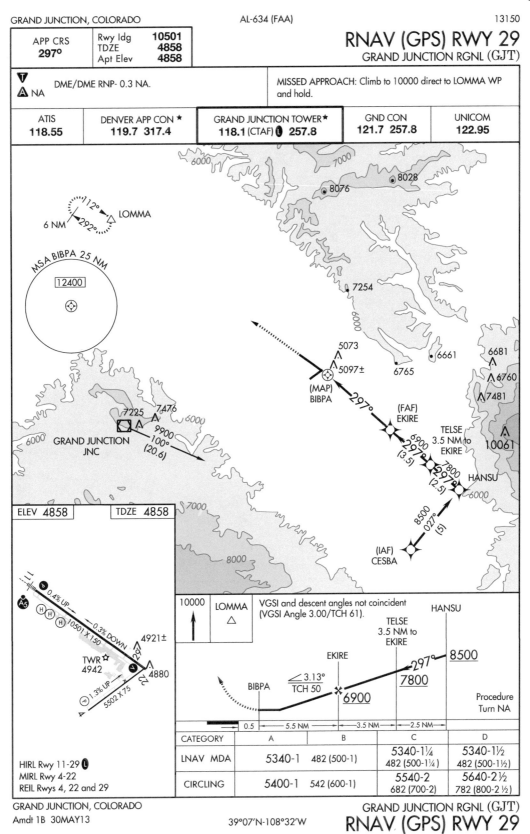

FIGURE 158.—ILS RWY 11 (GJT).

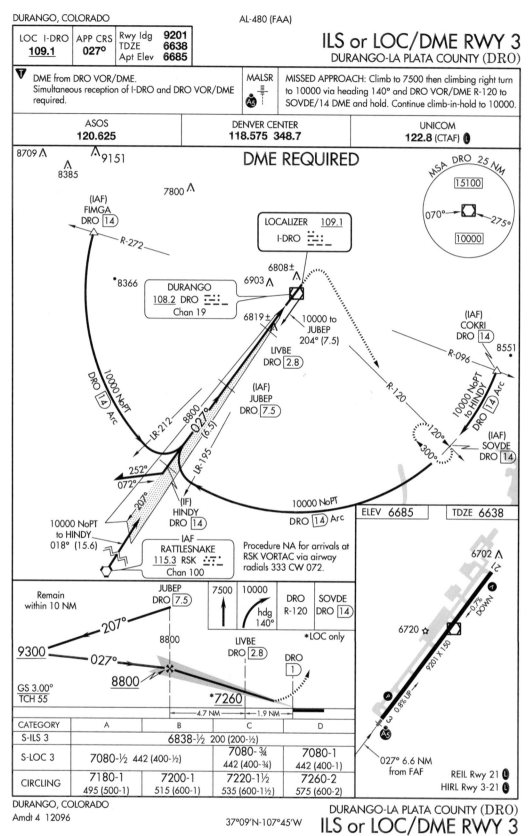

DURANGO, COLORADO

AL-480 (FAA)

ILS or LOC/DME RWY 3
DURANGO-LA PLATA COUNTY (DRO)

LOC I-DRO **109.1**	APP CRS **027°**	Rwy Idg	**9201**
		TDZE	**6638**
		Apt Elev	**6685**

DME from DRO VOR/DME.
Simultaneous reception of I-DRO and DRO VOR/DME required.

MALSR

MISSED APPROACH: Climb to 7500 then climbing right turn to 10000 via heading 140° and DRO VOR/DME R-120 to SOVDE/14 DME and hold. Continue climb-in-hold to 10000.

| ASOS
120.625 | DENVER CENTER
118.575 348.7 | UNICOM
122.8 (CTAF) |

DME REQUIRED

CATEGORY	A	B	C	D
S-ILS 3		6838-½ 200 (200-½)		
S-LOC 3	7080-½ 442 (400-½)		7080-¾ 442 (400-¾)	7080-1 442 (400-1)
CIRCLING	7180-1 495 (500-1)	7200-1 515 (600-1)	7220-1½ 535 (600-1½)	7260-2 575 (600-2)

DURANGO, COLORADO
Amdt 4 12096

37°09'N-107°45'W

DURANGO-LA PLATA COUNTY (DRO)
ILS or LOC/DME RWY 3

FIGURE 159.—ILS/DME RWY 3 (DRO).

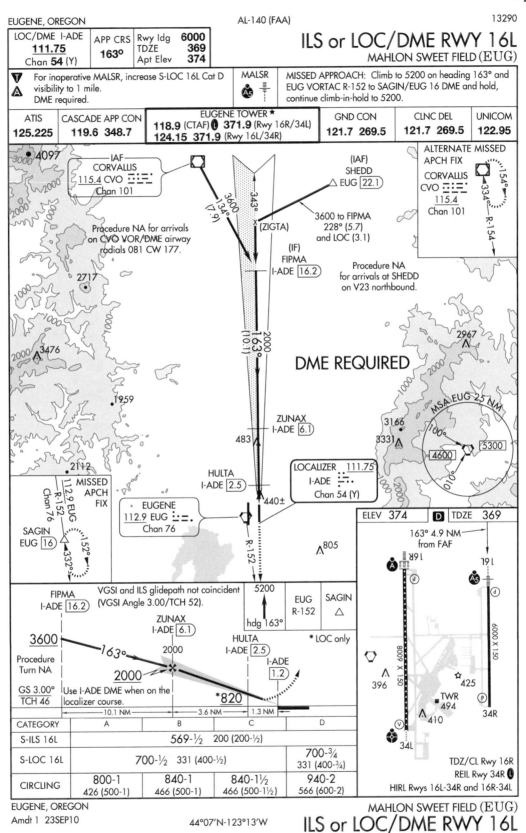

FIGURE 160.—ILS or LOC/DME RWY 16L (EUG).

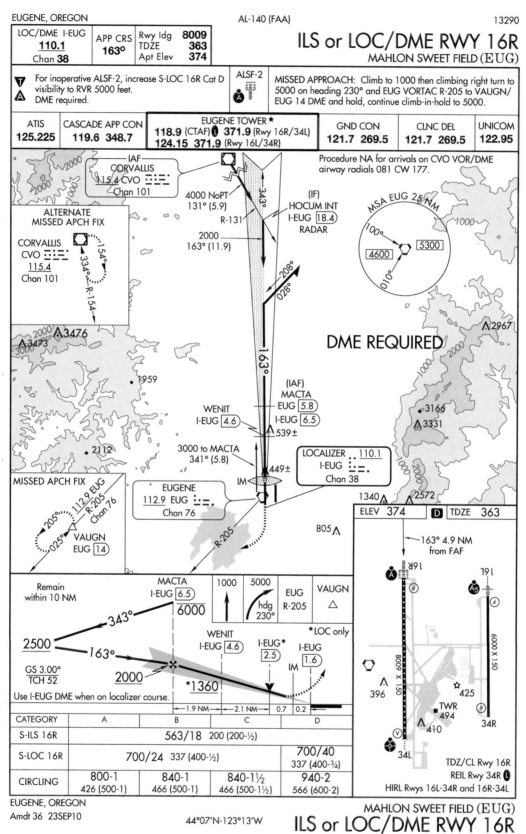

EUGENE, OREGON   AL-140 (FAA)   13290

| LOC/DME I-EUG **110.1** Chan **38** | APP CRS **163°** | Rwy Idg **8009** TDZE **363** Apt Elev **374** | **ILS or LOC/DME RWY 16R** MAHLON SWEET FIELD (EUG) |

For inoperative ALSF-2, increase S-LOC 16R Cat D visibility to RVR 5000 feet. DME required.

ALSF-2

MISSED APPROACH: Climb to 1000 then climbing right turn to 5000 on heading 230° and EUG VORTAC R-205 to VAUGN/ EUG 14 DME and hold, continue climb-in-hold to 5000.

| ATIS **125.225** | CASCADE APP CON **119.6 348.7** | EUGENE TOWER ★ **118.9** (CTAF) **371.9** (Rwy 16R/34L) **124.15 371.9** (Rwy 16L/34R) | GND CON **121.7 269.5** | CLNC DEL **121.7 269.5** | UNICOM **122.95** |

EUGENE, OREGON
Amdt 36 23SEP10

44°07'N-123°13'W

MAHLON SWEET FIELD (EUG)
ILS or LOC/DME RWY 16R

EUGENE

MAHLON SWEET FLD (EUG)   7 NW   UTC–8(–7DT)   N44°07.48´ W123°12.72´

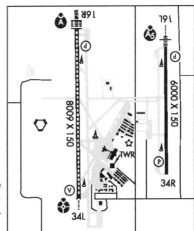

KLAMATH FALLS
H–1B, L–1B
IAP, AD

374   B   S4   **FUEL** 100LL, JET A   OX 1, 2, 3, 4   TPA—1174(800)   Class I, ARFF Index B
NOTAM FILE EUG
RWY 16R–34L: H8009X150 (ASPH–GRVD)   S–75, D–200, 2D–400
HIRL   CL
RWY 16R: ALSF2. TDZL. PAPI(P4L)—GA 3.0° TCH 50´.
RWY 34L: ODALS. VASI(V4L)—GA 3.0° TCH 53´.
RWY 16L–34R: H6000X150 (ASPH–GRVD)   S–105, D–175, 2D–240
HIRL
RWY 16L: MALSR. PAPI(P4L)—GA 3.0° TCH 52´.
RWY 34R: REIL. PAPI(P4L)—GA 3.0° TCH 50´.
RUNWAY DECLARED DISTANCE INFORMATION
RWY 16L: TORA–6000   TODA–6000   ASDA–6000   LDA–6000
RWY 16R: TORA–8009   TODA–8009   ASDA–8009   LDA–8009
RWY 34L: TORA–8009   TODA–8009   ASDA–8009   LDA–8009
RWY 34R: TORA–6000   TODA–6000   ASDA–6000   LDA–6000
AIRPORT REMARKS: Attended continuously. Migratory waterfowl and other
birds on and invof arpt. PPR for unscheduled air carrier ops with more
than 30 passenger seats call 541–682–5430. ARFF svcs unavailable
0000–0500 local except PPR 541–682–5430. No access to Rwy 34L
byd Twy A9. Helicopters ldg and departing avoid overflying the airline
passenger terminal and ramp located E of Rwy 16R–34L. Helipad west
of Rwy 16R restricted, PPR phone 541–682–5430. Twys H and K unavailable to acft 21,000 pounds single weight and
40,000 pounds dual gross weight. Terminal apron closed to acft except scheduled air carriers and flights with prior
permission. PAPI Rwy 16R and Rwy 16L and 34R and VASI Rwy 34L opr 24 hrs. When twr clsd HIRL Rwy 16L–34R
and Rwy 16R–34L preset medium ints. When twr clsd ACTIVATE ALSF2 Rwy 16R, ODALS Rwy 34L MALSR Rwy 16L
and REIL Rwy 34R—CTAF.
WEATHER DATA SOURCES: ASOS (541) 461–3114 **HIWAS** 112.9 EUG.
COMMUNICATIONS: CTAF 118.9 **ATIS** 125.225 541–607–4699 **UNICOM** 122.95
EUGENE RCO 122.3 (MC MINNVILLE RADIO)
®**CASCADE APP/DEP CON** 119.6 (340°–159°) 120.25 (160°–339°) (1400–0730Z‡)
®**SEATTLE CENTER APP/DEP CON** 125.8 (0730–1400Z‡)
EUGENE TOWER 118.9 (Rwy 16R– 34L) 124.15 (Rwy 16L– 34R) (1400–0730Z‡) **GND CON** 121.7 **CLNC DEL** 121.7
AIRSPACE: CLASS D svc 1400–0730Z‡ other times CLASS E.
RADIO AIDS TO NAVIGATION: NOTAM FILE EUG.
EUGENE (H) VORTACW 112.9   EUG   Chan 76   N44°07.25´ W123°13.37´   at fld. 364/20E.   **HIWAS.**
ILS/DME 111.75   I–ADE   Chan 54(Y)   Rwy 16L.   Class IE.
ILS/DME 110.1   I–EUG   Chan 38   Rwy 16R.   Class IIIE.   Unmonitored when ATCT clsd.

FLORENCE

FLORENCE MUNI (6S2)   1 N   UTC–8(–7DT)   N43°58.97´ W124°06.68´

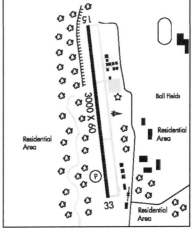

KLAMATH FALLS
L–1A

51   B   **FUEL** 100LL, JET A   TPA—1051(1000)   NOTAM FILE MMV
RWY 15–33: H3000X60 (ASPH)   S–12.5   MIRL   0.4% up NW
RWY 15: Hill. Rgt tfc.
RWY 33: PAPI(P2L)—GA 3.0° TCH 40´. Trees.
AIRPORT REMARKS: Attended 1630–0030Z‡. Birds, deer and wildlife on and
invof arpt. ACTIVATE MIRL Rwy 15–33—CTAF. PAPI Rwy 33 opr 24
hrs.
WEATHER DATA SOURCES: AWOS–3 118.225 (541) 997–8664.
COMMUNICATIONS: CTAF/UNICOM 122.8
RADIO AIDS TO NAVIGATION: NOTAM FILE OTH.
NORTH BEND (L) VORTACW 112.1   OTH   Chan 58   N43°24.93´
W124°10.11´   346° 34.1 NM to fld. 707/18E.   **HIWAS.**
VORTAC unusable:
012°–087° byd 30 NM blo 5,000´

FIGURE 162.—Excerpt from Chart Supplement.

(GNATS6.GNATS) 13290
GNATS SIX DEPARTURE
SL-251 (FAA)

ROGUE VALLEY INTL-MEDFORD (MFR)
MEDFORD, OREGON

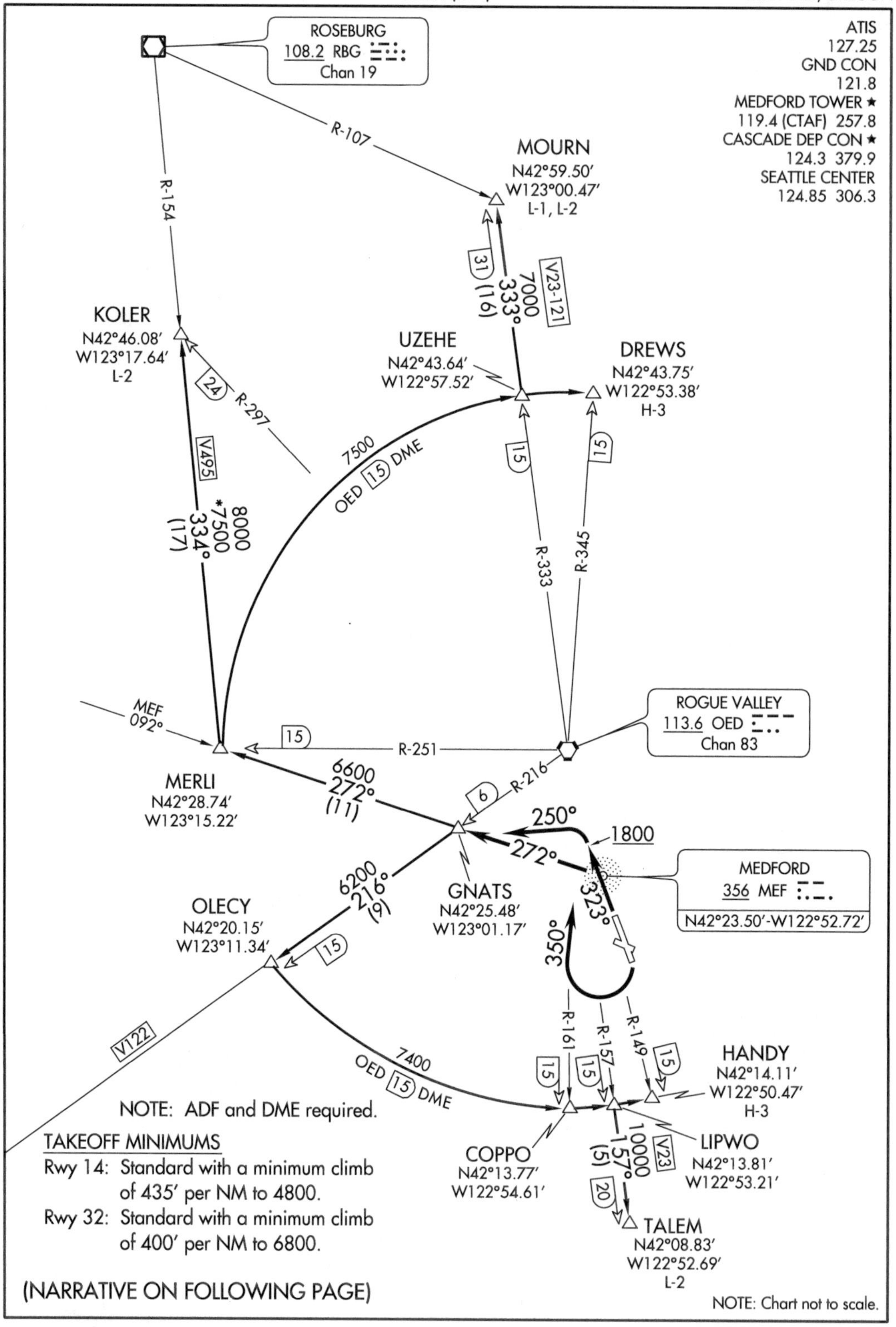

ATIS
127.25
GND CON
121.8
MEDFORD TOWER ★
119.4 (CTAF) 257.8
CASCADE DEP CON ★
124.3 379.9
SEATTLE CENTER
124.85 306.3

ROSEBURG
108.2 RBG
Chan 19

R-107

R-154

MOURN
N42°59.50'
W123°00.47'
L-1, L-2

31
333°
7000
V23-121

KOLER
N42°46.08'
W123°17.64'
L-2

24
R-297

V495

8000
*7500
334°
(17)

UZEHE
N42°43.64'
W122°57.52'

7500
OED 15 DME

15

15

DREWS
N42°43.75'
W122°53.38'
H-3

R-333

R-345

MEF
092°

15
R-251

MERLI
N42°28.74'
W123°15.22'

6600
272°
(11)

6
R-216

ROGUE VALLEY
113.6 OED
Chan 83

250°
272°
1800

323°

MEDFORD
356 MEF
N42°23.50'-W122°52.72'

OLECY
N42°20.15'
W123°11.34'

6200
216°
(9)

15

GNATS
N42°25.48'
W123°01.17'

350°

V122

7400
OED 15 DME

R-161

R-157

R-149

15

15

15

HANDY
N42°14.11'
W122°50.47'
H-3

NOTE: ADF and DME required.

TAKEOFF MINIMUMS
Rwy 14: Standard with a minimum climb
of 435' per NM to 4800.
Rwy 32: Standard with a minimum climb
of 400' per NM to 6800.

(NARRATIVE ON FOLLOWING PAGE)

COPPO
N42°13.77'
W122°54.61'

10000
157°
(5)

V23

20

LIPWO
N42°13.81'
W122°53.21'

TALEM
N42°08.83'
W122°52.69'
L-2

NOTE: Chart not to scale.

GNATS SIX DEPARTURE
(GNATS6.GNATS) 13290

MEDFORD, OREGON
ROGUE VALLEY INTL-MEDFORD (MFR)

FIGURE 163.—GNATS Six Departure (GNATS6.GNATS).

DEPARTURE ROUTE DESCRIPTION

<u>TAKEOFF RUNWAY 14:</u> Climbing right turn on heading 350° to intercept bearing 272° from MEF NDB to GNATS INT. Thence . . . .

<u>TAKEOFF RUNWAY 32:</u> Climb on heading 323° to 1800 then climbing left turn on heading 250° to intercept bearing 272° from MEF NDB to GNATS INT. Thence . . . .

. . . . via (transition) or (assigned route). Maintain 11000 or assigned lower altitude.

<u>COPPO TRANSITION (GNATS6.COPPO):</u> From over GNATS INT via OED VORTAC R-216 to OLECY DME, then via the OED VORTAC 15 DME Arc CCW to COPPO DME.

<u>DREWS TRANSITION (GNATS6.DREWS):</u> From over GNATS INT via MEF NDB 272° to MERLI INT, then via the OED VORTAC 15 DME Arc CW to DREWS DME.

<u>HANDY TRANSITION (GNATS6.HANDY):</u> From over GNATS INT via the OED VORTAC R-216 to OLECY DME, then via the OED VORTAC 15 DME Arc CCW to HANDY DME.

<u>KOLER TRANSITION (GNATS6.KOLER):</u> From over GNATS INT via MEF NDB 272° to MERLI INT, then via RBG VOR/DME R-154 to KOLER INT.

<u>MOURN TRANSITION (GNATS6.MOURN):</u> From over GNATS INT via MEF NDB 272° to MERLI INT, then via the OED VORTAC 15 DME Arc CW to UZEHE DME, then via OED VORTAC R-333 to MOURN INT.

<u>TALEM TRANSITION (GNATS6.TALEM):</u> From over GNATS INT via OED VORTAC R-216 to OLECY DME, then via the OED VORTAC 15 DME Arc CCW to LIPWO DME, then via OED VORTAC R-157 to TALEM DME.

FIGURE 164.—GNATS Six Departure (GNATS6.GNATS).

MEDFORD

ROGUE VALLEY INTL – MEDFORD (MFR) 3 N UTC–8(–7DT) N42°22.45´ W122°52.41´   KLAMATH FALLS
1335 B S4 **FUEL** 100LL, JET A OX 1, 3 TPA—See Remarks Class I, ARFF Index B   H–3B, L–2I
  NOTAM FILE MFR   IAP, AD

RWY 14–32: H8800X150 (ASPH–GRVD) S–200, D–200, 2S–175,
  2D–400 HIRL CL
  RWY 14: MALSR. TDZL. PAPI(P4L)—GA 3.0° TCH 73´. 0.4% up.
  RWY 32: REIL. PAPI(P4R)—GA 3.0° TCH 50´. 0.5% down. 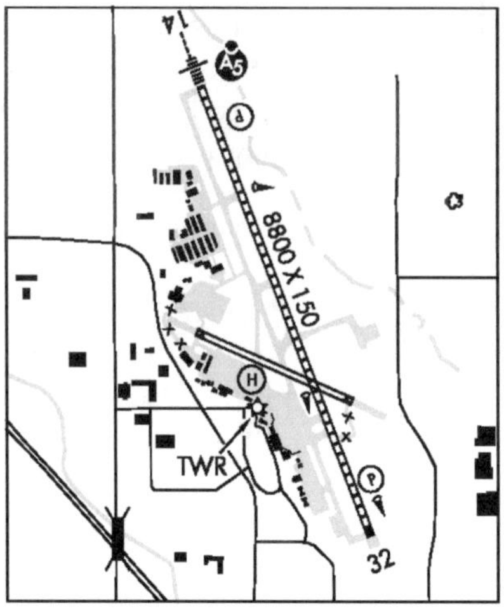
RUNWAY DECLARED DISTANCE INFORMATION
  RWY 14: TORA–8800 TODA–8800 ASDA–8800 LDA–8800
  RWY 32: TORA–8800 TODA–8800 ASDA–8800 LDA–8800
AIRPORT REMARKS: Attended 1300–0800Z‡. For fuel after hrs call
  541–779–5451, or 541–842–2254. Bird haz large flocks of
  migratory waterfowl in vicinity Nov–May. Terminal apron clsd to acft
  exc scheduled air carrier and flts with prior permission. PPR for
  unscheduled ops with more than 30 passenger seats, call arpt ops
  541–776–7228. Tran tie–downs avbl thru FBOs only. Rwy 32
  preferred for tkfs and ldgs when twr clsd. TPA—2304(969) for
  propeller acft, 2804(1469) for turbo acft. PAPI Rwy 14 and VASI
  Rwy 32 on continuously. ACTIVATE HIRL Rwy 14–32, MALSR Rwy
  14, REIL Rwy 32, TDZL Rwy 14, centerline lgts Rwy 14 and Rwy
  32, and twy lgts—CTAF. Ldg fee applies to all corporate acft and all
  other acft with weight exceeding 12,500 lbs.
WEATHER DATA SOURCES: ASOS (541) 776–1238 SAWRS.
COMMUNICATIONS: CTAF 119.4 **ATIS** 127.25 **UNICOM** 122.95
  MEDFORD RCO 122.65 (MC MINNVILLE RADIO)
®**CASCADE APP/DEP CON** 124.3 (1400–0730Z‡)
  SEATTLE CENTER APP/DEP CON 124.85 (0730–1400Z‡)
  TOWER 119.4 (1400–0500Z‡) **GND CON** 121.8
AIRSPACE: CLASS D svc 1400–0500Z‡ other times CLASS E.
VOR TEST FACILITY (VOT) 117.2
RADIO AIDS TO NAVIGATION: NOTAM FILE MFR.
  (H) VORTACW 113.6 OED Chan 83 N42°28.77´ W122°54.78´ 145° 6.6 NM to fld. 2083/19E. **HIWAS.**
  VOR portion unusable:
    260°–270° byd 35 NM blo 9,000´
    290°–300° byd 35 NM blo 8,500´
  MEDFORD NDB (MHW) 356 MEF N42°23.50´ W122°52.73´ 151° 1.1 NM to fld.
  NDB unusable:
    220°–240° byd 15 NM
  PUMIE NDB (LOM) 373 MF N42°27.06´ W122°54.80´ 143° 4.9 NM to fld. LOM unusable 260°–270° beyond 10 NM.
    Unmonitored when ATCT closed.
  ILS/DME 110.3 I–MFR Chan 40 Rwy 14. Class IA. LOM PUMIE NDB. LOM unusable 260°–270° beyond 10 NM.
    Unmonitored when ATCT closed. Localizer backcourse unusable byd 11 NM blo 7,000´, byd 13 NM blo 8,300´, byd
    17 NM blo 8,700´. Localizer backcourse unusable byd 20° left of course.

MEMALOOSE (See IMNAHA on page 122)

MILLER MEM AIRPARK (See VALE on page 145)

MONUMENT MUNI (12S) 1 NW UTC–8(–7DT) N44°49.89´ W119°25.78´   SEATTLE
2323 TPA—3323(1000) NOTAM FILE MMV
RWY 14–32: H2104X29 (ASPH)
  RWY 14: Hill.
AIRPORT REMARKS: Unattended. Intermittently clsd winters due to snow. Wildlife on and invof arpt. Rwy ends marked at each
  corner by a single white tire.
COMMUNICATIONS: CTAF 122.9

MULINO STATE (See PORTLAND–MULINO on page 137)

FIGURE 165.—Excerpt from Chart Supplement.

HOSSY   N34°25.35′ W93°11.38′   NOTAM FILE HOT.   MEMPHIS
   NDB (HW/LOM) 385   HO   050° 5.7 NM to Mem Fld.   L–17E

HOT SPRINGS

   MEMORIAL FLD   (HOT)   3 SW   UTC–6(–5DT)   N34°28.68′ W93°05.77′   MEMPHIS
     540   B   S4   **FUEL** 100LL, JET A   Class II, ARFF Index A   NOTAM FILE HOT   H–6I, L–17E
     RWY 05–23: H6595X150 (ASPH–GRVD)   S–75, D–125, 2S–158,   IAP
       2D–210, 2D/2D2–400   HIRL   0.6% up NE
       RWY 05: MALSR. Rgt tfc.
       RWY 23: PAPI(P4L)—GA 3.0° TCH 40′. Pole.
     RWY 13–31: H4098X100 (ASPH)   S–28, D–36, 2D–63   MIRL
       0.4% up NW
       RWY 13: REIL. Trees. Rgt tfc.
       RWY 31: Pole.
     RUNWAY DECLARED DISTANCE INFORMATION
       RWY 05: TORA–6595   TODA–6595   ASDA–6595   LDA–6595
       RWY 13: TORA–4100   TODA–4100   ASDA–4100   LDA–4100
       RWY 23: TORA–6595   TODA–6595   ASDA–6595   LDA–6595
       RWY 31: TORA–4100   TODA–4100   ASDA–4100   LDA–4100
     AIRPORT REMARKS: Attended 1100–0400Z‡. For fuel after hrs call
       501–617–0324 or 501–617–4908. Rwy 23 PAPI OTS indef.
       ACTIVATE HIRL Rwy 05–23, MIRL Rwy 13–31, MALSR Rwy 05,
       PAPI Rwy 23 and REIL Rwy 13—CTAF.
     WEATHER DATA SOURCES: ASOS 119.925 (501) 624–7633. HIWAS 110.0
       HOT.
     COMMUNICATIONS: CTAF/UNICOM 123.0
       RCO 122.1R 110.0T (JONESBORO RADIO)
   Ⓡ**MEMPHIS CENTER APP/DEP CON** 128.475
     AIRSPACE: CLASS E svc 1200–0400Z‡ other times CLASS G.
     RADIO AIDS TO NAVIGATION: NOTAM FILE HOT.
     HOT SPRINGS (L) VOR/DME 110.0   HOT   Chan 37   N34°28.72′ W93°05.44′   at fld. 529/4E.   **HIWAS.**
       VOR unusable:
         056°–140° byd 20 NM blo 6,500′
         141°–227° byd 20 NM blo 3,500′
         141°–227° byd 26 NM blo 5,500′
         228°–311° byd 20 NM blo 3,500′
         312°–345° byd 15 NM blo 5,500′
         312°–345° byd 32 NM blo 9,500′
         346°–055° byd 20 NM blo 3,500′
       DME unusable:
         310°–035° byd 10 NM blo 11,000′
         310°–035° byd 25 NM blo 12,000′
         310°–035° byd 30 NM blo 17,000′
     HOSSY NDB (LOM) 385   HO   N34°25.36′ W93°11.38′ 050° 5.7 NM to fld. Unmonitored.
     ILS/DME 111.5   I–HOT   Chan 52   Rwy 05.   Class IT.   LOM HOSSY NDB. ILS and LOM unmonitored.

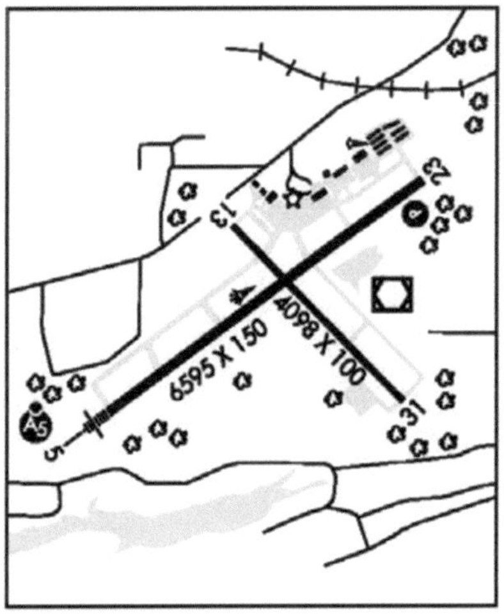

HOWARD CO   (See NASHVILLE on page 55)

FIGURE 166.—Chart Supplement (HOT).

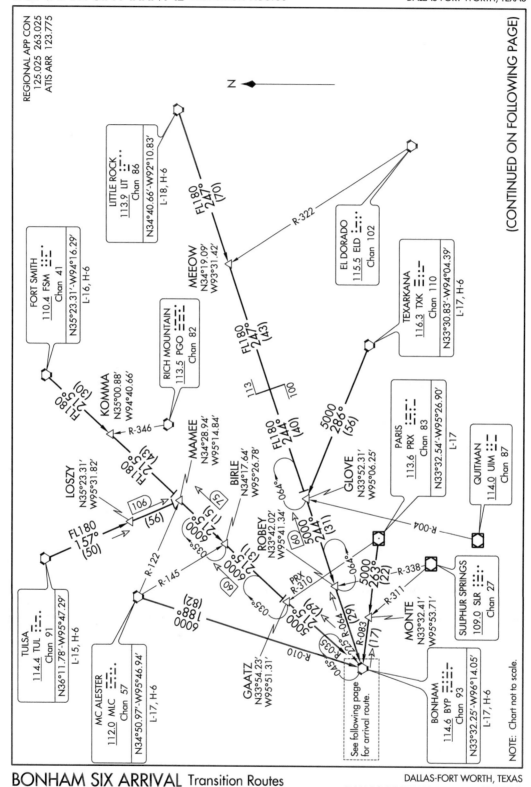

BONHAM SIX ARRIVAL Transition Routes
(BYP.BYP6) 13178

DALLAS-FORT WORTH, TEXAS
DALLAS-FORT WORTH INTL (DFW)

FIGURE 167.—BONHAM Six Arrival Transition Routes (BYP.BYP6) (DFW).

Appendix 2

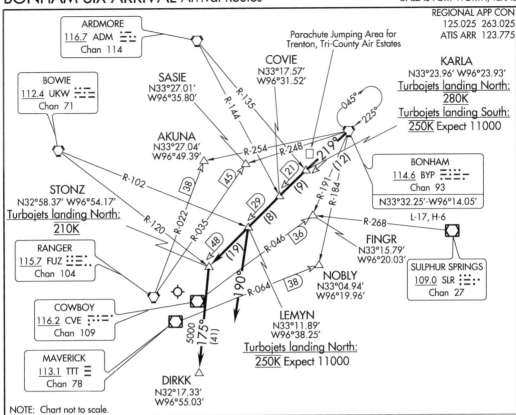

(BYP.BYP6) 13178
BONHAM SIX ARRIVAL Arrival Routes
ST-6039 (FAA)
DALLAS-FORT WORTH INTL (DFW)
DALLAS-FORT WORTH, TEXAS

NOTE: Chart not to scale.

ARRIVAL DESCRIPTION

FORT SMITH TRANSITION (FSM.BYP6): From over FSM VORTAC on FSM R-215 to
MAMEE INT, then on BYP R-035 to BYP VORTAC. Thence. . . .
LITTLE ROCK TRANSITION (LIT.BYP6): From over LIT VORTAC on LIT R-247 to MEEOW INT
then on LIT R-247 and BYP R-064 to GLOVE INT, then on BYP R-064 to BYP VORTAC. Thence. . .
MC ALESTER TRANSITION (MLC.BYP6): From over MLC VORTAC on MLC R-188
and BYP R-010 to BYP VORTAC. Thence. . . .
PARIS TRANSITION (PRX.BYP6): From over PRX VOR/DME on PRX R-263 to MONTE INT
then on BYP R-083 to BYP VORTAC. Thence. . . .
TEXARKANA TRANSITION (TXK.BYP6): From over TXK VORTAC on TXK R-286 to GLOVE INT
then on BYP R-064 to BYP VORTAC. Thence. . . .
TULSA TRANSITION (TUL.BYP6): From over TUL VORTAC on TUL R-157 to MAMEE
INT, then on BYP R-035 to BYP VORTAC. Thence. . . .

. . . . ALL AIRCRAFT: From over BYP VORTAC on BYP R-219, thence. . . .

ALL AIRCRAFT LANDING SOUTH: To LEMYN INT, expect vectors to final approach course.
JETS LANDING NORTH: FOR /E, /F, /G, and /R (RNP-2.0) EQUIPPED AIRCRAFT:
From over STONZ INT direct DIRKK, expect vector to final approach course prior to DIRKK, if
not received by DIRKK fly present heading.
ALL OTHERS: To STONZ depart STONZ heading 175° for vector to final approach course.
PROPS LANDING NORTH: Depart LEMYN INT heading 190°, expect vectors to final
approach course.

BONHAM SIX ARRIVAL Arrival Routes
(BYP.BYP6) 13178
DALLAS-FORT WORTH, TEXAS
DALLAS-FORT WORTH INTL (DFW)

FIGURE 168.—BONHAM Six Arrival Routes (BYP.BYP6) (DFW).

131

DALLAS

ADDISON (ADS)   9 N   UTC–6(–5DT)   N32°58.11´ W96°50.19´   DALLAS–FT WORTH
  645   B   S4   **FUEL** 100LL, JET A   OX 2, 3   TPA—See Remarks   LRA   NOTAM FILE ADS   COPTER
  RWY 15–33: H7203X100 (ASPH–GRVD)   S–60, D–120   HIRL   H–6H, L–17C, A
    RWY 15: MALSR. PAPI(P4R)—GA 3.0° TCH 60´. Thld dsplcd 979´.   IAP, AD
    Pole.
    RWY 33: REIL. PAPI(P4L)—GA 3.0° TCH 60´. Thld dsplcd 772´. Bldg.
  RUNWAY DECLARED DISTANCE INFORMATION
    RWY 15: TORA–7202   TODA–7202   ASDA–6592   LDA–5613
    RWY 33: TORA–7202   TODA–7202   ASDA–7202   LDA–6431
  AIRPORT REMARKS: Attended continuously. Birds on and invof arpt. No touch
    and go landings without arpt managers approval. Numerous 200´
    buildings within 1 mile East, and South of arpt, transmission towers and
    water tanks West of arpt. Noise sensitive areas surround arpt. Pilots
    requested to use NBAA std noise procedures. TPA—1600 (956) for light
    acft, 2000 (1356) for large acft. Be alert: Rwy holding position
    markings located at the west edge of Twy A. ACTIVATE HIRL Rwy
    15–33 and MALSR Rwy 15—CTAF. Flight Notification Service (ADCUS)
    available.
  WEATHER DATA SOURCES: AWOS–3 (972) 386–4855 LAWRS.
  COMMUNICATIONS: CTAF 126.0   ATIS 133.4 972–628–2439
    UNICOM 122.95
  ®**REGIONAL APP/DEP CON** 124.3
    TOWER 126.0 (1200–0400Z‡)   **GND CON** 121.6   **CLNC DEL** 119.55
  AIRSPACE: **CLASS D** svc 1200–0400Z‡, other times CLASS G.
  RADIO AIDS TO NAVIGATION: NOTAM FILE FTW.
    MAVERICK (H) VORW/DME 113.1   TTT   Chan 78   N32°52.15´ W97°02.43´   054° 11.9 NM to fld. 540/6E.
    All acft arriving DFW are requested to turn DME off until departure due to traffic overload of Maverick DME
    ILS/DME 110.1   I–ADS   Chan 38   Rwy 15.   Class IT.   Unmonitored when ATCT closed. DME also serves Rwy 33.
    ILS/DME 110.1   I–TBQ   Chan 38   Rwy 33.   Class IB.   Localizer unmonitored when ATCT closed. DME also serves
      Rwy 15.

AIR PARK–DALLAS (F69)   16 NE   UTC–6(–5DT)   N33°01.41´ W96°50.22´   DALLAS–FT WORTH
  695   S4   **FUEL** 100LL   TPA—1890(1195)   NOTAM FILE FTW   COPTER
  RWY 16–34: H3080X30 (ASPH)   LIRL(NSTD)   L–17C, A
    RWY 16: Thld dsplcd 300´. Pole.
    RWY 34: Tree. Rgt tfc.
  AIRPORT REMARKS: Uattended. For fuel call 972–248–4265 prior to arrival. Rwy 16–34 extensive cracking, loose asph and
    stones rwy. Rwy 16–34 NSTD LIRL, south 2780´ of rwy lgtd. Rwy 16 and Rwy 34 NSTD centerline marking incorrect
    size and spacing, dsplcd thld yellow. Rwy numbers 25´ tall. ACTIVATE LIRL Rwy 16–34—CTAF.
  COMMUNICATIONS: CTAF 122.9
  RADIO AIDS TO NAVIGATION: NOTAM FILE FTW.
    MAVERICK (H) VORW/DME 113.1   TTT   Chan 78   N32°52.15´ W97°02.43´   042° 13.8 NM to fld. 540/6E.
    All acft arriving DFW are requested to turn DME off until departure due to traffic overload of Maverick DME

AIRPARK EAST (1F7)   23 E   UTC–6(–5DT)   N32°48.78´ W96°21.12´   DALLAS–FT WORTH
  510   B   S4   NOTAM FILE FTW   COPTER
  RWY 13–31: H2630X30 (ASPH)   LIRL
    RWY 13: Tree. Rgt tfc.
    RWY 31: Tree.
  AIRPORT REMARKS: Unattended. ACTIVATE LIRL Rwy 13–31—122.9.
  COMMUNICATIONS: CTAF/UNICOM 122.7

FIGURE 169.—Excerpt from Chart Supplement (ADS).

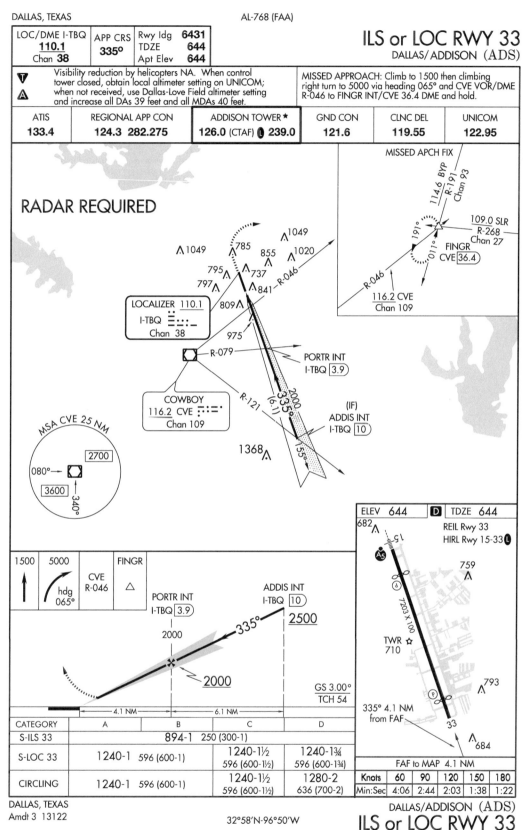

DALLAS, TEXAS   AL-768 (FAA)

LOC/DME I-TBQ	APP CRS	Rwy Idg	6431
110.1	**335°**	TDZE	**644**
Chan **38**		Apt Elev	**644**

ILS or LOC RWY 33
DALLAS/ADDISON (ADS)

Visibility reduction by helicopters NA. When control tower closed, obtain local altimeter setting on UNICOM; when not received, use Dallas-Love Field altimeter setting and increase all DAs 39 feet and all MDAs 40 feet.

MISSED APPROACH: Climb to 1500 then climbing right turn to 5000 via heading 065° and CVE VOR/DME R-046 to FINGR INT/CVE 36.4 DME and hold.

ATIS	REGIONAL APP CON	ADDISON TOWER ★	GND CON	CLNC DEL	UNICOM
133.4	**124.3 282.275**	**126.0** (CTAF) Ⓛ **239.0**	**121.6**	**119.55**	**122.95**

RADAR REQUIRED

MSA CVE 25 NM
2700
080° → 3600
340°

MISSED APCH FIX
114.6 BYP R-191 Chan 93
191°
011°
109.0 SLR R-268 Chan 27
FINGR CVE 36.4
R-046
116.2 CVE Chan 109

LOCALIZER 110.1
I-TBQ
Chan 38

PORTR INT I-TBQ 3.9

COWBOY 116.2 CVE Chan 109

R-079
R-121
R-046

ADDIS INT I-TBQ 10 (IF)

335° 2000 (6.1)
155°

1368

1049 785 1049
795 855 1020
797 737
841
809
975

| 1500 | 5000 | CVE R-046 | FINGR △ |
| ↑ | hdg 065° | | |

PORTR INT I-TBQ 3.9
ADDIS INT I-TBQ 10

2000
335°
2500
2000

GS 3.00° TCH 54

4.1 NM   6.1 NM

335° 4.1 NM from FAF

| ELEV 644 | Ⓓ | TDZE 644 |

REIL Rwy 33
HIRL Rwy 15-33 Ⓛ
682
A5
759
7203 x 100
TWR 710
793
33
684

CATEGORY	A	B	C	D
S-ILS 33		894-1 250 (300-1)		
S-LOC 33	1240-1 596 (600-1)		1240-1½ 596 (600-1½)	1240-1¾ 596 (600-1¾)
CIRCLING	1240-1 596 (600-1)		1240-1½ 596 (600-1½)	1280-2 636 (700-2)

FAF to MAP 4.1 NM

Knots	60	90	120	150	180
Min:Sec	4:06	2:44	2:03	1:38	1:22

DALLAS, TEXAS
Amdt 3 13122

32°58'N-96°50'W

DALLAS/ADDISON (ADS)
ILS or LOC RWY 33

FIGURE 170.—ILS or LOC RWY 33 (ADS).

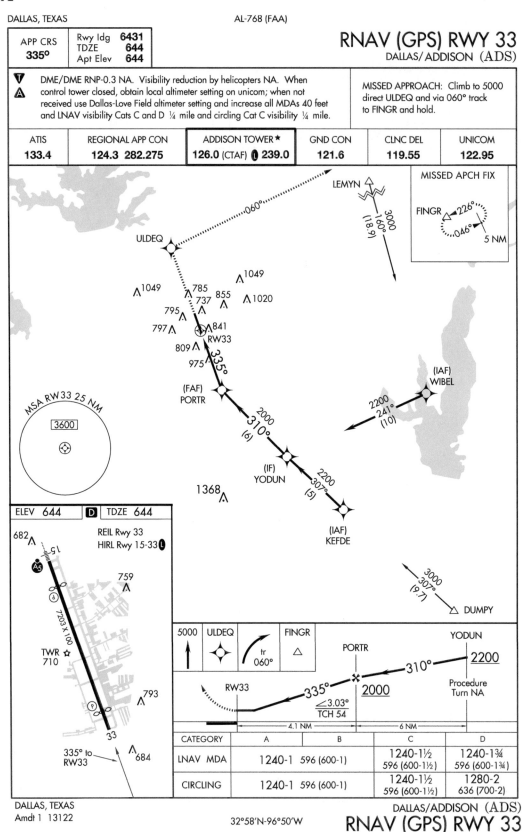

DALLAS, TEXAS   AL-768 (FAA)

APP CRS	Rwy Idg	**6431**
335°	TDZE	**644**
	Apt Elev	**644**

RNAV (GPS) RWY 33
DALLAS/ ADDISON (ADS)

DME/DME RNP-0.3 NA. Visibility reduction by helicopters NA. When control tower closed, obtain local altimeter setting on unicom; when not received use Dallas-Love Field altimeter setting and increase all MDAs 40 feet and LNAV visibility Cats C and D ¼ mile and circling Cat C visibility ¼ mile.

MISSED APPROACH: Climb to 5000 direct ULDEQ and via 060° track to FINGR and hold.

ATIS	REGIONAL APP CON	ADDISON TOWER ★	GND CON	CLNC DEL	UNICOM
133.4	**124.3 282.275**	**126.0** (CTAF) **239.0**	**121.6**	**119.55**	**122.95**

MISSED APCH FIX

FINGR 226° 046° 5 NM

MSA RW33 25 NM 3600

ELEV 644	**D**	TDZE 644

REIL Rwy 33
HIRL Rwy 15-33

TWR 710

7203 X 100

335° to RW33

5000	ULDEQ	tr 060°	FINGR

	5000	ULDEQ	FINGR	PORTR		YODUN

RW33 335° ∠3.03° TCH 54 PORTR 2000 310° YODUN 2200 Procedure Turn NA

4.1 NM   6 NM

CATEGORY	A	B	C	D
LNAV MDA	1240-1 596 (600-1)		1240-1½ 596 (600-1½)	1240-1¾ 596 (600-1¾)
CIRCLING	1240-1 596 (600-1)		1240-1½ 596 (600-1½)	1280-2 636 (700-2)

DALLAS, TEXAS
Amdt 1 13122

32°58'N-96°50'W

DALLAS/ADDISON (ADS)
RNAV (GPS) RWY 33

FIGURE 171.—RNAV (GPS) RWY 33 (ADS).

HELENA RGNL (HLN)(KHLN) P (ARNG)   2 NE   UTC–7(–6DT)   N46°36.41′ W111°58.97′   GREAT FALLS
    3877   B   S4   **FUEL** 80, 100, 100LL, JET A   OX 1, 3   LRA   Class I, ARFF Index B   NOTAM FILE HLN   H–1D, L–13C
     RWY 09–27: H9000X150 (ASPH–PFC)   S–100, D–160, 2S–175,   IAP, DIAP, AD
        2D–250   HIRL

        RWY 09: REIL. VASI(V4L)—GA 3.0° TCH 45′. Ground. 0.3% down.
        RWY 27: MALSR. VASI(V4L)—GA 3.0° TCH 47′. Rgt tfc.
     RWY 05–23: H4644X75 (ASPH–PFC)   S–21, D–30   MIRL   1.2% up SW
        RWY 05: Road.
        RWY 23: PAPI(P2L)—GA 3.0° TCH 49′. Fence. Rgt tfc.
     RWY 17–35: H2989X75 (ASPH–PFC)   S–21, D–30   MIRL   1.7% up SE
        RWY 35: Ground. Rgt tfc.
     MILITARY SERVICE: LGT When twr clsd, ACTIVATE–HIRL Rwy 09–27, MIRL
       Rwy 05–23 and 16–34, REIL Rwy 09, MALSR Rwy 27 – CTAF.   **FUEL**
       A+, J8 (C406–442–2190. Opr 1200–0600Z‡, OT $150 fee, 90 min
       PPR.) (NC–80, 100, 100LL)
     AIRPORT REMARKS: Attended 1200–0800Z‡. ARFF coverage provided for
       scheduled Part 121 air carriers only exc with prior approval, call
       406–442–2821. Ldg rights customs avbl call 406–449–5506. Rwy
       17–35 and Rwy 05–23 (exc between Twy F and Rwy 09–27) not avbl
       for air carrier use by acft with greater than 30 passenger seats. Twy A,
       Twy B, and Twy C between Twy A and Rwy 35 not avbl for air carrier
       use by acft with greater than 30 passenger seats. When twr clsd
       ACTIVATE HIRL Rwy 09–27, MIRL Rwy 05–23 and Rwy 17–35, REIL Rwy 09, MALSR Rwy 27—CTAF. Ldg fee for all
       commercial acft and all acft over 10,000 lbs. Flight Notification Service (ADCUS) avbl. NOTE: See SPECIAL NOTICE.
     MILITARY REMARKS: ARNG Opr Mon–Fri 1400–0030Z‡, exc holidays. Exercise caution while taxiing, AASF ramp not stressed
       for large acft. Ctc flt ops for ramp advisory 126.2, DSN 324–3055/56, C406–324–3055/56. No tran svc Sat, Sun,
       holidays or after 2300Z‡ Mon–Fri.
     WEATHER DATA SOURCES: ASOS (406) 443–4317
     COMMUNICATIONS: CTAF 118.3 ATIS 120.4 UNICOM 122.95
       RCO 122.55 255.4 (GREAT FALLS RADIO)
       APP/DEP CON 119.5 229.4 (1300–0500Z‡)
       SALT LAKE CENTER APP/DEP CON 133.4 285.4 (0500–1300Z‡)
       TOWER 118.3 257.8 (1300–0500Z‡) GND CON 121.9
       ARNG OPS 40.65 126.2 321.45
     AIRSPACE: CLASS D svc 1300–0500Z‡ other times CLASS E.
     RADIO AIDS TO NAVIGATION: NOTAM FILE HLN.
       (H) VORTACW 117.7   HLN   Chan 124   N46°36.41′ W111°57.21′   254° 1.2 NM to fld. 3823/16E.
       VOR portion unusable:
          035°–050° byd 35 NM blo 12,000′
          105°–165° byd 25 NM blo 17,000′
          165°–185° byd 25 NM blo 13,500′
          185°–230° byd 25 NM blo 17,500′
          203°–213° byd 22 NM blo 13,000′
          230°–270° byd 25 NM blo 12,500′
       TACAN AZIMUTH and DME unusable:
          035°–070° byd 35 NM blo 13,000′
          165°–185° byd 25 NM blo 13,500′
          250°–300° byd 25 NM blo 14,000′
          320°–035° byd 25 NM blo 13,000′
       TACAN DME unusable:
          035°–070° byd 35 NM blo 13,000′
          105°–150° byd 25 NM
          105°–210° byd 15 NM blo 11,100′
          105°–210° byd 20 NM blo 12,000′
          150°–165° byd 25 NM blo 17,000′
          165°–185° byd 25 NM blo 13,500′
          185°–210° byd 25 NM
          203°–213° byd 22 NM blo 13,000′
          210°–250° byd 15 NM blo 12,000′
          210°–250° byd 25 NM blo 17,500′
          250°–300° byd 25 NM blo 14,000′
          320°–035° byd 25 NM blo 13,000′
       TACAN AZIMUTH unusable:
          105°–150° byd 15 NM
          150°–165° byd 15 NM blo 17,000′
          185°–210° byd 15 NM
          210°–250° byd 15 NM blo 17,500′

CONTINUED ON NEXT PAGE

FIGURE 172.—Excerpt from Chart Supplement.

216   **TEXAS**

BIG SPRING MC MAHON–WRINKLE (BPG)   2 SW   UTC–6(–5DT)   N32°12.76´ W101°31.30´   **DALLAS–FT WORTH**
   2573   B   S4   **FUEL** 100LL, JET A   NOTAM FILE BPG   **H–6G, L–6H**
   RWY 17–35: H8802X100 (CONC)   S–60, D–150, 2D–200   MIRL   **IAP**
      RWY 17: SSALS. PAPI(P4L)—GA 3.0° TCH 45´. Rgt tfc.
      RWY 35: PAPI(P4L)—GA 3.0° TCH 36´.
   RWY 06–24: H4601X75 (ASPH)   MIRL   0.6% up NE
      RWY 06: PVASI(PSIL)—GA 2.97° TCH 47´. Rgt tfc.
      RWY 24: PVASI(PSIL)—GA 3.55° TCH 35´.
   AIRPORT REMARKS: Attended Mon–Sat 1400–2300Z‡. For fuel after hours
      call 432–267–8952 or 432–935–3395. Prairie dogs on rwys and twys.
      Extensive agricultural ops invof arpt. Sandhill Cranes crossing in the
      spring and fall. MIRL Rwy 06–24 and Rwy 17–35 preset low ints, to
      increase ints and ACTIVATE SSALS Rwy 17 and PVASI Rwy 06, Rwy
      24, and PAPI Rwy 17 and Rwy 35—CTAF.
   WEATHER DATA SOURCES: AWOS–3 118.025 (432) 263–3842.
   COMMUNICATIONS: CTAF/UNICOM 122.8
   RCO 122.4 (SAN ANGELO RADIO)
      FORT WORTH CENTER APP/DEP CON 133.7
   RADIO AIDS TO NAVIGATION: NOTAM FILE BPG.
      (L) **VORTACW** 114.3   BGS   Chan 90   N32°23.14´
      W101°29.02´   180° 10.5 NM to fld. 2670/11E.

BIGGS AAF (FORT BLISS) (BIF)(KBIF) A   5 NE   UTC–7(–6DT)   N31°50.97´ W106°22.80´   **EL PASO**
   3948   B   TPA—See Remarks   NOTAM FILE ABQ   Not insp.   **H–4L, L–6F**
   RWY 03–21: H13554X150 (PEM)   PCN 120 R/C/W/T   HIRL   **DIAP, AD**
      RWY 03: PAPI(P4L)—GA 3.0° TCH 71´.
      RWY 21: ALSF1. PAPI(P4L)—GA 3.0° TCH 71´. Rgt tfc. 0.3% down.
   MILITARY SERVICE: LGT When unattended ACTIVATE 3-step HIRL Rwy 03–21, High Intensity ALS Category I configuration with
      sequenced Flashers (code) Rwy 21 and PAPI Rwy 21–127.9.   **JASU** 4(A/M32A–86) 2(A/M32–95)   **FUEL** A+ (Atlantic
      Avn, 1200–0400Z‡ Mon–Sun, C915–779–2831, 1 hr prior notice, after hr C915–861–2390, after hr call out fee $100.)
      FLUID SP   **TRAN ALERT** 1300–0500Z‡ Mon–Sun, exc holidays.
   MILITARY REMARKS: Attended Mon–Sun 1300–0500Z‡, except holidays. See FLIP AP/1 Supplementary Arpt Remark. **RSTD** PPR
      all acft. 24 hr prior notice, ctc Airfield Ops DSN 621–8811/8330, C915–744–8811/8330. Twr and svcs avbl for all acft
      with PPR. PPR time valid +/— 1 hr. All acft ctc Afld Ops via PTD 30 min prior to arr. Twr and svcs unavbl before 1 hr
      prior to PPR sked arr. **CAUTION** El Paso Intl Rwy 22 2 NM SE can be mistaken for Rwy 21. Coyote hazard. **TFC PAT** Fixed
      Wing 5002(1054), Fixed Wing Category BCDE turbo prop 5502(1554), Rotary Wing 4502(554), Jet 6002(2054).
      NS ABTMT VFR west arr/dep via mountain pass 15 NM NW of Biggs AAF. Avoid VFR over flight of city. Fly 1500´ AGL,
      1500´ horizontal distance from mountain dwellings. **MISC** Approval required for access to ramp. Temporary storage of
      classified material avbl at Afld Ops. Intl garbage cap ltd. Expect delays unless placed in garbage bags prior to arrival.
      Hangar space extremely limited for transient acft. KBIF manual obsn and wx forecaster avbl Mon–Fri 1300–0500Z‡, clsd
      holidays. DSN 621–1215/1214, C915–744–1215/1214, OT 25th OWS, Davis Monthan AFB, DSN 228–6598/6599.
   COMMUNICATIONS: ATIS 120.0 254.3 (C915–772–9412) **PTD** 122.7
   Ⓡ **EL PASO APP CON** 119.15 353.5 (South of V16) 124.25 298.85 (North of V16)
      TOWER 127.9 342.25 (Mon–Sun 1300–0500Z‡, except holidays). Advisory svc twr freq other times.
   Ⓡ **EL PASO DEP CON** 121.3 263.0
      EL PASO CLNC DEL 125.0 379.1
   AIRSPACE: CLASS D svc 1300–0500Z‡ Mon–Sat except holidays other times CLASS E.
   RADIO AIDS TO NAVIGATION: NOTAM FILE ABQ.
      NEWMAN (L) VORTACW 112.4   EWM   Chan 71   N31°57.10´ W106°16.34´   210° 8.2 NM to fld. 4040/12E.
      DME portion unusable.
      220°–255° byd 25 NM blo 12,000´
   COMM/NAV/WEATHER REMARKS: Radar—See Terminal FLIP for Radar Minima.

BIRD DOG AIRFIELD (See KRUM on page 297)

BISHOP (See DECATUR on page 245)

FIGURE 172A.—Excerpt from Chart Supplement.

MONTANA

CONTINUED FROM PRECEDING PAGE

CAPITOL NDB (HW) 335   CVP   N46°36.40´ W111°56.23´   258° 1.9 NM to fld. NDB unmonitored when ATCT clsd.
HAUSER NDB (MHW) 386   HAU   N46°34.13´ W111°45.48´   268° 9.6 NM to fld. NDB unmonitored when HLN
    ATCT clsd.
ILS 110.1   I–HLN   Rwy 27.   Unmonitored when ATCT closed. Localizer backcourse unusable byd 22° rgt of course,
    unusable within 2.7 DME.

HINSDALE (6U5)   0 SE   UTC–7(–6DT)   N48°23.28´ W107°05.00´   BILLINGS
2220   NOTAM FILE GTF
RWY 07–25: 2200X75 (TURF)   LIRL(NSTD)   0.7% up W
   RWY 07: Road.
RWY 10–28: 2160X200 (TURF)   0.3% up W
   RWY 10: Road.
RWY 16–34: 1960X75 (TURF)   1.5% up S
   RWY 16: P–line.
   RWY 34: Fence.
AIRPORT REMARKS: Unattended. Rwys soft when wet. Hay bales and farm equipment adjacent to rwy. Rwys not clearly defined.
   Rwy 16–34, Rwy 07–25 and Rwy 10–28 marked with white cones full length of rwy. Rwy 16 p–lines marked with globes.
   Rwy 07–25 NSTD LIRL 335´ spacing between lgts, one thld lgt each end. For rwy lgts phone 406–364–2272/2387.
COMMUNICATIONS: CTAF 122.9

HOGELAND (6U6)   1 NW   UTC–7(–6DT)   N48°51.61´ W108°39.66´   BILLINGS
3139   B   NOTAM FILE GTF
RWY 07–25: 3140X60 (TRTD)   0.6% up W
RWY 16–34: 1230X50 (TURF)
   RWY 34: Bldg.
AIRPORT REMARKS: Unattended. Rwy 16–34 for emerg use only, road and drainage ditch parallel rwy on east side. Rwy 07–25
   patches of loose aggregate and grvl.
COMMUNICATIONS: CTAF 122.9

HOT SPRINGS (S09)   2 E   UTC–7(–6DT)   N47°36.75´ W114°36.81´   GREAT FALLS
2763   B   NOTAM FILE GTF
RWY 06–24: H3550X45 (ASPH–TRTD)   MIRL
   RWY 24: Thld dsplcd 411´. Road.
AIRPORT REMARKS: Unattended. Ultralights on and in vicinity of arpt. Occasional snow removal. Rwy 06–24 asph grvl
   composition full length. Rwy 24 has 411´ unlighted, 2169´ lgtd at ngt. Rwy 06–24 cones adjacent to MIRL full length
   and dsplcd thld marked with white cones. Rwy 06 and Rwy 24 numbers 4´x 8´ in measure, thld line and rwy lines NSTD.
COMMUNICATIONS: CTAF 122.9

HYSHAM (6U7)   2 E   UTC–7(–6DT)   N46°17.61´ W107°11.60´   BILLINGS
2624   B   NOTAM FILE GTF
RWY 07–25: H3060X45 (ASPH–TRTD)   LIRL
AIRPORT REMARKS: Unattended. 1030´ dirt extension east of Rwy 07 thld soft when wet. Rwy 07 basic markings NSTD
   numbers and stripes, markings are faded. Rwy 25 basic markings NSTD small numbers and stripes, markings are faded.
   Numerous rwy lgts inop. ACTIVATE LIRL Rwy 07–25—CTAF.
COMMUNICATIONS: CTAF 122.9

JORDAN (JDN)   2 NW   UTC–7(–6DT)   N47°19.73´ W106°57.16´   BILLINGS
2662   B   NOTAM FILE JDN   L–13D
RWY 10–28: H4300X75 (ASPH–PFC)   S–12.5   MIRL
   RWY 28: PAPI(P2L)—GA 3.0° TCH 29´.
AIRPORT REMARKS: Unattended. ACTIVATE MIRL Rwy 10–28 and PAPI Rwy 28—CTAF.
COMMUNICATIONS: CTAF 122.9
RADIO AIDS TO NAVIGATION: NOTAM FILE GGW.
   GLASGOW (H) VORW/DME 113.9   GGW   Chan 86   N48°12.92´ W106°37.53´   180° 54.8 NM to fld. 2283/14E.
   NDB (MHW) 263   JDN   N47°20.00´ W106°56.29´   at fld.   NOTAM FILE JDN. VFR only.

JUDITH MOUNTAIN   N47°13.03´ W109°13.31´   GREAT FALLS
RCO 122.2 (GREAT FALLS RADIO)   L–13D

FIGURE 173.—Excerpt from Chart Supplement.

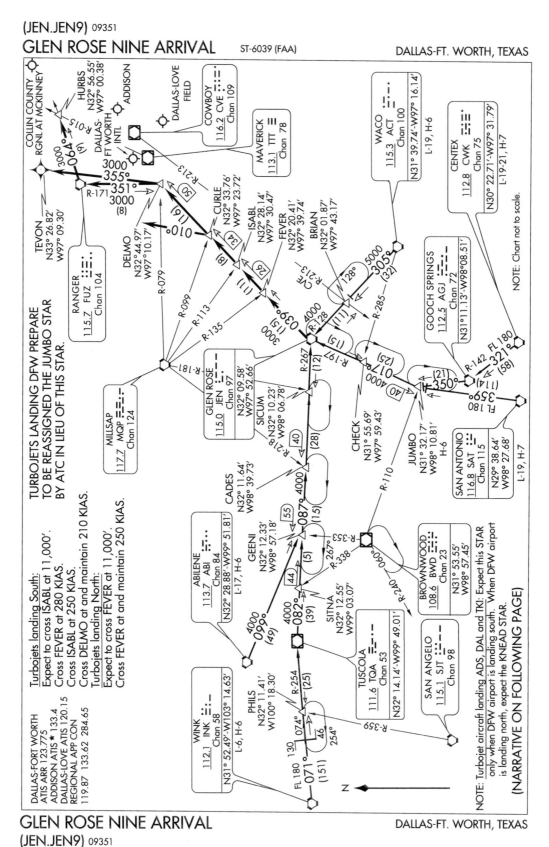

FIGURE 174.—GLEN ROSE Nine Arrival (JEN.JEN9).

(JEN.JEN9) 09351
GLEN ROSE NINE ARRIVAL   ST-6039 (FAA)   DALLAS-FT. WORTH, TEXAS

ARRIVAL DESCRIPTION

ABILENE TRANSITION (ABI.JEN9): From over ABI VORTAC via R-099 to GEENI INT,
then via JEN R-267 to JEN VORTAC. Thence. . . .
CENTEX TRANSITION (CWK.JEN9): From over CWK VORTAC via CWK R-321 and
AGJ R-142 to AGJ VORTAC, then via AGJ R-350 to JUMBO INT, then via JEN R-197 to
JEN VORTAC. Thence . . . .
JUMBO TRANSITION (JUMBO.JEN9): From over JUMBO INT via JEN R-197 to
JEN VORTAC. Thence . . . .
SAN ANTONIO TRANSITION (SAT.JEN9): From over SAT VORTAC via SAT R-359
to JUMBO INT, then via JEN R-197 to JEN VORTAC. Thence . . . .
WACO TRANSITION (ACT.JEN9): From over ACT VORTAC via ACT R-305 and
JEN R-128 to JEN VORTAC. Thence. . . .
WINK TRANSITION (INK.JEN9): From over INK VORTAC via INK R-071 and TQA
R-254 to TQA VOR/DME, then via TQA R-082 to GEENI INT, then via JEN R-267
to JEN VORTAC. Thence. . . .

. . . . ALL AIRCRAFT: From over JEN VORTAC via JEN R-039, thence . . . .

ALL AIRCRAFT LANDING NORTH: To CURLE INT, expect vectors to final approach course.

JETS LANDING SOUTH: To DELMO, depart DELMO heading 355°.
For /E, /F, /G and /R (RNP 2.0) EQUIPMENT SUFFIXED AIRCRAFT: From over
DELMO WP direct TEVON WP, expect vector to final approach course prior to
TEVON WP. If not received by TEVON fly present heading.
NON TURBOJETS LANDING SOUTH: To CURLE INT, depart CURLE heading 010°
for vectors to final approach course.

AIRCRAFT LANDING DAL, ADS, TKI: To DELMO INT, depart DELMO via FUZ R-171
to FUZ VORTAC then FUZ R-064 to HURBS INT, expect vectors to final approach course.

GLEN ROSE NINE ARRIVAL   DALLAS-FT. WORTH, TEXAS
(JEN.JEN9) 09351

FIGURE 175.—GLEN ROSE Nine Arrival (JEN.JEN9).

DALLAS–FORT WORTH

DALLAS/FORT WORTH INTL (DFW) 12 NW UTC–6(–5DT) N32°53.81′ W97°02.28′

607 B **FUEL** 100LL, JET A OX 1, 3 AOE Class I, ARFF Index E NOTAM FILE DFW

DALLAS–FT WORTH
COPTER
H–6H, L–17C, A
IAP, AD

RWY 17C–35C: H13401X150 (CONC–GRVD) S–120, D–200, 2S–175, 2D–600, 2D/2D2–850 HIRL CL

RWY 17C: ALSF2. TDZL. PAPI(P4L)—GA 3.0° TCH 74′.

RWY 35C: ALSF2. TDZL. PAPI(P4L)—GA 3.0° TCH 76′.

RWY 17R–35L: H13401X200 (CONC–GRVD) S–120, D–200, 2S–175, 2D–600, 2D/2D2–850 HIRL CL

RWY 17R: MALSR. TDZL. PAPI(P4L)—GA 3.0° TCH 68′.

RWY 35L: MALSR. TDZL. PAPI(P4L)—GA 3.0° TCH 63′.

RWY 18L–36R: H13400X200 (CONC–GRVD) S–120, D–200, 2S–175, 2D–600, 2D/2D2–850 HIRL CL

RWY 18L: MALSR. TDZL. PAPI(P4L)—GA 3.0° TCH 70′.

RWY 36R: MALSR. TDZL. PAPI(P4L)—GA 3.0° TCH 66′.

RWY 18R–36L: H13400X150 (CONC–GRVD) S–120, D–200, 2S–175, 2D–600, 2D/2D2–850 HIRL CL

RWY 18R: ALSF2. TDZL. PAPI(P4L)—GA 3.0° TCH 74′.

RWY 36L: MALSR. TDZL. PAPI(P4L)—GA 3.0° TCH 72′.

RWY 13R–31L: H9301X150 (CONC–GRVD) S–120, D–200, 2S–175, 2D–600, 2D/2D2–850 HIRL CL

RWY 13R: MALSR. TDZL. PAPI(P4L)—GA 3.0° TCH 71′.

RWY 31L: REIL. PAPI(P4L)—GA 3.13° TCH 72′.

RWY 13L–31R: H9000X200 (CONC–GRVD) S–120, D–200, 2S–175, 2D–600, 2D/2D2–850 HIRL CL

RWY 13L: REIL. PAPI(P4L)—GA 3.0° TCH 82′. Thld dsplcd 625′. 0.5% down.

RWY 31R: MALSR. TDZL. PAPI(P4L)—GA 3.0° TCH 69′. 0.5% up.

RWY 17L–35R: H8500X150 (CONC–GRVD) S–120, D–200, 2S–175, 2D–600, 2D/2D2–850 HIRL CL

RWY 17L: ALSF2. TDZL. PAPI(P4L)—GA 3.0° TCH 77′. Antenna. 0.6% up.

RWY 35R: ALSF2. TDZL. PAPI(P4R)—GA 3.0° TCH 73′. 0.6% down.

LAND AND HOLD–SHORT OPERATIONS

LDG RWY	HOLD–SHORT POINT	AVBL LDG DIST
RWY 17C	TWY B	10460
RWY 18R	TWY B	10100
RWY 35C	TWY EJ	9050
RWY 36L	TWY Z	10650

RUNWAY DECLARED DISTANCE INFORMATION

RWY 13L: TORA–9000 TODA–9000 ASDA–9000 LDA–8375

RWY 13R: TORA–9301 TODA–9301 ASDA–9301 LDA–9301

RWY 17C: TORA–13401 TODA–13401 ASDA–13401 LDA–13401

RWY 17L: TORA–8500 TODA–8500 ASDA–8500 LDA–8500

RWY 17R: TORA–13401 TODA–13401 ASDA–13401 LDA–13401

RWY 18L: TORA–13400 TODA–13400 ASDA–13400 LDA–13400

RWY 18R: TORA–13400 TODA–13400 ASDA–13400 LDA–13400

RWY 31L: TORA–9301 TODA–9301 ASDA–9301 LDA–9301

RWY 31R: TORA–8375 TODA–8375 ASDA–8375 LDA–8375

RWY 35C: TORA–13401 TODA–13401 ASDA–13401 LDA–13401

RWY 35L: TORA–13401 TODA–13401 ASDA–13401 LDA–13401

RWY 35R: TORA–8500 TODA–8500 ASDA–8500 LDA–8500

RWY 36L: TORA–13400 TODA–13400 ASDA–13400 LDA–13400

RWY 36R: TORA–13400 TODA–13400 ASDA–13400 LDA–13400

CONTINUED ON NEXT PAGE

FIGURE 176.—ILS-1 RWY 36L, Dallas-Fort Worth Intl.

244

TEXAS

CONTINUED FROM PRECEDING PAGE

AIRPORT REMARKS: Attended continuously. Rwy 17L–35R CLOSED 0400–1200Z‡ except PPR. Rwy 13R–31L CLOSED 0400–1200Z‡ except PPR. Rwy 13L–31R CLOSED 0400–1200Z‡ except PPR. Rwy 31R last 625´ CLOSED indef. Visual screen 20´ AGL 1180´ south AER 35C. Visual screen 22´ AGL 1179´ south AER 35L. ASDE–X SURVEILLANCE system in use: Pilots should opr transponders with mode C on all twys and rwys. PPR for acft with wingspan 215´ or greater (GROUP VI), call arpt ops 972–973–3112 for follow me services while taxiing to and from ramp and rwys. Rwy 13L, Rwy 17L, Rwy 31R, and Rwy 35R rwy visual range touchdown, midpoint and rollout avbl. Rwy 31L and Rwy 31R runway visual range touchdown and rollout avbl. Arpt under construction, PAEW in movement areas. Birds on and in vicinity of arpt. Tkf distance for Rwy 17L from Twy Q2 is 8196´. Tkf distance for Rwy 35R from Twy Q9 is 8196´. Tkf distance for Rwy 17R from Twy EG is 13082´ and from Twy EH is 12816´. Tkf distance for Rwy 35L from Twy EQ is 13084´ and from Twy EP is 12811´. Tkf distance for Rwy 36R from Twy WP is 12815´, from Twy WQ is 13082´. Tkf distance for Rwy 18L from Twy WG is 13082´, from Twy WH is 12815´. Tkf distance for Rwy 17C from Twy EG is 13,082´. Tkf distance for Rwy 18R from Twy WG is 13,082´. Land and hold–short signs on Rwy 17C at Twy B 10,460´ south of Rwy 17C thld, Rwy 18R at Twy B 10,100´ south of Rwy 18R thld, Rwy 35C at Twy EJ 9050´ north of Rwy 35C thld, Rwy 36L at Twy Z 10,650´ north of Rwy 36L thld, lgtd and marked with in–pavement pulsating white lgts. Twy G11 east of Twy G clsd to acft with wingspan 125´ and greater. Acft using gates D6–D17 must obtain approval from DFW ramp twr 129.95 prior to entering ramp and prior to pushback 1130–0430Z‡. Use extreme care at other times. Apron Terminal E ramp work in progress, ctc DFW ramp on 131.0 1530–1200Z‡ for Terminal E procedure change. Apron entrance/exit Points 32, 33, 34, 35, 36, 37, 38 and 39 clsd to acft with wingspan greater than 135´. Acft pushing back or powering back on Terminal B Apron have right of way. Frequent ground support equip under escort crossing Twys A and B at Twy HA. Apron entrance/exit points 5, 7, 42 and 44 clsd to acft with wingspan 118´ and greater. Apron entrance/exit points 42 and 44 clsd to acft with wingspan greater than 118´. Terminal B apron taxilane btn apron entrance/exit point taxilanes 110 and 115 clsd to acft with wingspan 118´ and greater. Apron entrance/exit points 22, 24, 105, 107 and 122 clsd to acft with wingspan 125´ and greater. Apron entrance/exit point 124 clsd to acft with wingspan 200´ and greater. Twy A5 clsd to acft with wingspan 171´ and greater. Twys may require judgemental oversteering for large acft. Apron entrance/exit points 52 and 53 clsd to acft with wingspan 171´ and greater. Acft exiting via apron entrance/exit points 42, 43 and 44 ctc Gnd Con prior to taxiing. PPR general aviation ops 0400–1200Z‡, call arpt ops 972–973–3112. PPR from arpt ops for general aviation acft to proceed to airline terminal gate except to general aviation facility. PPR from the primary tenant airlines to operate within the central terminal area. Proper minimum object free area distances may not be maintained for ramp/apron taxi lanes. Twy edge reflectors along all twys. Landing fee. Flight Notification Service (ADCUS) available. NOTE: See Land and Hold Short Operations, Intersection Departures During Periods of Darkness, Noise Abatement Procedures and Continuous Power Facilities.

WEATHER DATA SOURCES: ASOS (972) 453–0992 LLWAS.

COMMUNICATIONS: D–ATIS ARR 123.775 (972) 615–2701 **D–ATIS DEP** 135.925 (972) 615–2701 **UNICOM** 122.95

Ⓡ **RGNL APP CON** 125.025 133.525 (E) 119.875 133.625 (W)

DFW TOWER 126.55 127.5 (E) 124.15 134.9 (W) **GND CON** 121.65 121.8 (E) 121.85 (W)

CLNC DEL 128.25

Ⓡ **RGNL DEP CON** 118.55 (E) 126.475 (W) 124.825 (N) 125.125 (S)

AIRSPACE: CLASS B See VFR Terminal Area Chart

RADIO AIDS TO NAVIGATION: NOTAM FILE FTW.

    MAVERICK (H) VORW/DME 113.1　TTT　Chan 78　N32°52.15´ W97°02.43´　358° 1.7 NM to fld. 540/6E.

    ILS/DME 109.5　I–LWN　Chan 32　Rwy 13R.　Class IE.

    ILS/DME 110.3　I–FLQ　Chan 40　Rwy 17C.　Class IIIE.　DME also serves Rwy 35C.

    ILS/DME 111.75　I–PPZ　Chan 54(Y)　Rwy 17L.　Class IIIE.　DME also serves Rwy 35R.

    ILS/DME 111.35　I–JHZ　Chan 50(Y)　Rwy 17R.　Class IE.　DME also serves Rwy 35L.

    ILS/DME 110.55　I–CIX　Chan 42(Y)　Rwy 18L.　Class IE.　DME also serves Rwy 36R.

    ILS/DME 111.9　I–VYN　Chan 56　Rwy 18R.　Class IIIE.　DME also serves Rwy 36L.

    ILS/DME 110.9　I–RRA　Chan 46　Rwy 31R.　Class IE.

    ILS/DME 110.3　I–PKQ　Chan 40　Rwy 35C.　Class IIIE.　DME also serves Rwy 17C. OM/comlo also serves Rwy 35L.

    ILS/DME 111.35　I–UWX　Chan 50(Y)　Rwy 35L.　Class IE.　OM/comlo also serves Rwy 35R. LOC unusable byd 14 NM blo 3,400´. DME also serves Rwy 17R.

    ILS/DME 111.75　I–AJQ　Chan 54(Y)　Rwy 35R.　Class IIIE.　DME also serves Rwy 17L. LOC unusable byd 16 NM 5° right of course.

    ILS/DME 111.9　I–BXN　Chan 56　Rwy 36L.　Class ID.　DME also serves Rwy 18R. OM also serves Rwy 36R. LOC unusable byd 15 NM 5° right of course.

    ILS/DME 110.55　I–FJN　Chan 42(Y)　Rwy 36R.　Class IE.　OM also serves Rwy 36L. DME also serves Rwy 18L.

    COMM/NAV/WEATHER REMARKS: All acft arriving DFW are requested to turn DME off until dep due to tfc overload of Maverick DME.

DALLAS/FORT WORTH INTL (See DALLAS–FORT WORTH on page 243)

DAN E RICHARDS MUNI (See PADUCAH on page 325)

DAN JONES INTL (See HOUSTON on page 279)

FIGURE 176A.—ILS-1 RWY 36L, Dallas-Fort Worth Intl.

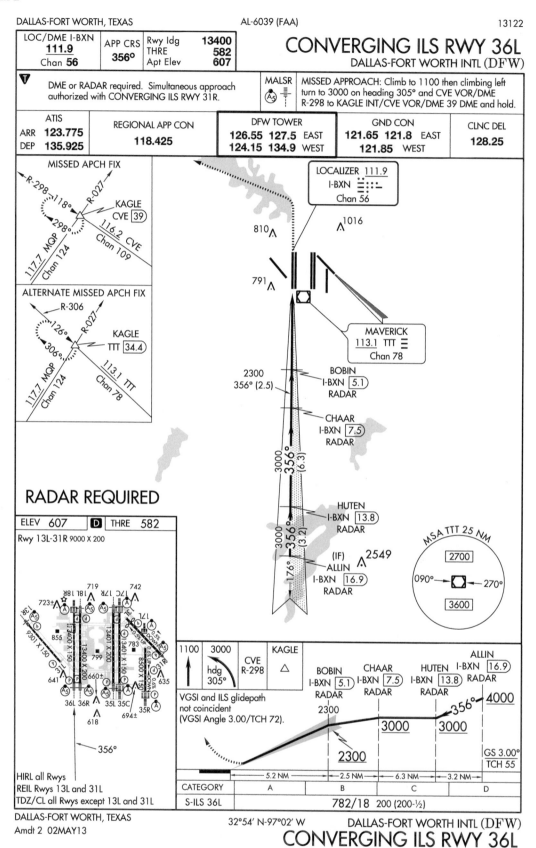

FIGURE 177.—Converging ILS RWY 36L (DFW).

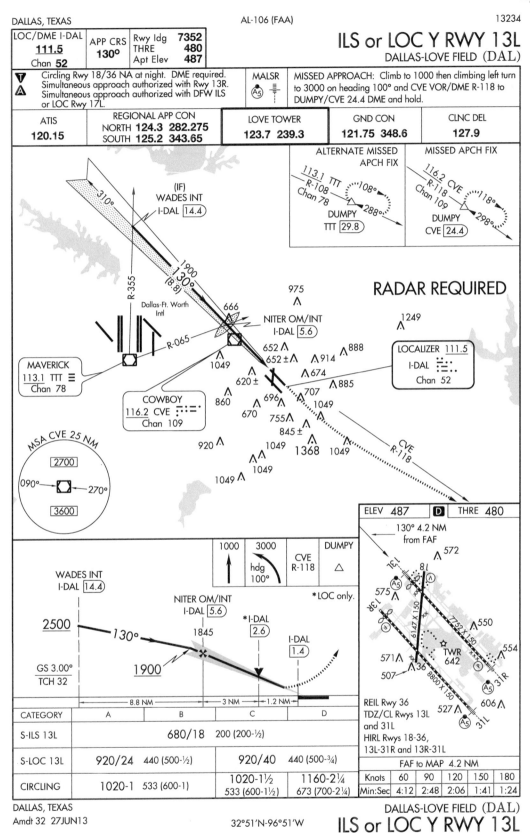

FIGURE 178.—ILS or LOC Y RWY 13L (DAL).

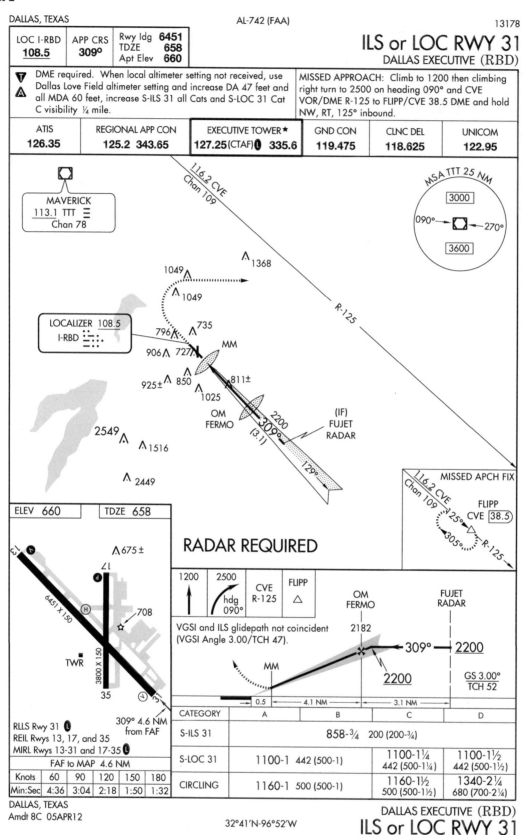

FIGURE 179.—ILS or LOC RWY 31 (RBD).

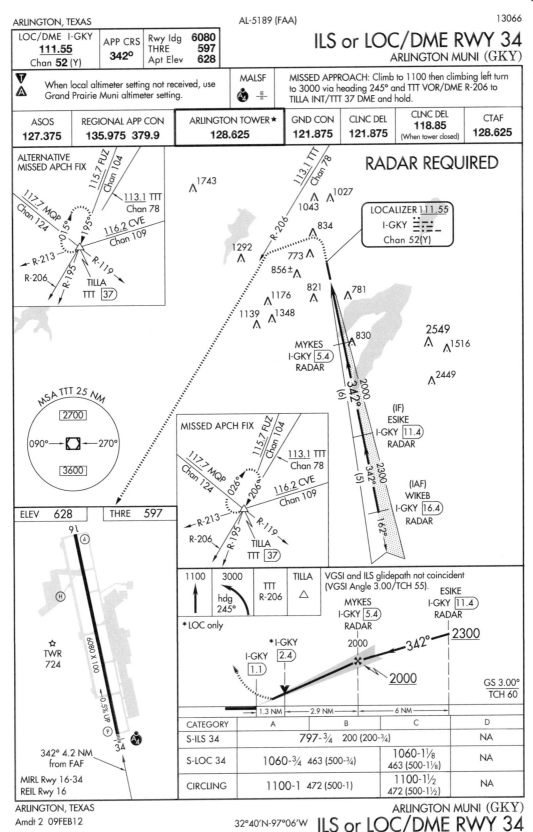

FIGURE 180.—ILS or LOC/DME RWY 34 (GKY).

208   TEXAS

ARCHER CITY MUNI (T39)   1 SE   UTC-6(-5DT)   N33°34.94′ W98°37.12′   DALLAS–FT WORTH
  1065   S2   NOTAM FILE FTW   L–17B
  RWY 17–35: H3200X60 (ASPH)   S–12.5
    RWY 17: Road.
  AIRPORT REMARKS: Unattended. Wildlife on and invof arpt. 70′ AGL drilling
    rig 700′ northwest of Rwy 17–35. Rwy 17–35 loose grvl, tall grass and
    pot holes on rwy.
  COMMUNICATIONS: CTAF 122.9
  RADIO AIDS TO NAVIGATION: NOTAM FILE SPS.
    WICHITA FALLS (H) VORTACW 112.7   SPS   Chan 74   N33°59.24′
      W98°35.61′   173° 24.3 NM to fld. 1133/10E.

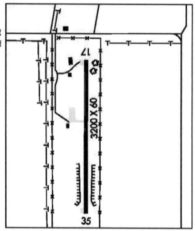

ARDYTH   N27°38.54′ W99°27.48′   NOTAM FILE SJT.   BROWNSVILLE
  NDB (MHW) 405   AGH   174° 5.9 NM to Laredo Intl.   L–20G

ARLEDGE FLD (See STAMFORD on page 351)

ARLINGTON MUNI (GKY)   4 S   UTC-6(-5DT)   N32°39.83′ W97°05.66′   DALLAS–FT WORTH
  628   B   S4   **FUEL** 100LL, JET A   OX 4   TPA—1628(1000)   NOTAM FILE GKY   COPTER
  RWY 16–34: H6080X100 (CONC)   S–60   MIRL   0.5% up NW   H–6H, L–17C, A
    RWY 16: REIL. PAPI(P4L)—GA 3.0° TCH 42′.   IAP, AD
    RWY 34: MALSF. PAPI(P4L)—GA 3.0° TCH 55′.
  AIRPORT REMARKS: Attended continuously. Self serve fuel with major credit
    card. Helicopter test facility at arpt mostly from private helipad
    adjoining ldg area. Extensive helicopter traffic west of rwy. Rwy 34
    PAPI unusable byd 8° right of centerline. MIRL Rwy 16–34 preset
    medium ints, higher ints by twr request. When twr clsd ACTIVATE
    MALSF Rwy 34—CTAF. PAPI Rwy 16 and Rwy 34 opr continuously.
  WEATHER DATA SOURCES: ASOS 127.375 (817) 557-0251.
  COMMUNICATIONS: CTAF 128.625
  ℝ **REGIONAL APP/DEP CON** 135.975
    TOWER 128.625 (1300–0300Z‡) **GND CON/CLNC DEL** 121.875
    CLNC DEL 118.85 (RGNL APP CON when twr clsd)
  AIRSPACE: CLASS D svc 1300–0300Z‡ other times CLASS G.
  RADIO AIDS TO NAVIGATION: NOTAM FILE FTW.
    MAVERICK (H) VORW/DME 113.1   TTT   Chan 78   N32°52.15′
      W97°02.43′   186° 12.6 NM to fld. 540/6E.
    All acft arriving DFW are requested to turn DME off until departure due
      to traffic overload of Maverick DME
    ILS/DME 111.55   I–GKY   Chan 52(Y)   Rwy 34.   Class IE.   LOC
      unusable byd 15° right of course. Unmonitored when ATCT clsd.

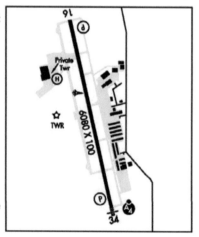

FIGURE 181.—Excerpt from Chart Supplement.

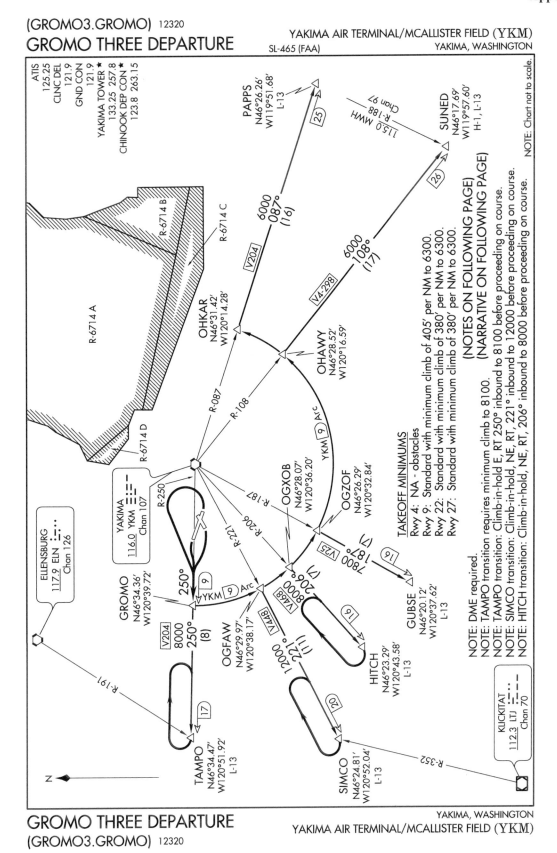

FIGURE 182.—GROMO Three Departure (GROMO3.GROMO).

GROMO THREE DEPARTURE
SL-465 (FAA)

YAKIMA AIR TERMINAL/MCALLISTER FIELD (YKM)
YAKIMA, WASHINGTON

DEPARTURE ROUTE DESCRIPTION

<u>TAKEOFF RUNWAY 9,27:</u> Climbing left turn thence. . . .

<u>TAKEOFF RUNWAY 22:</u> Climbing right turn thence. . . .

. . . . intercept and proceed via YKM R-250 to GROMO/YKM 9 DME, then on assigned transition.

<u>GUBSE TRANSITION (GROMO3.GUBSE):</u> From over GROMO DME Fix via YKM 9 DME Arc to OGZOF DME fix and YKM VORTAC R-187 to GUBSE DME fix.

<u>HITCH TRANSITION (GROMO3.HITCH):</u> From over GROMO DME Fix via YKM 9 DME Arc to OGXOB DME fix and YKM VORTAC R-206 to HITCH DME fix.

<u>PAPPS TRANSITION (GROMO3.PAPPS):</u> From over GROMO DME Fix via YKM 9 DME Arc to OKHAR DME fix and YKM VORTAC R-087 to PAPPS DME fix.

<u>SIMCO TRANSITION (GROMO3.SIMCO):</u> From over GROMO DME Fix via YKM 9 DME Arc to OGFAW DME fix and YKM VORTAC R-221 to SIMCO INT.

<u>SUNED TRANSITION (GROMO3.SUNED):</u> From over GROMO DME Fix via 9 DME Arc to OHAWY DME fix and KM R-108 to SUNED INT.

<u>TAMPO TRANSITION (GROMO3.TAMPO):</u> From over GROMO DME Fix via YKM VORTAC R-250 to TAMPO INT.

<u>TAKEOFF OBSTACLE NOTES</u>
Rwy 9: OL on building 27' from DER, 507' right of centerline, 34' AGL/1074' MSL.
Pole 388' from DER, 561' right of centerline, 34' AGL/1073' MSL.
Trees beginning 586' from DER, 550' right of centerline, up to 100' AGL/1139' MSL.
Rwy 22: Fence beginning 27' from DER, 435' right of centerline, up to 10' AGL/1085' MSL.
Trees beginning 570' from DER, 228' left of centerline, up to 100' AGL/1199' MSL.
Trees beginning 3195' from DER, 202' right of centerline, up to 100' AGL/1199' MSL.
Trees beginning 1 NM from DER, 732' left of centerline, up to 100' AGL/1239' MSL.
Rwy 27: Ant on building 398' from DER, 282' left of centerline, 15' AGL/1117' MSL.
Trees beginning 3893' from DER, 1341' right of centerline, up to 100' AGL/1239' MSL.

GROMO THREE DEPARTURE
(GROMO3.GROMO) 12208

YAKIMA, WASHINGTON
YAKIMA AIR TERMINAL/MCALLISTER FIELD (YKM)

FIGURE 183.—GROMO Three Departure (GROMO3.GROMO).

YAKIMA AIR TERMINAL/MCALLISTER FLD (YKM)   3 S   UTC–8(–7DT)   N46°34.09´ W120°32.64´   **SEATTLE**
  1099   B S4 **FUEL** 100LL, JET A   OX 1, 3   Class I, ARFF Index A   NOTAM FILE YKM   H–1C, L–13A
  RWY 09–27: H7604X150 (ASPH–GRVD) S–95, D–160, 2S–175, 2D–220, 2D/2D2–550 PCN 33 F/C/X/T   IAP, DIAP, AD
    HIRL   0.7% up W
    RWY 09: REIL. VASI(V4L)—GA 3.0° TCH 50´.
    RWY 27: MALSR. PAPI(P4L)—GA 3.0° TCH 57´.
  RWY 04–22: H3835X150 (ASPH–PFC) S–70, D–80, 2S–102, 2D–120 PCN 28 F/C/X/T   MIRL   0.5% up SW
    RWY 04: REIL. PAPI(P4L)—GA 3.0° TCH 57´.
    RWY 22: REIL. PAPI(P4L)—GA 3.0° TCH 45´.
  RUNWAY DECLARED DISTANCE INFORMATION
    RWY 04: TORA–3835   TODA–3835   ASDA–3835   LDA–3835
    RWY 09: TORA–7604   TODA–7604   ASDA–7604   LDA–7604
    RWY 22: TORA–3835   TODA–3835   ASDA–3535   LDA–3835
    RWY 27: TORA–7604   TODA–7604   ASDA–7604   LDA–7604
  AIRPORT REMARKS: Attended 1400–0400Z‡. Sfc conditions unmonitored 0800–1330Z‡. Be alert, birds invof Yakima River 5
    NM east of apch to Rwy 27. Reflectors on Twy C only. Rwy 04–22 some spalling and raveling. PPR for unscheduled air
    carrier ops with more than 30 passenger seats, call arpt manger 509–575–6149/6150. Twy B from apch end of Rwy 22
    to Twy A rstd to acft with wingspans 79´ or less. MIRL Rwy 04–22, REIL Rwy 04 and Rwy 22, PAPI Rwy 04 and Rwy
    22 OTS when twr clsd. Twy B1 and Twy B2 twy lgts OTS when twr clsd. Twy B lgts south of Rwy 09–27 OTS when twr
    clsd. When twr clsd ACTIVATE HIRL Rwy 09–27 and MALSR Rwy 27—CTAF.
  WEATHER DATA SOURCES: ASOS (509) 248–1502
  COMMUNICATIONS: CTAF 133.25 **ATIS** 125.25 **UNICOM** 122.95
    RCO 122.5 (SEATTLE RADIO)
  Ⓡ **CHINOOK APP/DEP CON** 123.8 (1400–0600Z‡)
  Ⓡ **SEATTLE CENTER APP/DEP CON** 132.6 (0600–1400Z‡)
    TOWER 133.25 (1400–0600Z‡) **GND CON** 121.9 **CLNC DEL** 121.9
  AIRSPACE: CLASS D svc 1400–0600Z‡ other times CLASS E.
  RADIO AIDS TO NAVIGATION: NOTAM FILE YKM.
    (H) VORTACW 116.0   YKM   Chan 107   N46°34.21´ W120°26.68´   247° 4.1 NM to fld. 984/21E.
    DME unusable:
      095°–115° byd 26 NM blo 8,000´
      095°–115° byd 35 NM
      115°–207° byd 20 NM blo 8,500´
      115°–207° byd 36 NM blo 10,000´
      207°–230° byd 20 NM blo 10,000´
      290°–315° byd 20 NM blo 11,000´
      315°–080° byd 12 NM blo 15,000´
    VOR portion unusable:
      025°–035° byd 5 NM blo 6,000´
      080°–105° byd 35 NM blo 6,000´
      105°–107° byd 25 NM blo 6,000´
      109°–135° byd 25 NM blo 6,000´
      135°–180° byd 30 NM blo 7,500´
      195°–225° byd 30 NM blo 8,500´
      305°–335° byd 30 NM blo 9,000´
      350°–080° byd 25 NM blo 9,000´
    DONNY NDB (LOM) 371   YK   N46°31.54´ W120°22.33´ 274° 7.6 NM to fld. Unmonitored when ATCT closed.
    ILS 110.1   I–YKM   Rwy 27.   LOM DONNY NDB. Unmonitored when ATCT closed.
  COMM/NAV/WEATHER REMARKS: During hrs twr is clsd all ops in vicinity of arpt rstd to acft with VHF radio capability, unless an
    emerg exist necessitating UHF equipped acft to land.

FIGURE 184.—Excerpt from Chart Supplement.

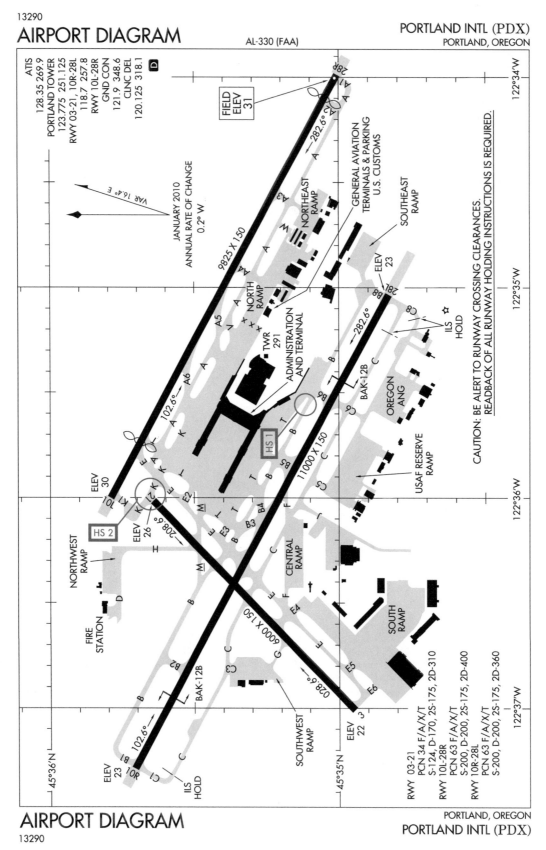

FIGURE 185.—Airport Diagram - Portland INTL (PDX).

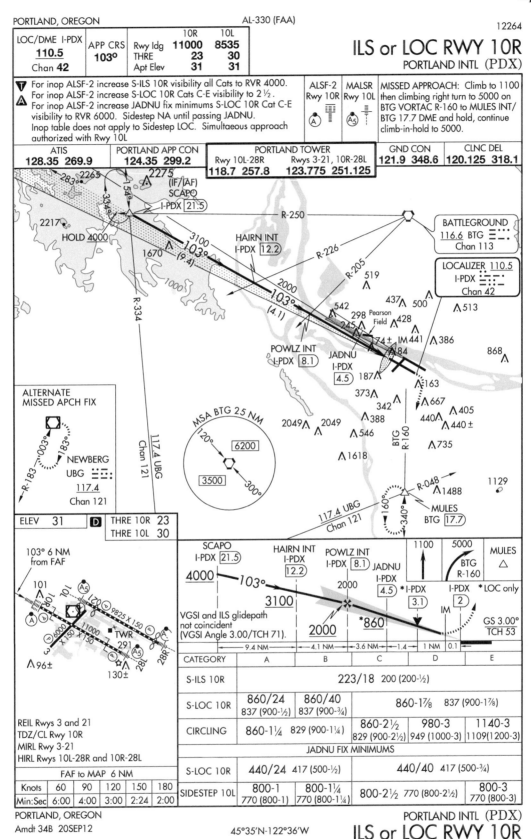

FIGURE 186.—ILS or LOC RWY 10R (PDX).

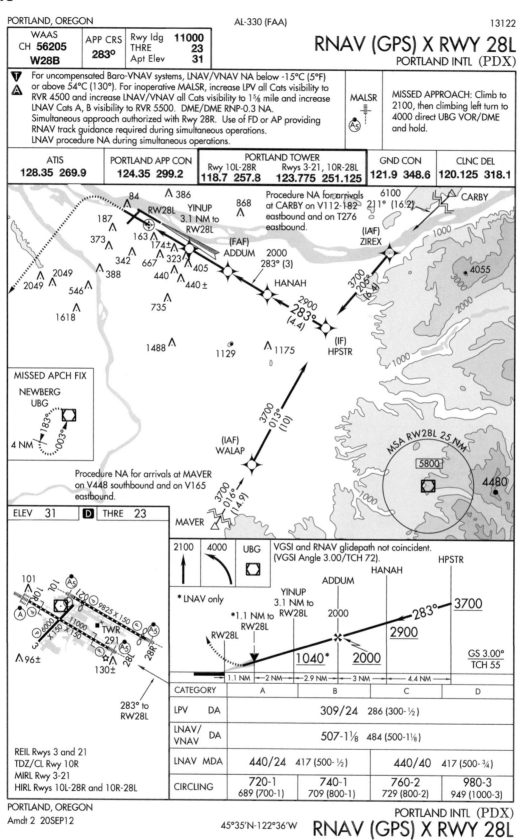

FIGURE 187.—RNAV (GPS) X RWY 28L (PDX).

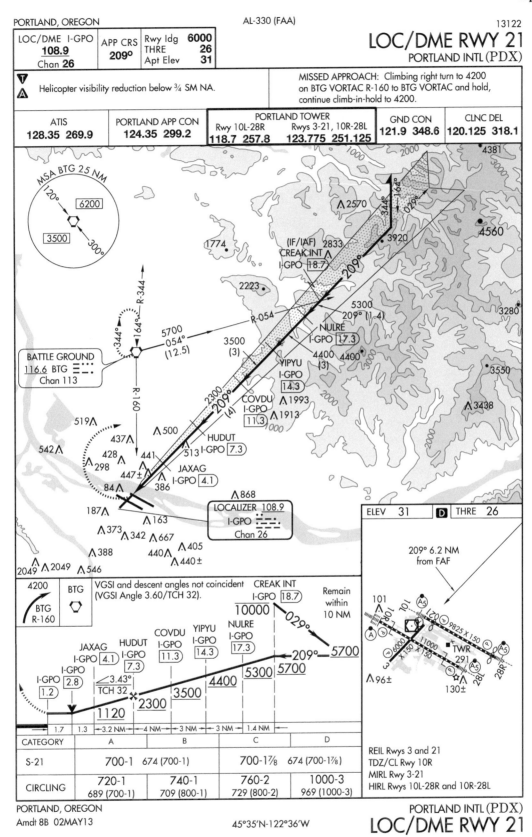

PORTLAND, OREGON · AL-330 (FAA) · 13122

LOC/DME RWY 21
PORTLAND INTL (PDX)

LOC/DME I-GPO 108.9 Chan 26	APP CRS 209°	Rwy Idg 6000 THRE 26 Apt Elev 31

Helicopter visibility reduction below ¾ SM NA.

MISSED APPROACH: Climbing right turn to 4200 on BTG VORTAC R-160 to BTG VORTAC and hold, continue climb-in-hold to 4200.

ATIS 128.35 269.9	PORTLAND APP CON 124.35 299.2	PORTLAND TOWER Rwy 10L-28R 118.7 257.8 · Rwys 3-21, 10R-28L 123.775 251.125	GND CON 121.9 348.6	CLNC DEL 120.125 318.1

CATEGORY	A	B	C	D
S-21	700-1	674 (700-1)	700-1⅞	674 (700-1⅞)
CIRCLING	720-1 689 (700-1)	740-1 709 (800-1)	760-2 729 (800-2)	1000-3 969 (1000-3)

REIL Rwys 3 and 21
TDZ/CL Rwy 10R
MIRL Rwy 3-21
HIRL Rwys 10L-28R and 10R-28L

PORTLAND, OREGON
Amdt 8B 02MAY13

45°35'N-122°36'W

PORTLAND INTL (PDX)
LOC/DME RWY 21

FIGURE 188.—LOC/DME RWY 21 (PDX).

(HABUT4.GVO) 13122
HABUT FOUR DEPARTURE SL-378 (FAA)

SANTA BARBARA MUNI (SBA)
SANTA BARBARA, CALIFORNIA

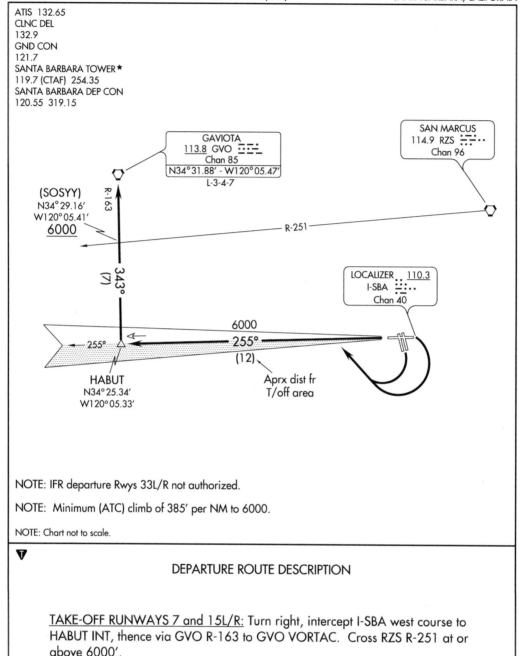

ATIS 132.65
CLNC DEL
132.9
GND CON
121.7
SANTA BARBARA TOWER★
119.7 (CTAF) 254.35
SANTA BARBARA DEP CON
120.55 319.15

GAVIOTA
113.8 GVO
Chan 85
N34°31.88' - W120°05.47'
L-3-4-7

SAN MARCUS
114.9 RZS
Chan 96

(SOSYY)
N34°29.16'
W120°05.41'
6000

R-163

R-251

343°
(7)

LOCALIZER 110.3
I-SBA
Chan 40

6000
255°
255°
(12)

HABUT
N34°25.34'
W120°05.33'

Aprx dist fr
T/off area

NOTE: IFR departure Rwys 33L/R not authorized.

NOTE: Minimum (ATC) climb of 385' per NM to 6000.

NOTE: Chart not to scale.

DEPARTURE ROUTE DESCRIPTION

<u>TAKE-OFF RUNWAYS 7 and 15L/R:</u> Turn right, intercept I-SBA west course to HABUT INT, thence via GVO R-163 to GVO VORTAC. Cross RZS R-251 at or above 6000'.

<u>TAKE-OFF RUNWAY 25:</u> Intercept I-SBA west course to HABUT INT, thence via GVO R-163 to GVO VORTAC. Cross RZS R-251 at or above 6000'.

HABUT FOUR DEPARTURE
(HABUT4.GVO) 13122

SANTA BARBARA, CALIFORNIA
SANTA BARBARA MUNI (SBA)

FIGURE 189.—HABUT Four Departure (HABUT4.GVO) (SBA).

SANTA BARBARA MUNI (SBA)   7 W   UTC–8(–7DT)   N34°25.57´ W119°50.49´   **LOS ANGELES**
    13   B   S4   **FUEL** 100LL, JET A   OX 1, 2, 3, 4   TPA—See Remarks   LRA   Class I, ARFF Index C   **H–4H, L–3D, 4F, 7A**
    NOTAM FILE SBA   **IAP, AD**
    RWY 07–25: H6052X150 (ASPH–PFC)   S–110, D–160, 2S–175,
      2D–245   HIRL
      RWY 07: MALSR. Tree. Rgt tfc.
      RWY 25: REIL. PAPI(P4L)—GA 3.0° TCH 50´. Fence.
    RWY 15R–33L: H4184X100 (ASPH)   S–48, D–63, 2S–80, 2D–100
      MIRL
      RWY 15R: REIL. Tree.
      RWY 33L: Tree. Rgt tfc.
    RWY 15L–33R: H4178X75 (ASPH)   S–35, D–41, 2S–80, 2D–63
      RWY 15L: Thld dsplcd 217´. Bldg.
      RWY 33R: Rgt tfc. 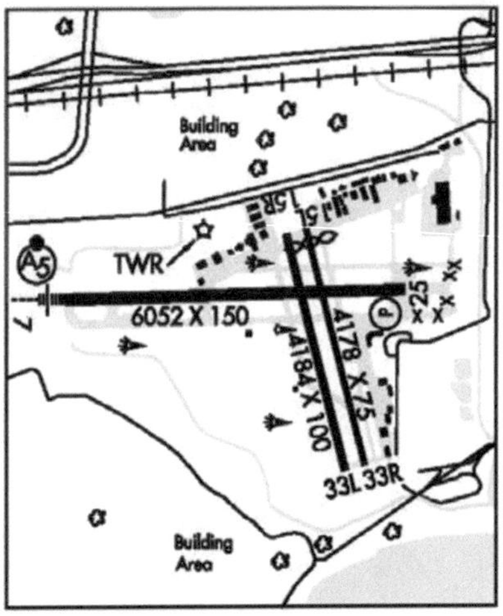
    AIRPORT REMARKS: Attended 1330–0600Z‡. 100LL fuel 24 hr credit card
      svc avbl. Fee for Jet A fuel after hrs call 805–964–6733 or 967–5608.
      Numerous flocks of birds on and invof arpt. Deep creek located 300´
      from rwy end Rwy 07, Rwy 33L and Rwy 33R. Rwy 15L–33R dalgt
      hrs only. Arpt has noise abatement procedures ctc arpt ops
      805–692–6005. Due to ltd ramp space at the airline terminal
      non–scheduled transport category acft with more than 30 passenger
      seats are required to ctc arpt ops 805–692–6005 24 hour PPR to
    arrival. Commercial airline ramp clsd to all General Aviation acft. No customs personnel or facilities are avbl and
    international acft will not be allowed to land unless an emerg exists. TPA—1003(990) small acft, 1503(1490) large acft.
    Pure jet touch/go or low approaches prohibited. When twr clsd ACTIVATE MIRL Rwy 15R–33L, REIL Rwy 15R—CTAF.
    MALSR Rwy 07, PAPI Rwy 25 and REIL Rwy 25 opr continuously. CTAF. Ldg fee for all PART 135 opr and transient acft
    with maximum gross weight 10,000 lbs or more. Fees collected at FBO.
    WEATHER DATA SOURCES: ASOS (805) 681–0583
    COMMUNICATIONS: CTAF 119.7 ATIS 132.65 UNICOM 122.95
    Ⓡ **APP/DEP CON** 120.55 (151°–329°) 125.4 (330°–150°) 124.15 127.725 (1400–0700Z‡)
    Ⓡ **L.A. CENTER APP/DEP CON** 119.05 (0700–1400Z‡)
      TOWER 119.7 (1400–0700Z‡) **GND CON** 121.7 **CLNC DEL** 132.9
    AIRSPACE: CLASS C svc ctc APP CON svc 1400–0700Z‡ other times CLASS E.
    RADIO AIDS TO NAVIGATION: NOTAM FILE HHR.
      SAN MARCUS (H) VORTAC 114.9   RZS   Chan 96   N34°30.57´ W119°46.26´   201° 6.1 NM to fld. 3623/14E.
        HIWAS.
      VOR unusable:
        140°–178° byd 27 NM
      GAVIOTA (L) VORTACW 113.8   GVO   Chan 85   N34°31.88´ W120°05.47´   101° 13.9 NM to fld. 2616/16E.
      VORTAC unusable:
        117°–137° byd 35 NM
        310°–095° byd 10 NM blo 8,500´
        360°–095° byd 20 NM blo 12,500´
      ILS/DME 110.3   I–SBA   Chan 40   Rwy 07.   Class IA.   Unmonitored when ATCT clsd.

SANTA CATALINA   N33°22.50´ W118°25.19´   NOTAM FILE HHR.   **LOS ANGELES**
    (L) **VORTACW** 111.4   SXC   Chan 51   352° 1.8 NM to Catalina. 2090/15E.   **H–4I, L–3E, 4G**

FIGURE 190.—Excerpt from Chart Supplement.

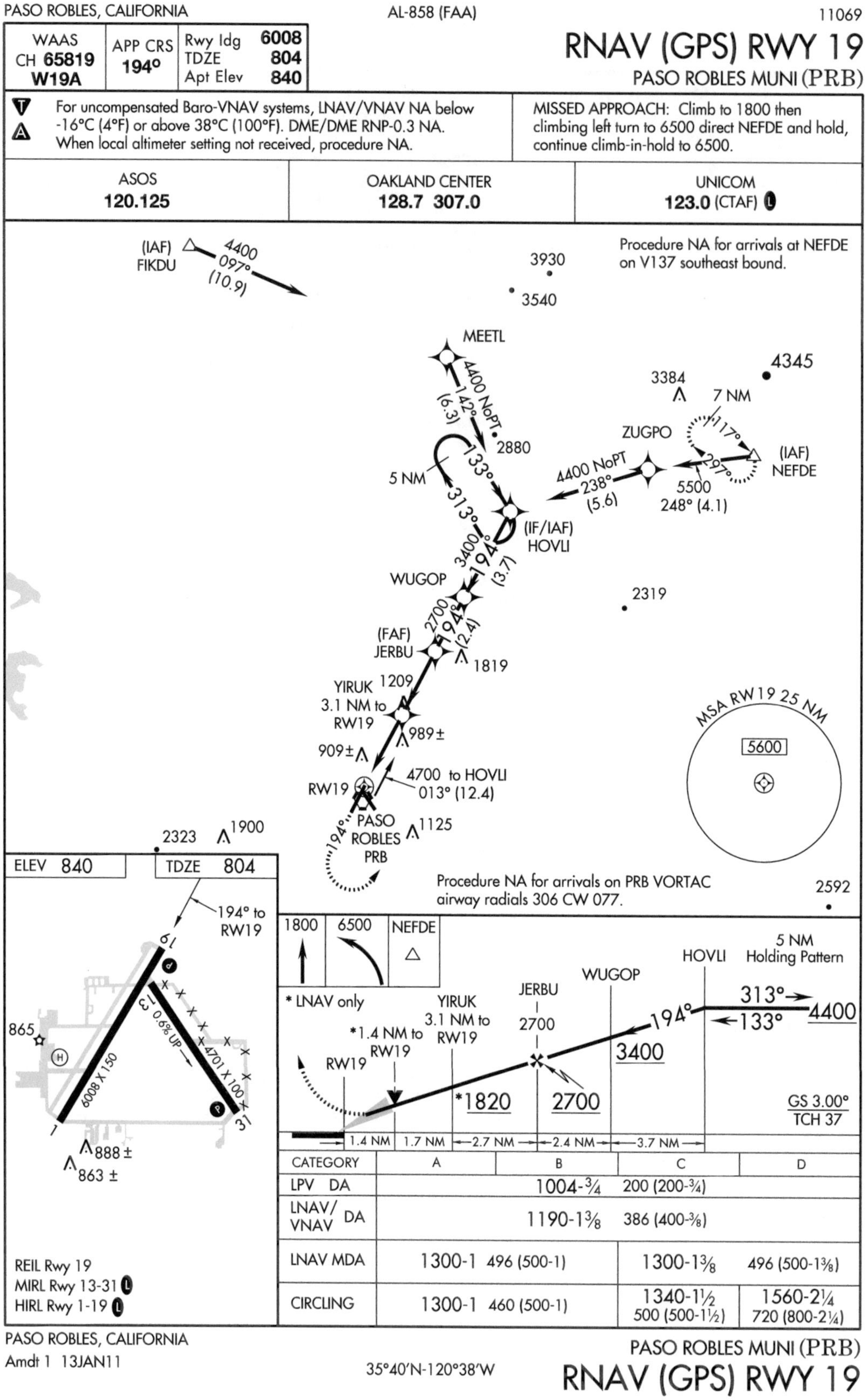
PASO ROBLES, CALIFORNIA
AL-858 (FAA)
11069
WAAS CH 65819 W19A
APP CRS 194°
Rwy ldg 6008
TDZE 804
Apt Elev 840
RNAV (GPS) RWY 19
PASO ROBLES MUNI (PRB)
For uncompensated Baro-VNAV systems, LNAV/VNAV NA below -16°C (4°F) or above 38°C (100°F). DME/DME RNP-0.3 NA. When local altimeter setting not received, procedure NA.
MISSED APPROACH: Climb to 1800 then climbing left turn to 6500 direct NEFDE and hold, continue climb-in-hold to 6500.
ASOS 120.125
OAKLAND CENTER 128.7 307.0
UNICOM 123.0 (CTAF)
(IAF) FIKDU
4400 097° (10.9)
3930
3540
Procedure NA for arrivals at NEFDE on V137 southeast bound.
MEETL
4400 NoPT 142° (6.3)
2880
133°
5 NM
313°
(IF/IAF) HOVLI
3400 194° (3.7)
4345
3384
7 NM
117°
ZUGPO
4400 NoPT 238° (5.6)
297°
5500 248° (4.1)
(IAF) NEFDE
WUGOP
2319
2700 194° (2.4)
(FAF) JERBU
1819
YIRUK 3.1 NM to RW19
1209
989±
909±
RW19
4700 to HOVLI 013° (12.4)
PASO ROBLES PRB
1125
194°
2323
1900
MSA RW19 25 NM
5600
Procedure NA for arrivals on PRB VORTAC airway radials 306 CW 077.
2592
ELEV 840
TDZE 804
194° to RW19
19
13
0.6% UP
4701 X 100
6008 X 150
31
1
865
888 ±
863 ±
REIL Rwy 19
MIRL Rwy 13-31
HIRL Rwy 1-19
1800
6500
NEFDE
* LNAV only
*1.4 NM to RW19
RW19
YIRUK 3.1 NM to RW19
JERBU 2700
WUGOP
HOVLI
5 NM Holding Pattern
313°
133°
4400
194°
3400
*1820
2700
GS 3.00° TCH 37
1.4 NM
1.7 NM
2.7 NM
2.4 NM
3.7 NM
CATEGORY A B C D
LPV DA 1004-¾ 200 (200-¾)
LNAV/VNAV DA 1190-1⅜ 386 (400-⅜)
LNAV MDA 1300-1 496 (500-1) 1300-1⅜ 496 (500-1⅜)
CIRCLING 1300-1 460 (500-1) 1340-1½ 500 (500-1½) 1560-2¼ 720 (800-2¼)
PASO ROBLES, CALIFORNIA
Amdt 1 13JAN11
35°40'N-120°38'W
PASO ROBLES MUNI (PRB)
RNAV (GPS) RWY 19

FIGURE 191.—RNAV (GPS) RWY 19 (PRB).

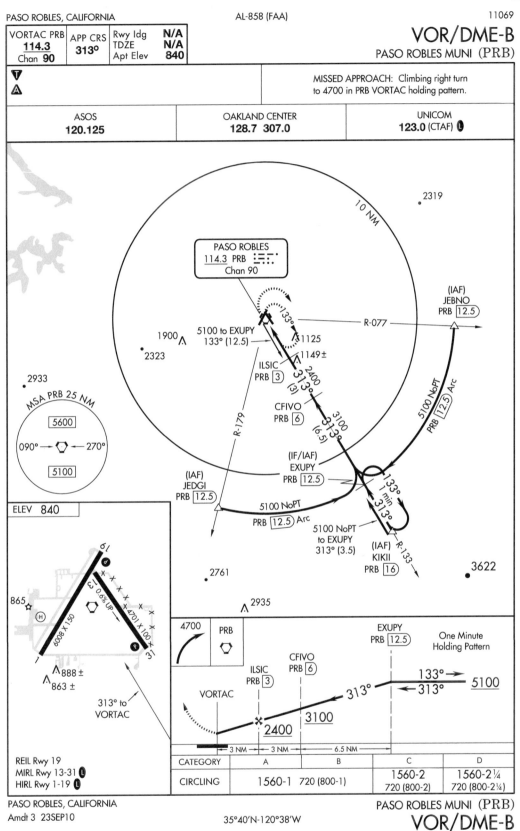

FIGURE 192.—VOR/DME-B (PRB).

Appendix 2

COLLEGE STATION

EASTERWOOD FLD (CLL) 3 SW UTC–6(–5DT) N30°35.32′ W96°21.83′   HOUSTON
321 B S4 **FUEL** 100LL, JET A Class I, ARFF Index A NOTAM FILE CLL   H–7C, L–19D, 21A
RWY 16–34: H7000X146 (ASPH–CONC–GRVD) S–70, D–90, 2S–114,   IAP, AD
2D–150 HIRL
RWY 16: VASI(V4R)—GA 3.0° TCH 51′. Tree.
RWY 34: MALSR.
RWY 10–28: H5158X150 (ASPH–GRVD) S–27, D–50, 2D–87 MIRL
RWY 10: VASI(V4L)—GA 3.0° TCH 50′. Tree.
RWY 28: REIL. VASI(V4L)—GA 3.0° TCH 54′. Tree.
RWY 04–22: H5150X150 (CONC) S–27, D–50, 2D–87
RWY 04: Tree.
RWY 22: Tree.
RUNWAY DECLARED DISTANCE INFORMATION
RWY 04: TORA–5149 TODA–5149 ASDA–5149 LDA–5149
RWY 10: TORA–5159 TODA–5159 ASDA–5159 LDA–5159
RWY 16: TORA–7000 TODA–7000 ASDA–7000 LDA–7000
RWY 22: TORA–5149 TODA–5149 ASDA–5149 LDA–5149
RWY 28: TORA–5159 TODA–5159 ASDA–5159 LDA–5159
RWY 34: TORA–7000 TODA–7000 ASDA–7000 LDA–7000
AIRPORT REMARKS: Attended 1200–0400Z‡. For fuel after hours PPR call
979–845–4811 or ctc Texas A and M University police
979–845–2345; late ngt fee. CLOSED to unscheduled air carrier ops
with more than 30 passenger seats except 24 hours PPR call arpt manager 979–845–4811. Rwy 04–22 day VFR ops
only. Rwy 10–28 mandatory hold short sign on Rwy 16–34 unlgtd. Itinerant acft park in front of twr, overnight parking
fee. Ldg fee scheduled FAR 135 and all FAR 121 ops. Rwy 04–22 and Twy E S of Rwy 10–28 not avbl for air carrier acft
with over 30 passenger seats. Rwy 16–34 first 1850′ Rwy 34 conc. PAEW adjacent all twys 1200–2200Z‡. When twr
clsd ACTIVATE HIRL Rwy 16–34 and MALSR Rwy 34—CTAF. MIRL Rwy 10–28 and REIL Rwy 28 preset low ints only.
WEATHER DATA SOURCES: ASOS (979) 846–1708 HIWAS 113.3 CLL.
COMMUNICATIONS: CTAF 118.5 ATIS 126.85 UNICOM 122.95
COLLEGE STATION RCO 122.65 122.2 (MONTGOMERY COUNTY RADIO).
Ⓡ HOUSTON APP/DEP CON 134.3
TOWER 118.5 (1400–0300Z‡) GND CON/CLNC DEL 128.7 CLNC DEL 120.4 (when twr clsd)
AIRSPACE: CLASS D svc 1400–0300Z‡ other times CLASS E.

VOR RECEIVER CHECK
TEXAS
VOR RECEIVER CHECKPOINTS

Facility Name (Arpt Name)	Freq/Ident	Type Check Pt. Gnd. AB/ALT	Azimuth from Fac. Mag	Dist. from Fac. N.M.	Checkpoint Description
Abilene (Abilene Rgnl)	113.7/ABI	A/2800	047	10.1	Over silos in center of Ft Phantom Lake.
Alice (Alice International)	114.5/ALI	G	272	0.5	On twy near FBO.
Borger (Hutchinson Co)	108.6/BGD	G	173	6.7	On twy intersection at N end of ramp.
Brownsville (Brownsville/South Padre Island Intl)	116.3/BRO	G	247	3.2	3.2 NM on hold line Rwy 13R.
Brownwood (Brownwood Rgnl)	108.6/BWD	A/2600	169	6.2	Over rotating bcn.
Childress Muni	117.6/CDS	G	353	3.7	At the apron and the twy from Rwy 04–22.
College Station (Easterwood Fld)	113.3/CLL	G	97	3.2	On west edge of parking ramp.
Corpus Christi (Alfred C 'Bubba' Thomas)	115.5/CRP	A/1000	318	9.3	Over Rwy 32 thld.
Corpus Christi (Corpus Christi Intl)	115.5/CRP	A/1100	187	7.5	Over grain elevator.
Daisetta (Liberty Muni)	116.9/DAS	A/1200	195	7.5	Over hangar S of arpt.
Dalhart (Dalhart Muni)	112.0/DHT	A/5000	176	4.1	Over water tower on arpt.
Eagle Lake (Eagle Lake)	116.4/ELA	A/1200	180	4.1	Over water tank 0.4 NM SW of arpt.

FIGURE 193.—Excerpts from Chart Supplement.

232   **TEXAS**

CONTINUED FROM PRECEDING PAGE

RADIO AIDS TO NAVIGATION: NOTAM FILE CLL.
    COLLEGE STATION (L) VORTACW 113.3   CLL   Chan 80   N30°36.30′ W96°25.24′   100° 3.1 NM to fld. 264/8E.
        HIWAS.
    DME unusable:
        101°–130° byd 25 NM blo 2,500′
        131°–148° byd 30 NM blo 2,500′
        149°–160° byd 30 NM blo 2,000′
        325°–349° byd 30 NM blo 2,500′
        350°–100° byd 25 NM blo 3,500′
    VOR portion unusable:
        131°–189° blo 7,000′
    ROWDY NDB (LOM) 260   CL   N30°29.62′ W96°20.26′ 341° 5.8 NM to fld. Unmonitored when ATCT clsd.
    ILS/DME 111.7   I–CLL   Chan 54   Rwy 34.   Class IB.   LOM ROWDY NDB. Unmonitored when ATCT clsd. DME
        unmonitored. Glideslope unusable for coupled apchs blo 1,050′ MSL.

COLLIN CO RGNL AT MC KINNEY (See DALLAS on page 241)

COLLINSVILLE

  SUDDEN STOP (T32)   1 NE   UTC–6(–5DT)   N33°34.29′ W96°54.43′   **DALLAS–FT WORTH**
    720   NOTAM FILE FTW
    RWY 17–35: 1550X60 (TURF)
      RWY 17: Trees.
      RWY 35: Road.
    AIRPORT REMARKS: Attended continuously. Student training prohibited.
    COMMUNICATIONS: CTAF 122.9

  COLORADO CITY (T88)   6 NW   UTC–6(–5DT)   N32°28.11′ W100°55.27′   **DALLAS–FT WORTH**
    2214   B   NOTAM FILE FTW   **H–6G, L–17A**
    RWY 17–35: H5479X60 (ASPH)   S–50   LIRL
      RWY 35: Tree.
    AIRPORT REMARKS: Attended irregularly. Rwy 17–35 pavement from Rwy 35
      thld lgts southward used as a twy and not maintained.
    COMMUNICATIONS: CTAF 122.9
    RADIO AIDS TO NAVIGATION: NOTAM FILE BPG.
      BIG SPRING (L) VORTACW 114.3   BGS   Chan 90   N32°23.14′
      W101°29.02′   069° 29.0 NM to fld. 2670/11E.

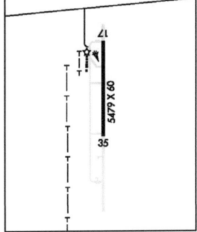

COLUMBUS

  ROBERT R WELLS JR (66R)   3 S   UTC–6(–5DT)   N29°38.49′ W96°30.96′   **HOUSTON**
    242   B   FUEL 100LL, JET A   NOTAM FILE CXO   **L–19D, 21A**
    RWY 15–33: H3800X60 (ASPH)   S–12.5   MIRL
      RWY 15: REIL. PAPI(P2L). Thld dsplcd 305′. Fence.
      RWY 33: REIL. PAPI(P2L). Thld dsplcd 177′. Brush.
    AIRPORT REMARKS: Unattended. Self svc fuel with major credit card. Ultra–light activity on and invof arpt. Rwy 33 REIL OTS
    indef. ACTIVATE MIRL Rwy 15–33—CTAF.
    COMMUNICATIONS: CTAF 122.9
    RADIO AIDS TO NAVIGATION: NOTAM FILE CXO.
      INDUSTRY (L) VORTACW 110.2   IDU   Chan 39   N29°57.36′ W96°33.73′   165° 19.0 NM to fld. 419/8E.

FIGURE 194.—Excerpts from Chart Supplement.

WESTHEIMER AIR PARK (OØ7)   20 W   UTC–6(–5DT)   N29°41.68´ W95°47.68´   HOUSTON
117   B   S2   **FUEL** 100LL   NOTAM FILE CXO
RWY 11–29: H2500X28 (CONC)   LIRL
   RWY 11: Trees.
   RWY 29: Tree.
AIRPORT REMARKS: Attended 1400–0000Z‡. 90´ P–line 1500´ from Rwy 11 thld. Grass in cracks on rwy sfc. ACTIVATE
   rotating bcn—CTAF. ACTIVATE LIRL Rwy 11–29—CTAF.
COMMUNICATIONS: CTAF/UNICOM 122.7

WILLIAM P HOBBY (HOU)   8 SE   UTC–6(–5DT)   N29°38.73´ W95°16.73´   HOUSTON
46   B   S2   **FUEL** 100LL, JET A, A1   OX 1, 2, 3, 4   LRA   Class I, ARFF Index C   COPTER
   NOTAM FILE HOU   H–7C, L–19E, 21A, GOMW
RWY 04–22: H7602X150 (CONC–GRVD)   S–75, D–200, 2S–168,   IAP, AD
   2T–461, 2D–400, 2D/D1–444, C5–717   HIRL   CL
   RWY 04: ALSF2. TDZL. PAPI(P4R)—GA 3.0° TCH 57´.
   RWY 22: MALS. VASI(V4L)—GA 3.0° TCH 52´. Pole.
RWY 12R–30L: H7602X150 (ASPH–GRVD)   S–75, D–195, 2S–168,
   2T–461, 2D–220, 2D/D1–444, C5–717   HIRL   CL
   RWY 12R: MALSR. TDZL. PAPI(P4R)—GA 3.0° TCH 52´. Thld dsplcd
   1034´. Pole.
   RWY 30L: TDZL. REIL. PAPI(P4L)—GA 3.0° TCH 71´. Road.
RWY 17–35: H6000X150 (ASPH–CONC–GRVD)   S–75, D–121, 2S–153,
   2D–195   MIRL
   RWY 17: VASI(V4L)—GA 3.0° TCH 38´. Antenna.
   RWY 35: REIL. VASI(V4R)—GA 3.0° TCH 41´. Bldg.
RWY 12L–30R: H5148X100 (CONC–GRVD)   S–30, D–45, 2D–80   MIRL
   RWY 12L: PAPI(P4L)—GA 3.0° TCH 60´.
RUNWAY DECLARED DISTANCE INFORMATION

RWY 04: TORA–7602	TODA–7602	ASDA–7602	LDA–7602
RWY 12L: TORA–5148	TODA–5148	ASDA–5148	LDA–5148
RWY 12R: TORA–7602	TODA–7602	ASDA–7602	LDA–6568
RWY 17: TORA–6000	TODA–6000	ASDA–6000	LDA–6000
RWY 22: TORA–7602	TODA–7602	ASDA–7602	LDA–7602
RWY 30L: TORA–7602	TODA–7602	ASDA–7602	LDA–7602
RWY 30R: TORA–5148	TODA–5148	ASDA–5148	LDA–5148
RWY 35: TORA–6000	TODA–6000	ASDA–6000	LDA–6000

Rwy 12L-30R: 5148 X 100

AIRPORT REMARKS: Attended continuously. Arpt CLOSED to acft with wingspan over 125´ except 24 hours PPR, call arpt
   manager 713–640–3000. Numerous birds on and invof arpt. ASDE–X Surveillance System in use: pilots should operate
   transponders with Mode C on all twys and rwys. Customs ramp has multiple obstructions, recommend large acft use
   customs overflow ramp. Acft in tkf position on Rwy 22 be alert for possible radio interference or null on frequency 118.7.
   Use upper antenna if so equipped. Rwy 04 runway visual range touchdown, midfield, rollout avbl. Rwy 22 runway visual
   range touchdown, midfield, rollout avbl. Rwy 12R runway visual range touchdown avbl. Rwy 30L runway visual range
   touchdown avbl. Twy G centerline to parked acft on W side only 68´. Twy G centerline to edge of adjacent svc vehicle
   road on W side only 48´. Due to complex rwy configuration, when taxiing to thlds 12L and 12R and 17 check compass
   heading before departing. Acft southbound on Twy C to Rwy 30L thld use extreme care, Twy C makes a 45° dogleg to the
   left crossing Twy K. PAPI Rwy 30L unusable byd 8° left and right of course. Flight Notification Service (ADCUS) available.
   NOTE: See Special Notices—U.S. Special Customs Requirement.
WEATHER DATA SOURCES: ASOS (713) 847–1462 TDWR.
COMMUNICATIONS: D–ATIS 124.6 (713) 847–1491 UNICOM 122.95
   HOBBY RCO 122.35 (MONTGOMERY COUNTY RADIO)
  Ⓡ HOUSTON APP CON 134.45 (South) 124.35 (West) 120.05 (East)
   HOBBY TOWER 118.7
   HOUSTON GND CON 121.9 **CLNC DEL** 125.45 **PRE–TAXI CLNC** 125.45
  Ⓡ HOUSTON DEP CON 134.45 (South) 123.8 (West) 119.7 (North)
AIRSPACE: CLASS B See VFR Terminal Area Chart
VOR TEST FACILITY (VOT) 108.4
RADIO AIDS TO NAVIGATION: NOTAM FILE HOU.
   HOBBY **(H) VORW/DME** 117.1   HUB   Chan 118   N29°39.34´ W95°16.60´   at fld. 47/5E.
   ILS/DME 109.9   I–HUB   Chan 36   Rwy 04.   Class IIIE.   DME also serves Rwy 22.
   ILS/DME 111.3   I–PRQ   Chan 50   Rwy 12R.   Class IE.   DME also serves Rwy 30L.
   LOC/DME 109.9   I–OIB   Chan 36   Rwy 22.   DME also serves Rwy 04. DME unusable byd 17° right of course.
   ILS/DME 111.3   I–UPU   Chan 50   Rwy 30L.   Class IE.   DME also serves Rwy 12R.

HOUSTON MCJ   N29°42.83´ W95°23.80´   HOUSTON
AWOS–3 119.575   H–7C, L–19E, 21A, GOMW

FIGURE 195.—Excerpt from Chart Supplement.

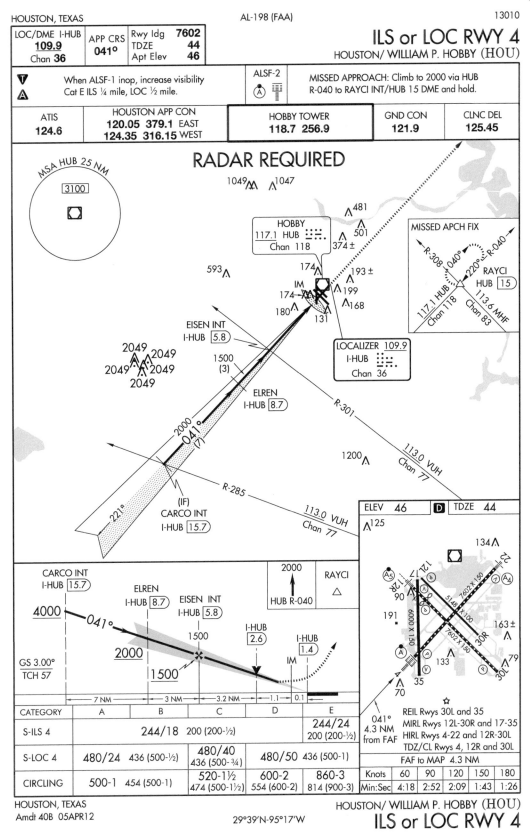

LOC/DME I-HUB	APP CRS	Rwy ldg	7602
109.9	**041°**	TDZE	**44**
Chan **36**		Apt Elev	**46**

ILS or LOC RWY 4
HOUSTON/ WILLIAM P. HOBBY (HOU)

When ALSF-1 inop, increase visibility Cat E ILS ¼ mile, LOC ½ mile.

ALSF-2

MISSED APPROACH: Climb to 2000 via HUB R-040 to RAYCI INT/HUB 15 DME and hold.

| ATIS | HOUSTON APP CON | HOBBY TOWER | GND CON | CLNC DEL |
| **124.6** | **120.05 379.1** EAST
124.35 316.15 WEST | **118.7 256.9** | **121.9** | **125.45** |

RADAR REQUIRED

MSA HUB 25 NM
3100

HOBBY
117.1 HUB
Chan 118

MISSED APCH FIX

R-308 040° R-040

220°

RAYCI
HUB 15

117.1 HUB
Chan 118

113.6 MHF
Chan 83

LOCALIZER 109.9
I-HUB
Chan 36

EISEN INT
I-HUB 5.8

ELREN
I-HUB 8.7

R-301

113.0 VUH
Chan 77

1500
(3)

2000
(7)

041°

221°

(IF)
CARCO INT
I-HUB 15.7

R-285

113.0 VUH
Chan 77

ELEV 46   D   TDZE 44

REIL Rwys 30L and 35
MIRL Rwys 12L-30R and 17-35
HIRL Rwys 4-22 and 12R-30L
TDZ/CL Rwys 4, 12R and 30L

| CARCO INT I-HUB 15.7 | ELREN I-HUB 8.7 | EISEN INT I-HUB 5.8 | I-HUB 2.6 | I-HUB 1.4 | 2000 HUB R-040 | RAYCI |

4000 041° 2000 1500 1500

GS 3.00°
TCH 57

041°
4.3 NM
from FAF

FAF to MAP 4.3 NM

CATEGORY	A	B	C	D	E
S-ILS 4	244/18 200 (200-½)				244/24 200 (200-½)
S-LOC 4	480/24 436 (500-½)		480/40 436 (500-¾)	480/50 436 (500-1)	
CIRCLING	500-1 454 (500-1)		520-1½ 474 (500-1½)	600-2 554 (600-2)	860-3 814 (900-3)

Knots	60	90	120	150	180
Min:Sec	4:18	2:52	2:09	1:43	1:26

HOUSTON, TEXAS
Amdt 40B 05APR12

29°39'N-95°17'W

HOUSTON/ WILLIAM P. HOBBY (HOU)
ILS or LOC RWY 4

FIGURE 196.—ILS or LOC RWY 4 (HOU).

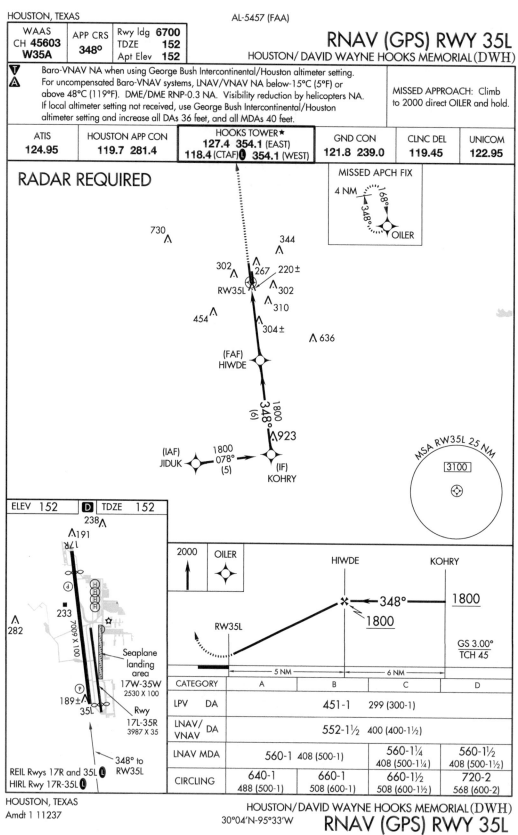

FIGURE 197.—RNAV (GPS) RWY 35L(DWH).

84   **LOUISIANA**

LAFAYETTE RGNL (LFT)   2 SE   UTC–6(–5DT)   N30°12.30′ W91°59.27′   HOUSTON
   42   B   S4   **FUEL** 100LL, JET A   OX 1, 4   Class I, ARFF Index B   NOTAM FILE LFT   H–7D, L–21B, 22E, GOMC
   RWY 04R–22L: H8001X150 (ASPH–GRVD)   S–140, D–170, 2S–175,   IAP, AD
    2D–290   HIRL
     RWY 04R: REIL. PAPI(P4L)—GA 3.0° TCH 53′. Pole. Rgt tfc.
     RWY 22L: MALSR. PAPI(P4L)—GA 3.0° TCH 52′. Thld dsplcd 342′.
    Trees.
   RWY 11–29: H5401X148 (ASPH–GRVD)   S–85, D–110, 2S–140,
    2D–175   MIRL
     RWY 11: REIL. PAPI(P4L)—GA 3.0° TCH 35′. Trees. Rgt tfc.
     RWY 29: REIL. PAPI(P4L)—GA 3.0° TCH 35′. Tree.
   RWY 04L–22R: H4099X75 (ASPH)   S–25, D–32   MIRL
     RWY 04L: REIL. PAPI(P2L)—GA 3.0° TCH 26′. Tree.
     RWY 22R: REIL. PAPI(P2L)—GA 3.0° TCH 27′. Tree. Rgt tfc.
   RUNWAY DECLARED DISTANCE INFORMATION

RWY 04L: TORA–4099	TODA–4099	ASDA–4099	LDA–4099
RWY 04R: TORA–8001	TODA–8001	ASDA–8001	LDA–8001
RWY 11: TORA–5401	TODA–5401	ASDA–5401	LDA–5401
RWY 22L: TORA–8001	TODA–8001	ASDA–8001	LDA–7659
RWY 22R: TORA–4099	TODA–4099	ASDA–4099	LDA–4099
RWY 29: TORA–5401	TODA–5401	ASDA–5401	LDA–5401

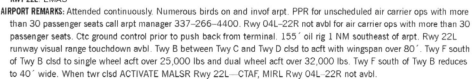

   ARRESTING GEAR/SYSTEM
    RWY 04R: EMAS
    RWY 22L: EMAS
   AIRPORT REMARKS: Attended continuously. Numerous birds on and invof arpt. PPR for unscheduled air carrier ops with more
    than 30 passenger seats call arpt manager 337–266–4400. Rwy 04L–22R not avbl for air carrier ops with more than 30
    passenger seats. Ctc ground control prior to push back from terminal. 155′ oil rig 1 NM southeast of arpt. Rwy 22L
    runway visual range touchdown avbl. Twy B between Twy C and Twy D clsd to acft with wingspan over 80′. Twy F south
    of Twy B clsd to single wheel acft over 25,000 lbs and dual wheel acft over 32,000 lbs. Twy F south of Twy B reduces
    to 40′ wide. When twr clsd ACTIVATE MALSR Rwy 22L—CTAF, MIRL Rwy 04L–22R not avbl.
   WEATHER DATA SOURCES: ASOS (337) 237–8153 **HIWAS** 109.8 LFT.
   COMMUNICATIONS: CTAF 118.5 ATIS 134.05 UNICOM 122.95
    RCO 122.35 (DE RIDDER RADIO)
  ® **APP/DEP CON** 121.1 (020°–210°) 128.7 (211°–019°) (1130–0430Z‡)
  ® **HOUSTON CENTER APP/DEP CON** 126.35 (0430–1130Z‡)
    TOWER 118.5 (1130–0430Z‡) **GND CON** 121.8 **CLNC DEL** 125.55
   AIRSPACE: CLASS C svc ctc APP CON svc 1130–0430Z‡ other times CLASS E.
   RADIO AIDS TO NAVIGATION: NOTAM FILE LFT.
    (L) VORTACW 109.8   LFT   Chan 35   N30°11.63′ W91°59.55′   at fld. 36/3E.   **HIWAS.**
    LAFFS NDB (LOM) 375   LF   N30°17.36′ W91°54.48′ 216° 6.5 NM to fld. Unmonitored when ATCT clsd.
    ILS/DME 110.9   I–TYN   Chan 46   Rwy 04R.   Class IE.
    ILS/DME 109.5   I–LFT   Chan 32   Rwy 22L.   Class IE.   LOM LAFFS NDB. ILS and LOM unmonitored when ATCT clsd.
    ASR (1130–0430Z‡)

• • • • • • • • • • • • • • • • • • • •

   HELIPAD H1: H50X50 (ASPH)
    HELIPAD H1: RLLS.
   HELIPORT REMARKS: Rwy H1 circular pad. Helipad H1 perimeter lgts. Heliport ops to/from helipad between Twys B and F and
    the terminal ramp, avoid overflight of the terminal and other buildings in the 270°–020° quadrant from the helipad.
    Lead–in lgts two ingress paths. Helicopter parking pads avbl.

LAFFS   N30°17.36′ W91°54.48′   NOTAM FILE LFT.   HOUSTON
   NDB (LOM) 375   LF   216° 6.5 NM to Lafayette Rgnl. Unmonitored when ATCT clsd.   L–21B, 22E

FIGURE 198.—Excerpt from Chart Supplement.

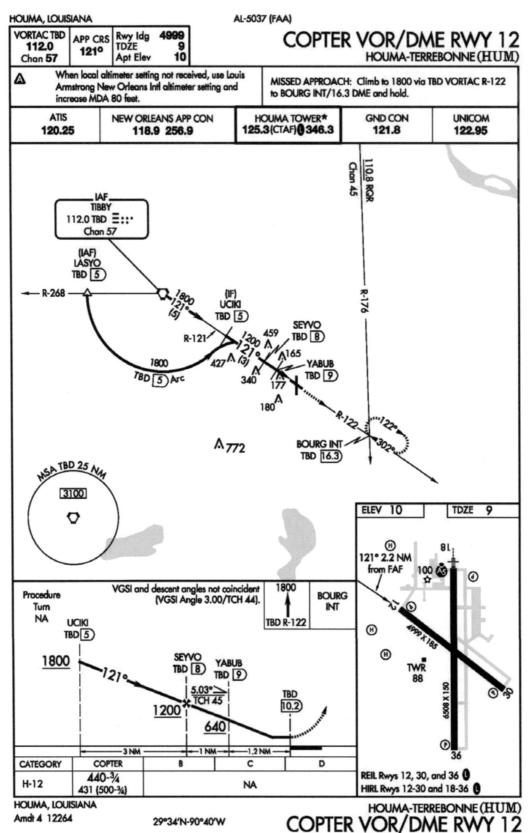

FIGURE 199.—COPTER VOR/DME RWY 12 (HUM).

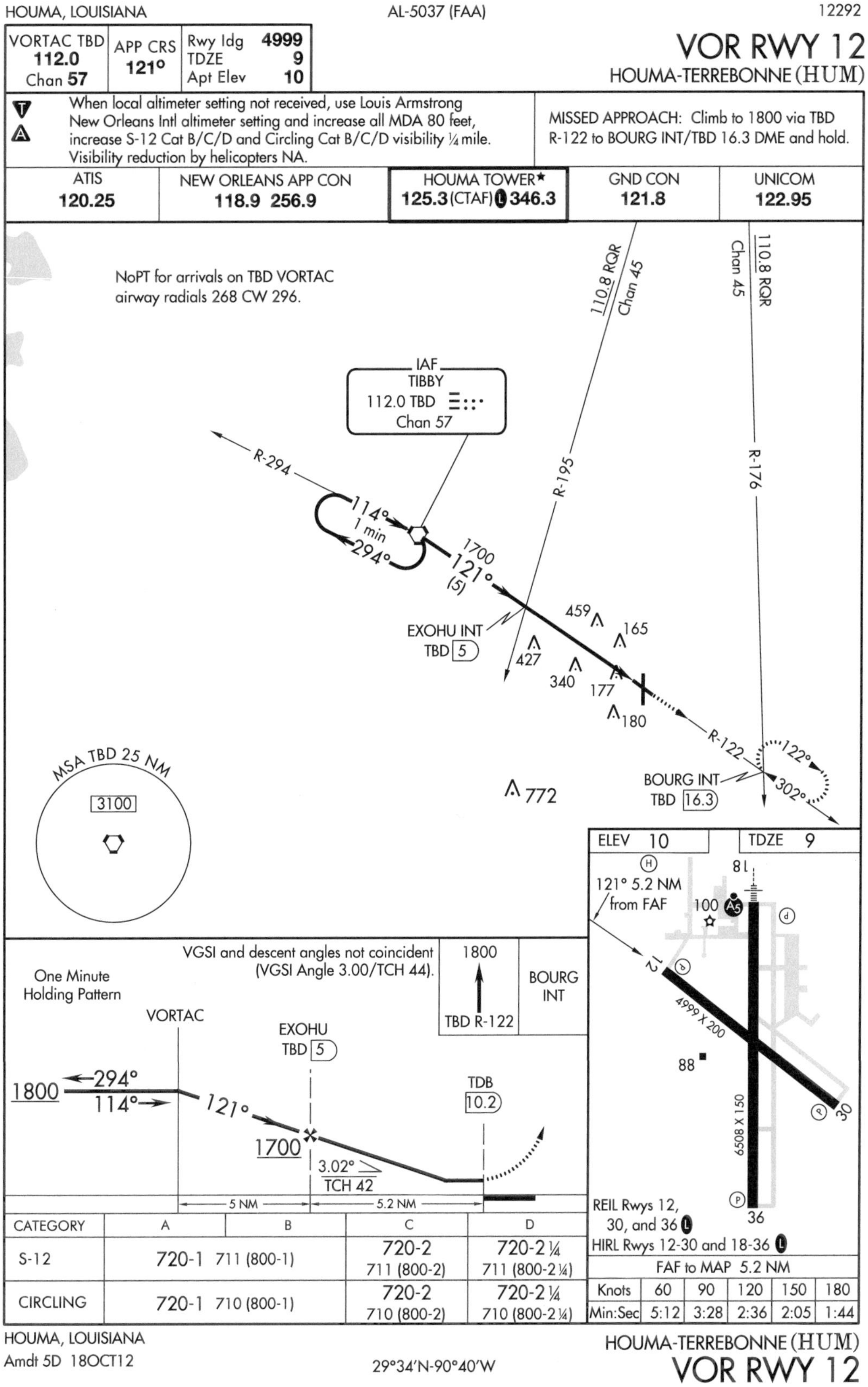

HOUMA, LOUISIANA　　　　　　　　AL-5037 (FAA)　　　　　　　　12292

VORTAC TBD **112.0** Chan **57**	APP CRS **121°**	Rwy Idg **4999** TDZE **9** Apt Elev **10**

VOR RWY 12
HOUMA-TERREBONNE (HUM)

▽ ⚠ When local altimeter setting not received, use Louis Armstrong New Orleans Intl altimeter setting and increase all MDA 80 feet, increase S-12 Cat B/C/D and Circling Cat B/C/D visibility ¼ mile. Visibility reduction by helicopters NA.

MISSED APPROACH: Climb to 1800 via TBD R-122 to BOURG INT/TBD 16.3 DME and hold.

ATIS **120.25**	NEW ORLEANS APP CON **118.9 256.9**	HOUMA TOWER★ **125.3** (CTAF) ◐ **346.3**	GND CON **121.8**	UNICOM **122.95**

NoPT for arrivals on TBD VORTAC airway radials 268 CW 296.

IAF
TIBBY
112.0 TBD ☰∷∙
Chan 57

R-294
114°
1 min
294°
121°
1700
(5)

R-195
110.8 RQR Chan 45
110.8 RQR Chan 45
R-176

EXOHU INT
TBD 5

459
165
427
340 177
180
772

R-122
122°
302°

BOURG INT
TBD 16.3

MSA TBD 25 NM
3100

ELEV 10		TDZE 9

121° 5.2 NM from FAF
100
88
4999 X 200
6509 X 150

REIL Rwys 12, 30, and 36 ◐
HIRL Rwys 12-30 and 18-36 ◐

One Minute Holding Pattern

VGSI and descent angles not coincident (VGSI Angle 3.00/TCH 44).

1800
TBD R-122
BOURG INT

VORTAC
294°
114°
1800
121°
EXOHU TBD 5
1700
3.02°
TCH 42
TDB 10.2

5 NM　　5.2 NM

FAF to MAP 5.2 NM

CATEGORY	A	B	C	D
S-12	720-1 711 (800-1)		720-2 711 (800-2)	720-2¼ 711 (800-2¼)
CIRCLING	720-1 710 (800-1)		720-2 710 (800-2)	720-2¼ 710 (800-2¼)

Knots	60	90	120	150	180
Min:Sec	5:12	3:28	2:36	2:05	1:44

HOUMA, LOUISIANA
Amdt 5D 18OCT12

29°34'N-90°40'W

HOUMA-TERREBONNE (HUM)
VOR RWY 12

FIGURE 200.—VOR RWY 12 (HUM).

Appendix 2

HOUMA—TERREBONNE (HUM) 3 SE UTC–6(–5DT) N29°33.99′ W90°39.63′   NEW ORLEANS
9 B S4 **FUEL** 100LL, JET A OX 1, 2, 3, 4 TPA—1009(1000) NOTAM FILE HUM   H–7D, L–21B, 22F
 RWY 18–36: H6508X150 (CONC–GRVD) S–50, D–70, 2S–89, 2D–137   IAP, AD
  HIRL 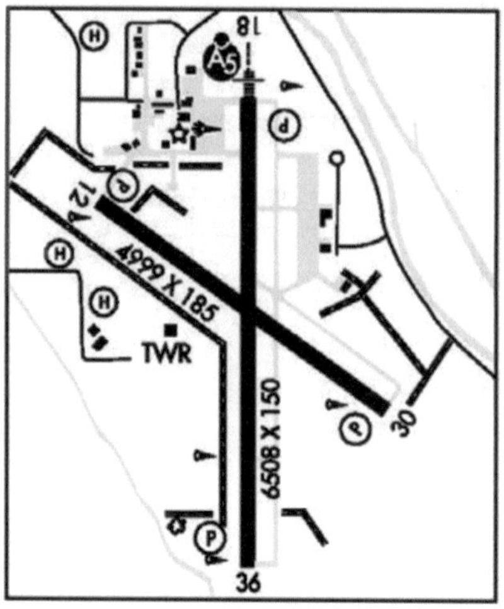
  RWY 18: MALSR. PAPI(P2L)—GA 3.0° TCH 52′. Trees.
  RWY 36: REIL. PAPI(P2L)—GA 3.0° TCH 50′. Trees.
 RWY 12–30: H4999X185 (CONC) S–50, D–70, 2S–89, 2D–137 HIRL
  RWY 12: REIL. PAPI(P2L)—GA 3.0° TCH 44′. Trees.
  RWY 30: REIL. PAPI(P2L)—GA 3.0° TCH 39′.
 AIRPORT REMARKS: Attended 1200–0100Z‡. Fuel avbl 24 hrs with credit
  card. Birds on and invof arpt. Numerous birds 500′AGL and blo 2.8 NM
  south southwest AER 36, avoidance advised. Extensive helicopter ops
  south thru west of arpt. Rwy 12–30 surface skid resistance fair when
  wet. ACTIVATE HIRL Rwy 12–30 and Rwy 18–36 and MALSR Rwy 18
  and REIL Rwy 12, Rwy 30 and Rwy 36—CTAF.
 WEATHER DATA SOURCES: AWOS–3PT 120.25 (985) 876–4055. LAWRS.
 COMMUNICATIONS: CTAF 125.3 ATIS 120.25 UNICOM 122.95
  RCO 122.45 (DE RIDDER RADIO)
 Ⓡ NEW ORLEANS APP/DEP CON 118.9
  TOWER 125.3 (1200–0100Z‡) GND CON 121.8
 AIRSPACE: CLASS D svc 1200–0100Z‡ other times CLASS G.
 RADIO AIDS TO NAVIGATION: NOTAM FILE DRI.
  TIBBY (L) VORTAC 112.0 TBD Chan 57 N29°39.86′ W90°49.75′ 122° 10.6 NM to fld. 10/2E.
  VORTAC unusable:
   byd 30 NM blo 2,000′
  TACAN DME unusable:
   byd 30 NM blo 2,000′
  HOUMA NDB(LOM) 219 HU N29°39.80′ W90°39.58′ 179° 5.8 NM to fld. LOM unmonitored. Unmonitored when ATCT
   clsd.
  ILS 108.5 I–HUM Rwy 18. LOM HOUMA NDB. LOM unmonitored. Unmonitored when ATCT clsd.

IDA'S HELIPORT (L87) 0 N UTC–6(–5DT) N33°00.26′ W93°53.59′   MEMPHIS
286 NOTAM FILE DRI
HELIPAD H1: H40X40 (CONC)
HELIPORT REMARKS: Attended continuously. Helipad H1 perimeter lgts. Helipad H1 100′ water twr 300′ E and 149′ radio
 twr 500′ S of pad. For perimeter lgts call 318–284–3231. Helipad H1 apch 180°–departure 000°.
COMMUNICATIONS: CTAF 122.9

INDEPENDENCE IPN N28°05.10′ W87°59.15′
AWOS–3 118.125 Winds unreliable.

JEANERETTE
LE MAIRE MEM (2R1) 1 S UTC–6(–5DT) N29°53.94′ W91°39.96′   HOUSTON
14 B FUEL 100LL NOTAM FILE DRI   L–21B, 22F
RWY 04–22: H3000X75 (ASPH) S–6 MIRL
 RWY 04: REIL. PAPI(P2L)—GA 3.0° TCH 50′. Trees.
 RWY 22: REIL. PAPI(P2L)—GA 3.0° TCH 50′. Thld dsplcd 603′. Tree.
AIRPORT REMARKS: Unattended. For arpt attended call 337–365–7202. Fuel avbl 24 hrs self svc with credit card. MIRL Rwy
 04–22 and REIL Rwys 04 and 22 preset low ints dusk to dawn, to incr ints ACTIVATE–CTAF.
COMMUNICATIONS: CTAF 122.9
RADIO AIDS TO NAVIGATION: NOTAM FILE LFT.
 LAFAYETTE (L) VORTACW 109.8 LFT Chan 35 N30°11.63′ W91°59.55′ 133° 24.5 NM to fld. 36/3E. HIWAS.

FIGURE 201.—Excerpt from Chart Supplement.

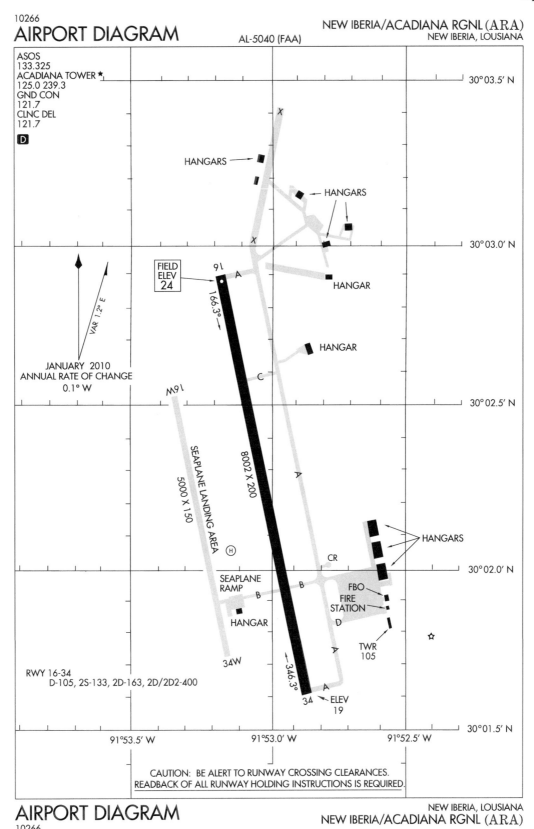

10266
AIRPORT DIAGRAM
AL-5040 (FAA)

NEW IBERIA/ACADIANA RGNL (ARA)
NEW IBERIA, LOUSIANA

ASOS
133.325
ACADIANA TOWER ★
125.0 239.3
GND CON
121.7
CLNC DEL
121.7

D

VAR 1.2° E

JANUARY 2010
ANNUAL RATE OF CHANGE
0.1° W

FIELD
ELEV
24

166.3°

8002 X 200

SEAPLANE LANDING AREA

5000 X 150

16W

34W

SEAPLANE
RAMP

HANGAR

346.3°

34 — ELEV
19

HANGARS

HANGARS

HANGAR

HANGAR

HANGARS

FBO
FIRE
STATION

TWR
105

CR

RWY 16-34
D-105, 2S-133, 2D-163, 2D/2D2-400

CAUTION: BE ALERT TO RUNWAY CROSSING CLEARANCES.
READBACK OF ALL RUNWAY HOLDING INSTRUCTIONS IS REQUIRED.

30° 03.5' N
30° 03.0' N
30° 02.5' N
30° 02.0' N
30° 01.5' N

91°53.5' W   91°53.0' W   91°52.5' W

AIRPORT DIAGRAM
10266

NEW IBERIA, LOUSIANA
NEW IBERIA/ACADIANA RGNL (ARA)

Figure 202.—Airport Diagram: New Iberia/Acadiana RGNL (ARA).

90   **LOUISIANA**

NATCHITOCHES RGNL (IER)   2 S   UTC–6(–5DT)   N31°44.14´ W93°05.95´   HOUSTON
    121   B   S4   **FUEL** 100LL, JET A1+   NOTAM FILE IER   H–6I, L–22E
    RWY 17–35: H5003X150 (ASPH)   S–30   MIRL   IAP
      RWY 17: REIL. PAPI(P4L)—GA 3.0° TCH 45´. Tree.
      RWY 35: ODALS. PAPI(P4L)—GA 3.0° TCH 43´. Trees.
    RWY 07–25: H4000X100 (ASPH)   S–21   MIRL
      RWY 07: Trees.
      RWY 25: P–line.
    AIRPORT REMARKS: Attended dawn–dusk. For arpt attendant after hrs call
      318–471–2106. Fuel avbl 24 hr with credit card. MIRL Rwy 17–35
      and REIL Rwy 17 preset low ints dusk to dawn, to increase ints and
      ACTIVATE MIRL Rwy 07–25—CTAF. Rwy 35 ODALS operate low ints
      continuously, to increase ints ACTIVATE—CTAF.
    WEATHER DATA SOURCES: AWOS–3 119.025 (318) 352–1575.
    COMMUNICATIONS: CTAF/UNICOM 122.8
  Ⓡ POLK APP/DEP CON 125.4
     GCO 135.075 (FORT POLK APCH AND DE RIDDER FSS)
    RADIO AIDS TO NAVIGATION: NOTAM FILE AEX.
     ALEXANDRIA (H) VORTACW 116.1   AEX   Chan 108   N31°15.40´
      W92°30.06´   310° 42.0 NM to fld. 80/3E.   **HIWAS.**
     VOR unusable:
       035°–065° blo 2,000´
       066°–094° byd 35 NM blo 3,000´
       185°–200° byd 35 NM blo 3,000´
       201°–214° byd 35 NM blo 2,000´
       215°–260° blo 2,000´
       261°–285° byd 35 NM blo 2,000´
       357°–034° byd 35 NM blo 3,000´
     NDB (MHW) 407   OOC   N31°39.45´ W93°04.66´   343° 4.8 NM to fld.   NOTAM FILE IER.
     LOC 110.5   I–IER   Rwy 35.   LOC unmonitored 0000–1200Z‡.

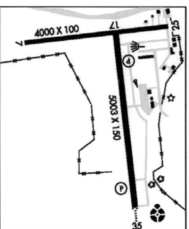

NEW IBERIA
   ACADIANA RGNL (ARA)   4 NW   UTC–6(–5DT)   N30°02.27´ W91°53.03´   HOUSTON
    24   B   S2   **FUEL** 100LL, JET A   OX 4   TPA—1024(1000)   Class IV, ARFF Index A   H–7D, L–21B, 22E, GOMC
    NOTAM FILE ARA   IAP, AD
    RWY 16–34: H8002X200 (CONC)   D–105, 2S–133, 2D–163,
     2D/2D2–400   HIRL
      RWY 16: ODALS. PAPI(P4L)—GA 3.0° TCH 51´.
      RWY 34: MALSR. PAPI(P4L)—GA 3.0° TCH 52´. Rgt tfc.
    RUNWAY DECLARED DISTANCE INFORMATION
      RWY 16: TORA–8002   TODA–8002   ASDA–8002   LDA–8002
      RWY 34: TORA–8002   TODA–8002   ASDA–8002   LDA–8002
    AIRPORT REMARKS: Attended 1300–0300Z‡. For fuel after hrs call
     337–367–1401, FAX 337–367–1404. Seaplane landing area (water
     channel) West of and adjacent/parallel to runway. Rwy 16W–34W
     seaway edge lgts green; thld lgts amber. Bird activity on and invof arpt.
     ARFF PPR for more than 30 passenger seats call arpt manager
     337–365–7202. Rotor wing movement and landing area between the
     rwy and seaway. Intensive helicopter training. When twr closed HIRL
     Rwy 16–34 preset low ints, to increase ints and ACTIVATE MALSR Rwy
     34—CTAF.
    WEATHER DATA SOURCES: ASOS 133.325 (337) 365–0128.
    COMMUNICATIONS: CTAF 125.0 UNICOM 122.95
  Ⓡ LAFAYETTE APP/DEP CON 121.1 (1130–0430Z‡)
     HOUSTON CENTER APP/DEP CON 126.35 (0430–1130Z‡)
     TOWER 125.0 (1200–0300Z‡) GND CON 121.7 CLNC DEL 121.7
     LAFAYETTE CLNC DEL 118.05
    AIRSPACE: CLASS D svc 1200–0300Z‡ other times CLASS G.

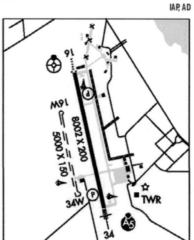

CONTINUED ON NEXT PAGE

FIGURE 203.—Excerpt from Chart Supplement.

LOUISIANA

CONTINUED FROM PRECEDING PAGE

RADIO AIDS TO NAVIGATION: NOTAM FILE LFT.

    LAFAYETTE (L) VORTACW 109.8   LFT   Chan 35   N30°11.63′ W91°59.55′   146° 10.9 NM to fld. 36/3E.   **HIWAS.**

    ACADI NDB (MHW/LOM) 269   AR   N29°57.38′ W91°51.80′   345° 5.0 NM to fld.   NOTAM FILE ARA.

    ILS 108.9 I–ARA Rwy 34. Class IA. LOM ACADI NDB.

• • • • • • • • • • • • • • • • • • •

WATERWAY 16W–34W: 5000X150 (WATER)   MIRL

    WATERWAY 16W: Rgt tfc.

RUNWAY DECLARED DISTANCE INFORMATION

    RWY 16W: TORA–5000 TODA–5000 ASDA–5000 LDA–5000

    RWY 34W: TORA–5000 TODA–5000 ASDA–5000 LDA–5000

SEAPLANE REMARKS: Waterway 16–34 seaway edge lgts green, thld lgts amber. ACTIVATE seaway edge lgts Waterway
16–34—122.7. 3 clicks on 7 clicks off.

NEW ORLEANS

LAKEFRONT (NEW)   4 NE   UTC–6(–5DT)   N30°02.55′ W90°01.70′   **NEW ORLEANS**

   7   B S4 **FUEL** 100LL, JET A OX 1, 3 LRA NOTAM FILE NEW   **H–7E, 8F, L–21B, 22F, GOMC**

   RWY 18R–36L: H6879X150 (ASPH–GRVD) S–60, D–175, 2S–175,   **IAP, AD**

      2D–200, 2D/2D2–350 MIRL

    RWY 18R: MALSF. PAPI(P4L)—GA 3.0° TCH 51′. Thld dsplcd 239′.
Pier. Rgt tfc.

    RWY 36L: REIL. PAPI(P4L)—GA 3.0° TCH 50′. Thld dsplcd 820′. Wall.

   RWY 18L–36R: H3697X75 (ASPH) S–35, D–55, 2D–80 MIRL

    RWY 18L: REIL.

    RWY 36R: REIL. PAPI(P4L)—GA 3.0° TCH 45′. Bldg. Rgt tfc.

   RWY 09–27: H3114X75 (ASPH) S–50, D–80, 2S–102, 2D–100 MIRL

    RWY 09: REIL. PAPI(P4L)—GA 3.0° TCH 40′. Berm.

    RWY 27: PAPI(P4R)—GA 3.0° TCH 40′. Road. Rgt tfc.

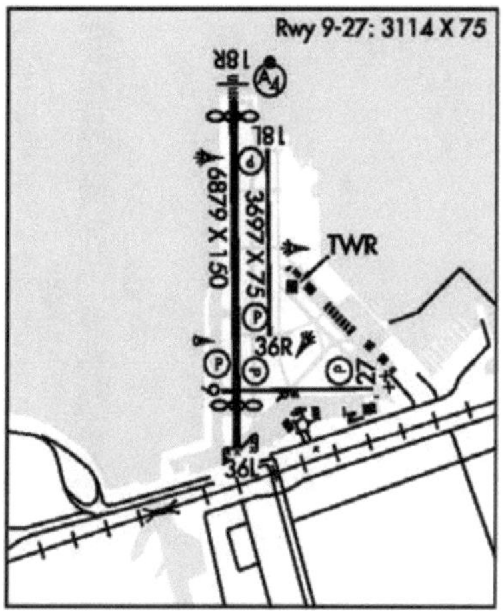

   RUNWAY DECLARED DISTANCE INFORMATION

    RWY 09: TORA–3113 TODA–3113 ASDA–3113 LDA–3113

    RWY 18L: TORA–3697 TODA–3697 ASDA–3697 LDA–3697

    RWY 18R: TORA–6880 TODA–6880 ASDA–6035 LDA–5510

    RWY 27: TORA–3113 TODA–3113 ASDA–3113 LDA–3113

    RWY 36L: TORA–6880 TODA–6880 ASDA–5955 LDA–5135

    RWY 36R: TORA–3697 TODA–3697 ASDA–3697 LDA–3697

AIRPORT REMARKS: Attended continuously. For field conditions after 2200Z‡
ctc arpt manager on 504–914–5721. Birds on and invof arpt. Boats as
high as 80′ pass within 400′ of Rwy 09 thld. Rwy 18R–36L few low spots near intersection of Rwy 09–27 holding water.
When twr clsd MIRL Rwy 18R–36L preset med ints and twy lgts for Twys A, B, D, E, F and H preset on medium. ARFF
capability equivalent to Index B. Acft transporting any items listed in Part 175 title 49 PPR to land. Landing fee. Landing
fee waived with minimum fuel purchase. Flight Notification Service (ADCUS) temporarily not available. NOTE: See Special
Notices—U.S. Special Customs Requirement.

WEATHER DATA SOURCES: ASOS (504) 245–4366 LAWRS.

COMMUNICATIONS: CTAF 119.9 ATIS 124.9

   NEW ORLEANS RCO 122.6 (DE RIDDER RADIO)

® **NEW ORLEANS APP/DEP CON** 133.15 (North) 123.85 (South)

   TOWER 119.9 (1400–0000Z‡) **GND CON** 121.7 **CLNC DEL** 127.4 (NEW ORLEANS APP/DEP CON when twr clsd)

AIRSPACE: CLASS D svc 1400–0000Z‡ other times CLASS E.

RADIO AIDS TO NAVIGATION: NOTAM FILE NEW.

   HARVEY (H) VORTACW 114.1   HRV   Chan 88   N29°51.01′ W90°00.18′   351° 11.6 NM to fld. 2/2E.

    VORTAC unusable:

      004°–125° byd 30 NM blo 2,000′

      126°–136° byd 25 NM blo 3,000′

      137°–174° byd 30 NM blo 2,000′

      175°–190° byd 30 NM blo 3,000′

      191°–239° byd 30 NM blo 2,000′

      240°–255° byd 25 NM blo 6,000′

      256°–279° byd 30 NM blo 2,000′

      280°–290° byd 30 NM

      291°–352° byd 30 NM blo 2,000′

      353°–003° byd 30 NM blo 3,000′

    ILS/DME 111.3 I–NEW Chan 50 Rwy 18R.

FIGURE 203A.—Excerpt from Chart Supplement.

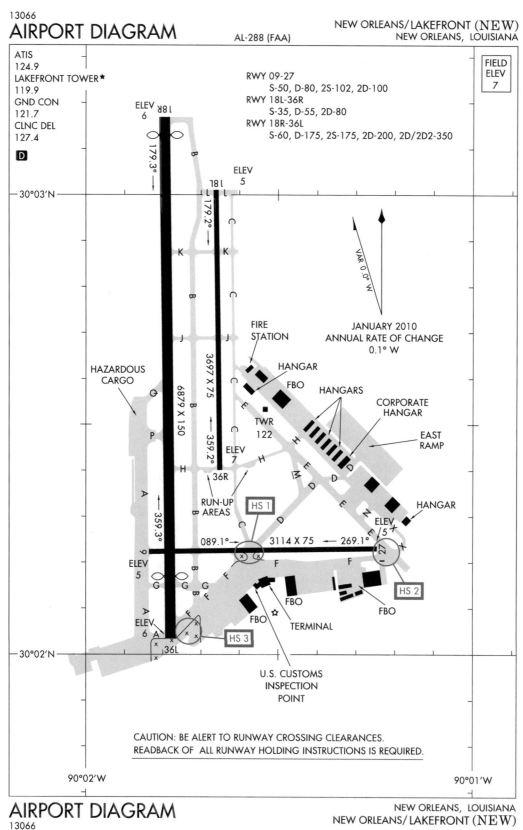

13066

AIRPORT DIAGRAM

AL-288 (FAA)

NEW ORLEANS/LAKEFRONT (NEW)
NEW ORLEANS, LOUISIANA

ATIS
124.9
LAKEFRONT TOWER★
119.9
GND CON
121.7
CLNC DEL
127.4
Ⓓ

FIELD
ELEV
7

RWY 09-27
S-50, D-80, 2S-102, 2D-100
RWY 18L-36R
S-35, D-55, 2D-80
RWY 18R-36L
S-60, D-175, 2S-175, 2D-200, 2D/2D2-350

JANUARY 2010
ANNUAL RATE OF CHANGE
0.1° W

VAR 0.0° W

FIRE STATION
HANGAR
FBO
HANGARS
CORPORATE HANGAR
EAST RAMP
HANGAR

HAZARDOUS CARGO

TWR 122

RUN-UP AREAS

HS 1

HS 2

HS 3

FBO
FBO
TERMINAL
FBO
FBO

U.S. CUSTOMS INSPECTION POINT

CAUTION: BE ALERT TO RUNWAY CROSSING CLEARANCES.
READBACK OF ALL RUNWAY HOLDING INSTRUCTIONS IS REQUIRED.

AIRPORT DIAGRAM

13066

NEW ORLEANS, LOUISIANA
NEW ORLEANS/LAKEFRONT (NEW)

FIGURE 204.—Airport Diagram: New ORLEANS/LAKEFRONT (NEW).

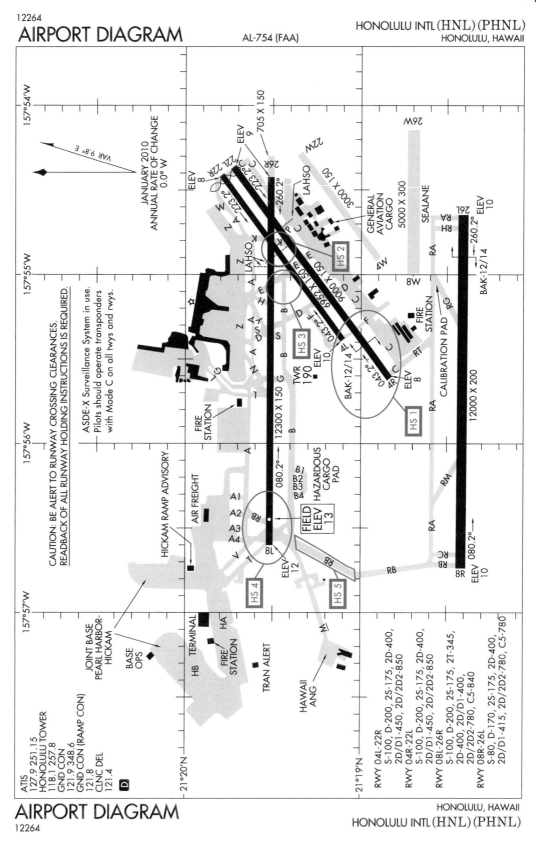

FIGURE 205.—Airport Diagram: Honolulu Intl (HNL) (PHNL).

- -

HONOLULU INTL (JOINT BASE PEARL HARBOR–HICKAM)   (HNL)(PHNL)   3 NW   UTC–10   HAWAIIAN–MARIANA
N21°19.12′ W157°55.35′   P–1C, 2G
13   B   S4   **FUEL** 80, 100, JET A, A1+, B   OX 1, 2, 3, 4   TPA—See Remarks   IAP
LRA   Class I, ARFF Index E   NOTAM FILE HNL
RWY 08L–26R: H12300X150 (ASPH–GRVD)   S–100, D–200, 2S–175, 2T–345, 2D–400, 2D/D1–400,
D2D/2D2–780   HIRL
  RWY 08L: MALSR. PAPI(P4L)—GA 3.0° TCH 80′.
  RWY 26R: REIL. PAPI(P4L)—GA 3.0 TCH 71′.
RWY 08R–26L: H12000X200 (ASPH–GRVD)   S–80, D–170, 2S–175, 2D–400, D/2D2–780   HIRL
  RWY 08R: REIL. PAPI(P4L)—GA 3.25° TCH 99′.
  RWY 26L: MALSF. PAPI(P4L)—GA 3.0° TCH 75′. 3 cranes.
RWY 04R–22L: H9000X150 (ASPH–GRVD)   S–100, D–200, 2S–175, 2D–400, D/2D2–850   HIRL
  RWY 04R: MALSR. PAPI(P4L)—GA 3.0° TCH 71′. Tree.
  RWY 22L: REIL. PAPI(P4L)—GA 3.44° TCH 80′. Stack.
RWY 04L–22R: H6952X150 (ASPH)   S–100, D–200, 2S–175, 2D–400, D/2D2–850   MIRL
  RWY 04L: REIL. PAPI(P4L)—GA 3.0° TCH 50′.   **RWY 22R:** REIL. Antenna. Thld dsplcd 150′.
LAND AND HOLD-SHORT OPERATIONS

LDG RWY	HOLD-SHORT POINT	AVBL LDG DIST
RWY 04L	08L–26R	3700
RWY 04R	08L–26R	6250
RWY 08L	04L–22R	9300

RUNWAY DECLARED DISTANCE INFORMATION

RWY 04R:	TORA–9000	TODA–9000	ASDA–8950	LDA–8950
RWY 22L:	TORA–9000	TODA–9000	ASDA–8937	LDA–8937

ARRESTING GEAR/SYSTEMS
  RWY 04R BAK–14 BAK–12B (1500′)

HOOK MB 60 (200′) → **RWY 26R**
BAK–14 BAK 12B(B) (1500) **RWY 26L**

AIRPORT REMARKS: Attended continuously. 80 and 100 octane fuel avbl thru FBO. Bird strike hazard all runways. Mil acft opr during Bird Watch Condition MODERATE (initial tkof or full stop ldg only, no multiple IFR/VFR approaches) and SEVERE (tkof and ldg prohibited w/o 15 OG/CC approval or 154 OG/CC approval for HIANG acft) ctc HIK ramp, PTD, 15 WG command post, 735 AMC command post, 154 WG command post for current conditions. See FLIP AP/3 Supplementary arpt information, route and area rstd, and Oakland FIR flt haz. Use caution for obstruction 76′ from Twy M centerline on Oceanside, approximately 200′ from parking apron. Crane 290′ AGL approximately 2,600′ north of Rwy 08L, 2500′ west of Inter Island Terminal 1630–0330Z daily. PAEW 600′–1300′E Rwy 22L and Rwy 22R thld, 1700–0130Z Mon–Fri. Rwys CLOSED 1730–0630 every month as follows: Rwy 04R–22L first Tue; Rwy 08R–26L second Tue; and Rwy 08L–26R third Tue. Rwy 08R–26L 200′ pavement width with lgts outside, pavement striped 150′ wide. Thld of Rwy 08L difficult to determine due to Twy T. All jet acft ctc ramp control prior to engine start at gate or hard stand. Foreign object debris hazard exists on all movement areas east of Twy S. Fighter acft exercise extreme caution when taxiing. To minimize foreign object damage potential, all acft should use minimum thrust, especially outboard engines, when taxiing past the F–22 alert facility on Twy T. Twys G and L between Twy A and Inter–Island ramp clsd to wide–bodied and 4–engine turbo–jet acft under power without PPR from arpt ops manager 808–836–6428 Mon–Fri 1745–0230Z. Twy K not a high speed exit twy. Wide body and 4 engine turbojets ldg on Rwy 04R roll to end of rwy, no left turn at Twy K without approval. Tfc pattern overhead altitude 2000(1987), restricted to HIANG acft. Rwy 04R–22L and Rwy 08R–26L sfc grvd within 10′ of A–G system. Potential for fighter acft tail hook skip exists. Due to sensitivities of citizens, fighter acft and water–augmented acft dep only authorized from Mon–Sat 1700–0700Z, and Sun and holidays 1800–0700Z. All request for waivers will be sent to the 15/OG/CC at least 5 working days in advance. Waivers will be granted on extreme necessary. If short notice mission essential waivers are necessary, ctc 15OG/CC by phone thru 15 WG Comd Post (15 WG/CP). 15 WG Comd Post will pass approval to Hickam flight svc and Hickam ramp advisory. Tfc pattern altitude for small acft entering from NW 800(787). Tfc pattern altitude for small acft entering from S 1000(987). Tfc pattern altitude for large acft entering from N 1500(1487). No F–16 transient support avbl in accordance with Area Control Center LSET flash safety 06–02. Transient F–16 units should provide their own maintenance support. PPR all acft units planning to stage ops from Hickam AFB must ctc 15 OSS/OSX DSN 315–449–1596/1597 at least 60 days prior to arrival. All military acft rqr Customs/Agriculture/Immigration inspection must ctc 15 WG command post or if Air Mobility Command ctc Hickam AMCC, no later than 3 hrs prior to arrival with departure location estimated block time, number of aircrew, Civilian/Military Passengers/Foreign Nationals/and Distinguished Visitor codes. JBPH–H is PPR to all non–AMC acft and AMC trng msn (QEN, KEN, PEN, AEN, and ANC C130's). All tran acft not on an AMC/TWCF msn and home stn acft terminating at JBPH–H, will provide a 3 hr out call (COMM 808–448–6900) as well as a 20–30 min out call on 292.5 to the 15 WG/CP (KOA CONTROL). All transient acft, not on an Air Mobility Command mission, will provide a 2–3 hr out call, as well as 20–30 minute out call on 292.5 to the 15 WG/CP (KOA Control). 15 WG can provide eqpt but crews must provide own pers when needed. Upon arrival, crews will proceed directly to Command Post (Bldg 2050) and complete an outbound setup sheet to facilitate departure requirements. No COMSEC material avbl thru Hickam Airfield Ops. Transient aircrews should plan to arrive with appropriate amount of COSMEC to complete entire mission. Arfld

CONTINUED ON NEXT PAGE

FIGURE 206.—Excerpt from Chart Supplement.

This page is intentionally left blank

(STELA.STELA1) 16259

ST-460 (FAA)

STELA ONE ARRIVAL

WINDSOR LOCKS, CONNECTICUT

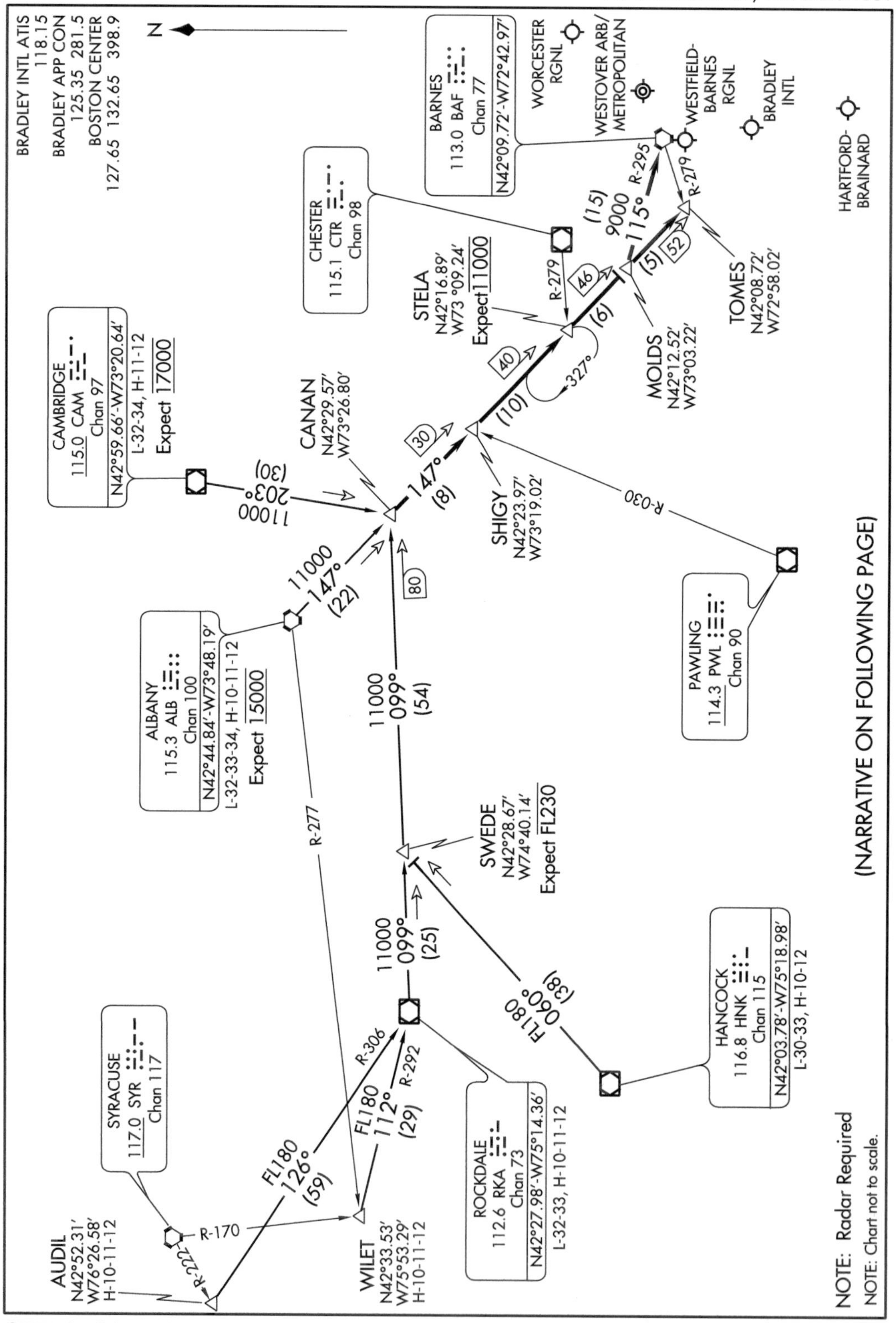

STELA ONE ARRIVAL

WINDSOR LOCKS, CONNECTICUT

(STELA.STELA1) 31MAY12

FIGURE 208.—STELA One Arrival (STELA.STELA1).

(STELA.STELA1) 16259

ST-460 (FAA)

STELA ONE ARRIVAL

WINDSOR LOCKS, CONNECTICUT

ARRIVAL ROUTE DESCRIPTION

ALBANY TRANSITION (ALB.STELA1): From over ALB VORTAC via ALB R-147 to CANAN INT. Thence. . . .
AUDIL TRANSITION (AUDIL.STELA1): From over AUDIL INT via RKA R-306 to RKA VOR/DME, then via RKA R-099 to CANAN INT. Thence. . . .
CAMBRIDGE TRANSITION (CAM.STELA1): From over CAM VOR/DME via CAM R-203 to CANAN INT. Thence. . . .
HANCOCK TRANSITION (HNK.STELA1): From over HNK VOR/DME via HNK R-060 to SWEDE INT, then via RKA R-099 to CANAN INT. Thence. . . .
WILET TRANSITION (WILET.STELA1): From over WILET INT via RKA R-292 to RKA VOR/DME, then via RKA R-099 TO CANAN INT. Thence. . . .

KBDL and KHFD ARRIVALS: From over CANAN INT via ALB R-147 to TOMES INT. Expect radar vectors to final approach course prior to TOMES INT.

KBAF, KCEF and KORH ARRIVALS: From over CANAN INT via ALB R-147 to MOLDS INT. Then via BAF R-295 to BAF VORTAC. Expect radar vectors to final approach course prior to BAF VORTAC.

STELA ONE ARRIVAL

WINDSOR LOCKS, CONNECTICUT

(STELA.STELA1) 31MAY12

FIGURE 209.—STELA One Arrival (STELA.STELA1).

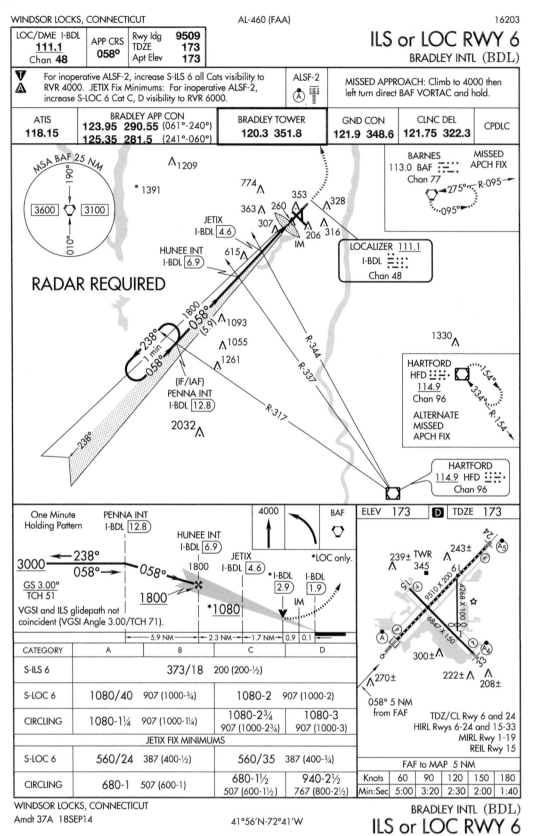

FIGURE 210.—ILS or LOC RWY 6 (CAT I) (BDL).

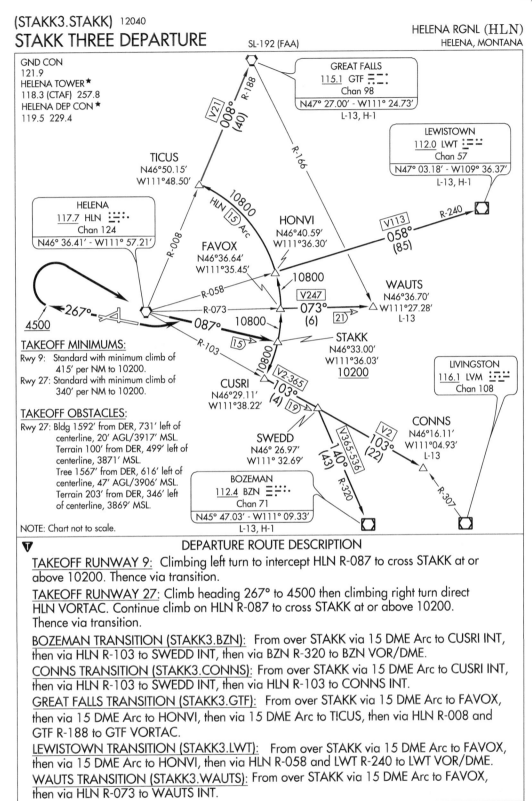

(STAKK3.STAKK) 12040
STAKK THREE DEPARTURE
SL-192 (FAA)

HELENA RGNL (HLN)
HELENA, MONTANA

GND CON
121.9
HELENA TOWER ★
118.3 (CTAF) 257.8
HELENA DEP CON ★
119.5 229.4

GREAT FALLS
115.1 GTF
Chan 98
N47° 27.00' - W111° 24.73'
L-13, H-1

LEWISTOWN
112.0 LWT
Chan 57
N47° 03.18' - W109° 36.37'
L-13, H-1

TICUS
N46°50.15'
W111°48.50'

HELENA
117.7 HLN
Chan 124
N46° 36.41' - W111° 57.21'

HONVI
N46°40.59'
W111°36.30'

FAVOX
N46°36.64'
W111°35.45'

WAUTS
N46°36.70'
W111°27.28'
L-13

STAKK
N46°33.00'
W111°36.03'
10200

LIVINGSTON
116.1 LVM
Chan 108

CUSRI
N46°29.11'
W111°38.22'

CONNS
N46°16.11'
W111°04.93'
L-13

SWEDD
N46° 26.97'
W111° 32.69'

BOZEMAN
112.4 BZN
Chan 71
N45° 47.03' - W111° 09.33'
L-13, H-1

TAKEOFF MINIMUMS:
Rwy 9: Standard with minimum climb of
415' per NM to 10200.
Rwy 27: Standard with minimum climb of
340' per NM to 10200.

TAKEOFF OBSTACLES:
Rwy 27: Bldg 1592' from DER, 731' left of
centerline, 20' AGL/3917' MSL.
Terrain 100' from DER, 499' left of
centerline, 3871' MSL.
Tree 1567' from DER, 616' left of
centerline, 47' AGL/3906' MSL.
Terrain 203' from DER, 346' left
of centerline, 3869' MSL.

NOTE: Chart not to scale.

DEPARTURE ROUTE DESCRIPTION

TAKEOFF RUNWAY 9: Climbing left turn to intercept HLN R-087 to cross STAKK at or above 10200. Thence via transition.

TAKEOFF RUNWAY 27: Climb heading 267° to 4500 then climbing right turn direct HLN VORTAC. Continue climb on HLN R-087 to cross STAKK at or above 10200. Thence via transition.

BOZEMAN TRANSITION (STAKK3.BZN): From over STAKK via 15 DME Arc to CUSRI INT, then via HLN R-103 to SWEDD INT, then via BZN R-320 to BZN VOR/DME.

CONNS TRANSITION (STAKK3.CONNS): From over STAKK via 15 DME Arc to CUSRI INT, then via HLN R-103 to SWEDD INT, then via HLN R-103 to CONNS INT.

GREAT FALLS TRANSITION (STAKK3.GTF): From over STAKK via 15 DME Arc to FAVOX, then via 15 DME Arc to HONVI, then via 15 DME Arc to TICUS, then via HLN R-008 and GTF R-188 to GTF VORTAC.

LEWISTOWN TRANSITION (STAKK3.LWT): From over STAKK via 15 DME Arc to FAVOX, then via 15 DME Arc to HONVI, then via HLN R-058 and LWT R-240 to LWT VOR/DME.

WAUTS TRANSITION (STAKK3.WAUTS): From over STAKK via 15 DME Arc to FAVOX, then via HLN R-073 to WAUTS INT.

STAKK THREE DEPARTURE
(STAKK3.STAKK) 12040

HELENA, MONTANA
HELENA RGNL (HLN)

FIGURE 211.—STAKK Three Departure (STAKK3.STAKK) (HLN).

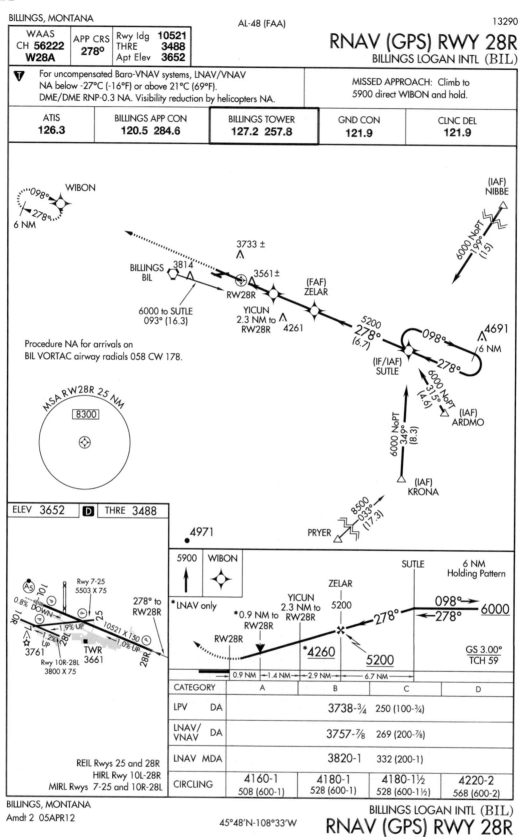

BILLINGS, MONTANA
Amdt 2 05APR12

45°48'N-108°33'W

FIGURE 212.—RNAV (GPS) RWY 28R (BIL).

Appendix 2

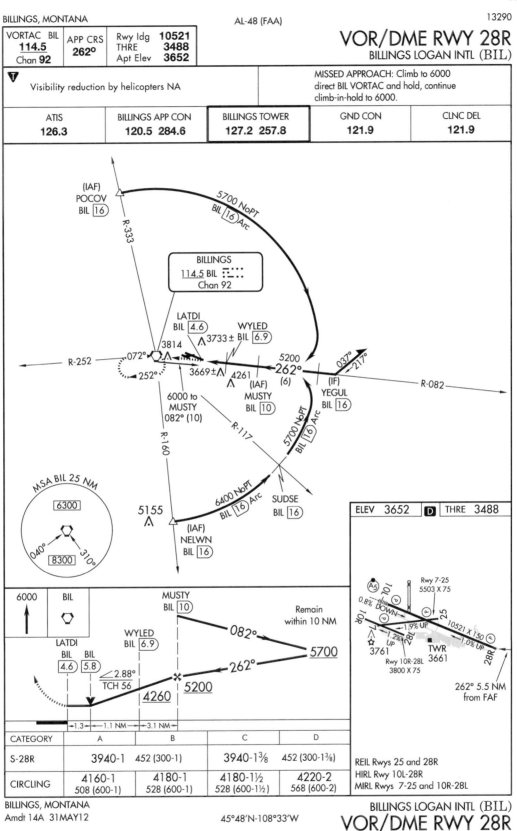

FIGURE 213.—VOR/DME RWY 28R (BIL).

179

BILLINGS LOGAN INTL (BIL) 2 NW UTC–7(–6DT) N45°48.46´ W108°32.57´   **BILLINGS**
  3652   B S4 **FUEL** 100LL, JET A   OX 1, 2, 3, 4   ARFF Index—See Remarks   NOTAM FILE BIL   **H–1E, L–13D**
  RWY 10L–28R: H10521X150 (ASPH–GRVD) S–130, D–170, 2S–175,   **IAP AD**
    2D–285   HIRL

    RWY 10L: MALSR. PAPI(P4L)—GA 3.0° TCH 51´. 0.8% down.
    RWY 28R: REIL. PAPI(P4R)—GA 3.0° TCH 56´. Ground. 1.0% up.
  RWY 07–25: H5503X75 (ASPH–GRVD) S–12.5 MIRL 1.9% up SW
    RWY 07: PAPI(P4L)—GA 3.0° TCH 31´. Ground.
    RWY 25: REIL. PAPI(P4R)—GA 3.0° TCH 36´.
  RWY 10R–28L: H3800X75 (ASPH) S–12.5 MIRL 1.2% up NW
    RWY 10R: Ground.

Rwy 10R–28L: 3800 X 75
Rwy 7-25: 5503 X 75

RUNWAY DECLARED DISTANCE INFORMATION
    RWY 07: TORA–5503 TODA–5503 ASDA–5503 LDA–5503
    RWY 10L: TORA–10521 TODA–10521 ASDA–10521 LDA–10521
    RWY 10R: TORA–3800 TODA–3800 ASDA–3800 LDA–3800
    RWY 25: TORA–5503 TODA–5503 ASDA–5503 LDA–5503
    RWY 28L: TORA–3800 TODA–3800 ASDA–3800 LDA–3800
    RWY 28R: TORA–10521 TODA–10521 ASDA–10521 LDA–10521
AIRPORT REMARKS: Attended continuously. Rwy 07–25 and Rwy 10R–28L
  CLOSED to acft over 12,500 lbs. No customs, remote acft parking, ltd
  ground handling svc. Migratory waterfowl invof arpt. Twy D 35´ wide
  clsd to acft over 12,500 lbs. Class I, ARFF Index C. PPR unscheduled
  air carrier ops with more than 30 passenger seats ctc arpt ops 406–657–8496. ARFF Index B from 0900–1300Z‡. 180°
  turns Rwy 10L–28R by acft over 25,000 lbs prohibited. For MIRL Rwy 10R–28L and Rwy 07–25, HIRL Rwy 10L–28R,
  MALSR Rwy 10L and REIL Rwy 25 and Rwy 28R ctc twr.
WEATHER DATA SOURCES: ASOS (406) 248–2773 LLWAS.
COMMUNICATIONS: ATIS 126.3   UNICOM 122.95
  RCO 122.55 (GREAT FALLS RADIO)
Ⓡ **APP/DEP CON** 119.2 (EAST)   120.5 (WEST)
  TOWER 127.2   **GND CON** 121.9   **CLNC DEL** 121.9
  PRE TAXI CLNC 121.9
AIRSPACE: CLASS C svc ctc **APP CON**
RADIO AIDS TO NAVIGATION: NOTAM FILE BIL.
  (H) VORTACW 114.5   BIL   Chan 92   N45°48.51´ W108°37.48´   077° 3.4 NM to fld. 3811/14E.
  SAIGE NDB (LOM) 251   BI   N45°51.13´ W108°41.67´ 099° 6.9 NM to fld.
  ILS 110.3 I–BIL Rwy 10L.   Class IB.   LOM SAIGE NDB.
  ILS/DME 111.5 I–BMO Chan 52 Rwy 28R.   Class IA.   Localizer unusable beyond 20° left and right of course.

BLACK BUTTE NORTH (See WINIFRED on page 106)

BOULDER (3U9)   2 S   UTC–7(–6DT)   N46°12.70´ W112°06.46´   **GREAT FALLS**
  4968   NOTAM FILE GTF
  RWY 11–29: 3675X72 (TURF)   1.6% up W
    RWY 11: Hill.
    RWY 29: Road.
  AIRPORT REMARKS: Unattended. No snow removal. Rwy 11–29 thlds marked with faded red cones, edges marked with white
    cones. –2´ drainage ditch +1´ berm W side of rwy full length, 43´ from Rwy 11–29 centerline.
  COMMUNICATIONS: CTAF 122.9

BOWMAN FLD (See ANACONDA on page 62)

FIGURE 214.—Excerpt from Chart Supplement.

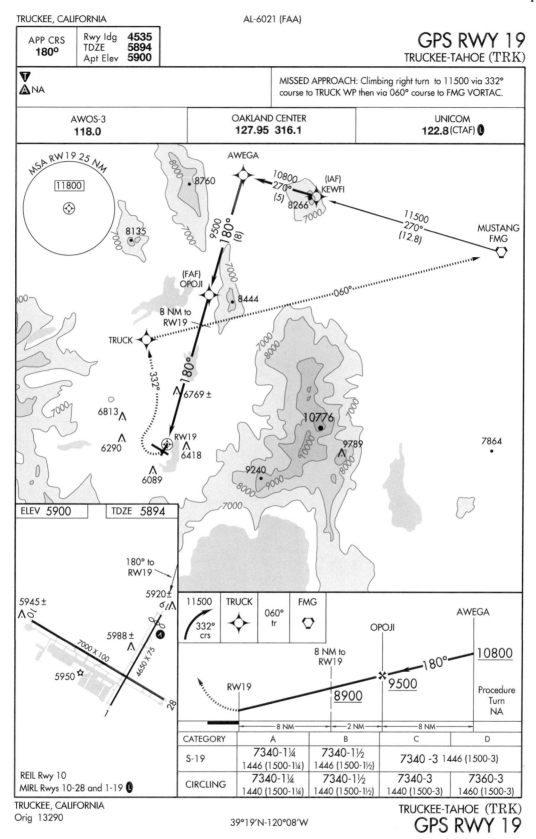

FIGURE 215.—GPS RWY 19 (TRK).

(RENO9.FMG) 16035

RENO NINE DEPARTURE

SL-346 (FAA)

RENO/TAHOE INTL (RNO)
RENO, NEVADA

TOP ALTITUDE:
FL190

ATIS
135.8 363.0
CLNC DEL
124.9 370.85
GND CON
121.9 348.6
RENO TOWER
118.7 257.8

TAKEOFF MINIMUMS

Rwy 7: NA- Obstacles.
Rwy 16L: Standard with minimum climb of 730' per NM to 10900,
or 600-1¼ with minimum climb of 352' per NM to 10900.
Rwy 16R: Standard with minimum climb of 460' per NM to 10900,
or 300-1 with minimum climb of 395' per NM to 10900.
Rwy 25: Standard with minimum climb of 500' per NM to 9700.
Rwys 34L/R: Standard with mimimum climb of 480' per NM to 8700,
or 500-1½ with minimum climb of 430' per NM to 8700.

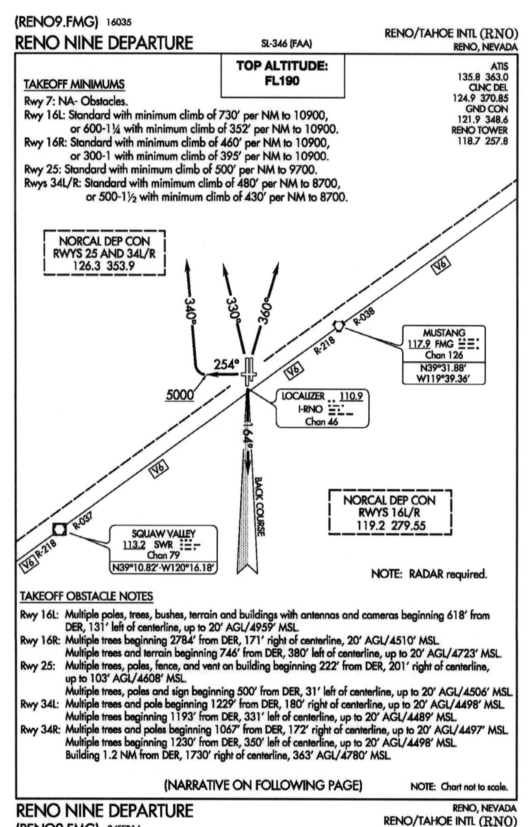

NORCAL DEP CON
RWYS 25 AND 34L/R
126.3 353.9

340°   330°   360°

254°

5000'

164°

BACK COURSE

MUSTANG
117.9 FMG
Chan 126
N39°31.88'
W119°39.36'

R-038

R-218

V6

LOCALIZER 110.9
I-RNO
Chan 46

R-037

SQUAW VALLEY
113.2 SWR
Chan 79
N39°10.82'-W120°16.18'

V6 R-218

NORCAL DEP CON
RWYS 16L/R
119.2 279.55

NOTE: RADAR required.

TAKEOFF OBSTACLE NOTES

Rwy 16L: Multiple poles, trees, bushes, terrain and buildings with antennas and cameras beginning 618' from
DER, 131' left of centerline, up to 20' AGL/4959' MSL.
Rwy 16R: Multiple trees beginning 2784' from DER, 171' right of centerline, 20' AGL/4510' MSL.
Multiple trees and terrain beginning 746' from DER, 380' left of centerline, up to 20' AGL/4723' MSL.
Rwy 25: Multiple trees, poles, fence, and vent on building beginning 222' from DER, 201' right of centerline,
up to 103' AGL/4608' MSL.
Multiple trees, poles and sign beginning 500' from DER, 31' left of centerline, up to 20' AGL/4506' MSL.
Rwy 34L: Multiple trees and pole beginning 1229' from DER, 180' right of centerline, up to 20' AGL/4498' MSL.
Multiple trees beginning 1193' from DER, 331' left of centerline, up to 20' AGL/4489' MSL.
Rwy 34R: Multiple trees and poles beginning 1067' from DER, 172' right of centerline, up to 20' AGL/4497' MSL.
Multiple trees beginning 1230' from DER, 350' left of centerline, up to 20' AGL/4498' MSL.
Building 1.2 NM from DER, 1730' right of centerline, 363' AGL/4780' MSL.

(NARRATIVE ON FOLLOWING PAGE)

NOTE: Chart not to scale.

RENO NINE DEPARTURE

(RENO9.FMG) 04FEB16

RENO, NEVADA
RENO/TAHOE INTL (RNO)

FIGURE 216.—RENO Nine Departure (RENO9.FMG) (RNO).

(RENO9.FMG) 16035

RENO NINE DEPARTURE SL-346 (FAA)

RENO/TAHOE INTL (RNO)
RENO, NEVADA

DEPARTURE ROUTE DESCRIPTION

TAKEOFF RUNWAYS 16L/R: Climb on heading 164° and I-RNO localizer south course. Thence. . . .

TAKEOFF RUNWAY 25: Climb heading 254° to 5000 then climbing right turn heading 340°. Thence. . . .

TAKEOFF RUNWAYS 34L/R: Climb heading 330° CW 360° as assigned by ATC. Thence. . . .

. . . .All aircraft maintain FL190 or assigned altitude. Expect clearance to requested altitude 5 minutes after departure. Expect RADAR vectors to assigned route/fix.

LOST COMMUNICATIONS: If not in contact with departure control within one minute after takeoff, maintain assigned heading until passing 10000, thence. . . .

. . . .RUNWAYS 16L/R DEPARTURES: Turn left direct FMG VORTAC, then via assigned route.

. . . .RUNWAYS 25 and 34L/R DEPARTURES: Turn right direct FMG VORTAC, then via assigned route.

RENO NINE DEPARTURE

(RENO9.FMG) 04FEB16

RENO, NEVADA
RENO/TAHOE INTL (RNO)

FIGURE 216A.—RENO Nine Departure (RENO9.FMG) (RNO).

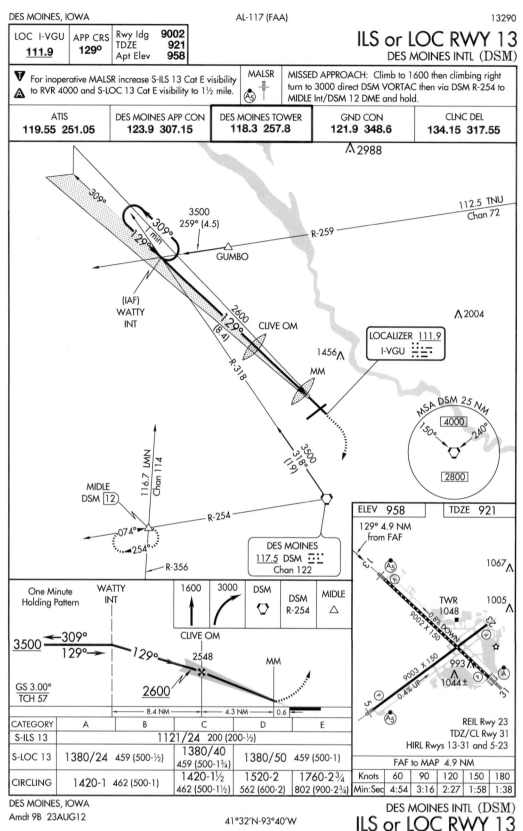

FIGURE 217.—ILS or LOC RWY 13 (DSM).

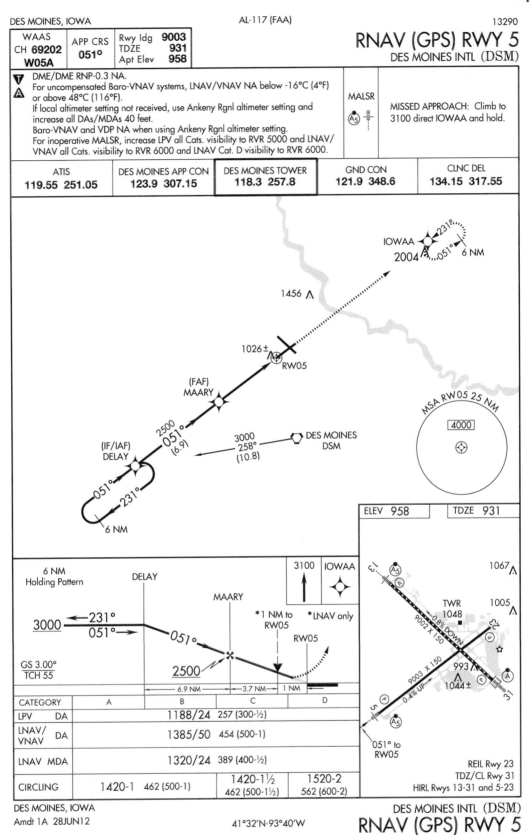

FIGURE 218.—RNAV (GPS) RWY 5 (DSM).

Appendix 2

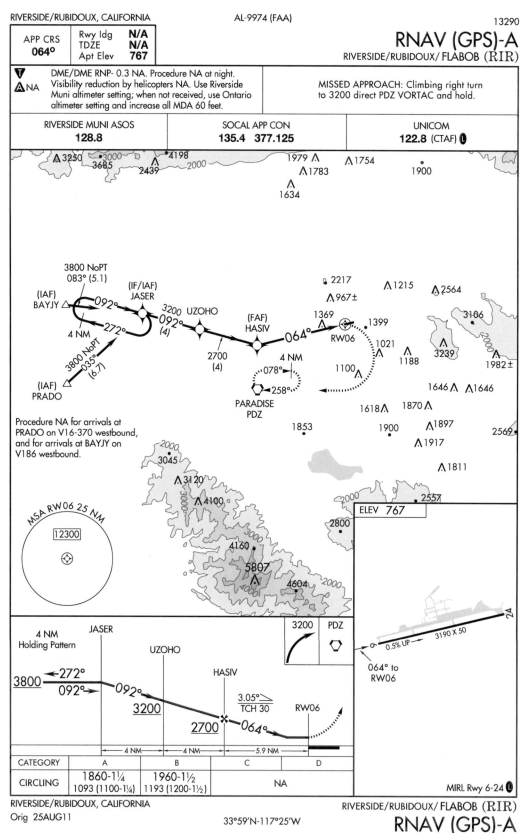

RNAV (GPS)-A
RIVERSIDE/RUBIDOUX/ FLABOB (RIR)

APP CRS 064°	Rwy Idg **N/A** TDZE **N/A** Apt Elev **767**

▼ ⚠NA DME/DME RNP- 0.3 NA. Procedure NA at night. Visibility reduction by helicopters NA. Use Riverside Muni altimeter setting; when not received, use Ontario altimeter setting and increase all MDA 60 feet.

MISSED APPROACH: Climbing right turn to 3200 direct PDZ VORTAC and hold.

RIVERSIDE MUNI ASOS **128.8**	SOCAL APP CON **135.4 377.125**	UNICOM **122.8** (CTAF) Ⓛ

3250 3000 •4198   1979 ⋀   ⋀1754
3685   •2439   2000   1900
                                ⋀1783
                              ⋀
                              1634

3800 NoPT
083° (5.1)
(IAF)
BAYJY △ ─092°─   (IF/IAF)
                  JASER
        ─272°─   3200 UZOHO   (FAF)   1369
4 NM   092°   HASIV   ─064°─ ⋀
                      (4)   RW06
3800 NoPT   2700   4 NM   1399
035°   (4)   078°   1021
(6.7)   258°   1100
(IAF)
PRADO   PARADISE
                               PDZ

⌂ 2217   ⋀1215   ⋀2564
⋀ 967±   3106
              ⋀   ⋀
              1188   3239   1982±
                    1646 ⋀ ⋀1646
        1618⋀   1870 ⋀
1853   1900   ⋀1897   2569•
                ⋀1917
                    ⋀1811

Procedure NA for arrivals at PRADO on V16-370 westbound, and for arrivals at BAYJY on V186 westbound.

2000
3045
⋀ 3120
⋀ 4100
                    •2557
              4160 •   2800
              5807
                  4604   2000

MSA RW06 25 NM
[12300]

ELEV 767

4 NM
Holding Pattern   JASER

3800 ─272°─
      092°→ ─092°─ UZOHO
                    092°→
                    3200   HASIV
                          2700   ─064°─
                                          3.05°
                                          TCH 30   RW06

|← 4 NM →|← 4 NM →|←─ 5.9 NM ─→|

3200   PDZ
⬡

0.5% UP   3190 X 50   24

064° to
RW06
064° to RW06

CATEGORY	A	B	C	D
CIRCLING	1860-1¼ 1093 (1100-1¼)	1960-1½ 1193 (1200-1½)	NA	

MIRL Rwy 6-24 Ⓛ

FIGURE 219.—RNAV (GPS)-A (RIR).

TAKEOFF MINIMUMS AND (OBSTACLE) DEPARTURE PROCEDURES

13234

RIVERSIDE/RUBIDOUX, CA
FLABOB (RIR)
ORIG 11181 (FAA)

TAKEOFF MINIMUMS: **Rwy 6,** std. w/min. climb of 670' per NM to 4000 or 400-2 w/min. climb of 480' per NM to 4000 or 2100-3 for climb in visual conditions. **Rwy 24,** std. w/min. climb of 630' per NM to 3000 or 800-2¾ w/min. climb of 305' per NM to 4600 or 2100-3 for climb in visual conditions.

DEPARTURE PROCEDURE: **Rwy 6,** climb via heading 064° to 4000 then right turn direct PDZ VORTAC, or for climb in visual conditions cross Flabob Airport Southwest bound at or above 2700 then via PDZ R-039 to PDZ VORTAC. **Rwy 24,** climb via heading 244° and PDZ R-031 to PDZ VORTAC, or for climb in visual conditions cross Flabob airport Southwest bound at or above 2700 then via PDZ R-039 to PDZ VORTAC.

All aircraft climb in PDZ VORTAC holding pattern (hold East, right turns, 258° inbound) to cross PDZ VORTAC at or above MEA for direction of flight before proceeding on course.

NOTE: **Rwy 6,** trees beginning 3763' from DER, 1152' right of centerline, up to 40' AGL/1119' MSL. **Rwy 24,** antenna on tank 6193' from DER, 2057' right of centerline, 38' AGL/1237' MSL. Trees beginning 2494' from DER, 434' right of centerline, up to 40' AGL/1519' MSL. Pole 6261' from DER, 1950' right of centerline, 30' AGL/1230' MSL. Building 1.52 NM from DER, 1154' right of centerline, up to 29' AGL/1369' MSL. Antenna on tank 1.26 NM from DER, 2047' right of centerline, 54' AGL/1254' MSL. Tank 4043' from DER, 794' right of centerline, 66' AGL/961' MSL. Tree 1.79 NM from DER, 434' right of centerline, 58' AGL/1138' MSL.

SAN BERNARDINO, CA
SAN BERNARDINO INTL (SBD)
ORIG 93343 (FAA)

TAKEOFF MINIMUMS: **Rwy 6,** CAT A,B 2100-2 or std. with a min. climb of 340' per NM to 3700. CAT C,D 3100-2 or std. with a min. climb of 480' per NM to 4600.

DEPARTURE PROCEDURE: **Rwy 6,** climbing right turn. **Rwy 24,** climbing left turn. **All aircraft** climb direct PDZ VORTAC. Aircraft departing PDZ R-091 CW R-140 and R-231 CW R-280 climb on course. All others continue climb in PDZ holding pattern (Hold NE, right turns, 210° inbound) to cross PDZ VORTAC at or above: R-281 CW R-090, 7700; R-141 CW R-230, 4900.

SAN CLEMENTE ISLAND NALF (FREDERICK SHERMAN FLD)(KNUC)
SAN CLEMENTE ISLAND, CA 12208

Rwy 5: Diverse departures authorized 090° to 233° CCW.

Rwy 23: Diverse departures authorized 160° to 053° CW.

TAKE-OFF OBSTACLES: **Rwy 5,** Pylon 198' MSL, 44' from DER, 274' left of centerline. Terrain 192' MSL, 50' from DER, 500' right of centerline. Terrain 194' MSL, 264' from DER, 509' right of centerline. Terrain 209' MSL, 824' from DER, 721' right of centerline. Terrain 199' MSL, 957' from DER, 612' right of centerline.

SAN DIEGO, CA
BROWN FIELD MUNI (SDM)
AMDT 4 10154(FAA)

TAKEOFF MINIMUMS: **Rwy 8L,** std. w/ min. climb of 570' per NM to 3100. **Rwys 8R,26L,** NA - ATC.

DEPARTURE PROCEDURE: **Rwy 8L,** climbing left turn, thence...**Rwy 26R,** climbing right turn, thence... ...via heading 280° to intercept MZB R-160 to MZB VORTAC.

NOTE: **Rwy 26R,** tree 1284' from DER, 778' left of centerline, 52' AGL/561' MSL.

MONTGOMERY FIELD (MYF)
AMDT 3A 10210 (FAA)

TAKEOFF MINIMUMS: **Rwy 5,** 1500-2 or std. with a min. climb of 290' per NM to 1700.

DEPARTURE PROCEDURE: **Rwys 5, 10L/R,** climbing right turn. **Rwys 28L/R,** climbing left turn. **All aircraft** climb direct to MZB VORTAC. Aircraft departing MZB R-090 CW R-360 climb on course. All others climb in MZB holding pattern (W, right turns, 075° inbound) to cross MZB VORTAC at or above 1800.

NOTE: **Rwy 5,** trees and bushes beginning 244' from DER, 161' left of centerline, up to 99' AGL/524' MSL. Tree 1287' from DER, 103' right of centerline, up to 49' AGL/474' MSL. **Rwy 23,** tree, flag pole, and transmission towers beginning 1594' from DER, 82' right of centerline, up to 125' AGL/545' MSL. Transmission towers beginning 2627' from DER, 414' left of centerline up to 125' AGL/524' MSL. **Rwy 10L,** trees beginning 230' from DER, 494' left of centerline, up to 57' AGL/486' MSL. Trees beginning 1172' from DER, 591' right of centerline, up to 69' AGL/488' MSL. **Rwy 10R,** rod on electrical equipment 40' from DER, 66' left of centerline, 7' AGL/426' MSL. Trees beginning 2107' from DER, 199' right of centerline, up to 69' AGL/488' MSL. **Rwy 28L,** bushes and poles beginning 35' from DER, 160' right of centerline, up to 37' AGL/451' MSL. Trees beginning 1008' from DER, 7' left of centerline, up to 37' AGL/451' MSL. **Rwy 28R,** bushes, trees, and poles beginning 34' from DER, 162' left of centerline, up to 38' AGL/451' MSL. Trees, signs, and poles beginning 768' from DER, 98' right of centerline, up to 67' AGL/488' MSL.

13234

 TAKEOFF MINIMUMS AND (OBSTACLE) DEPARTURE PROCEDURES

FIGURE 220.—Takeoff Minimums and (Obstacle) Departure Procedures.

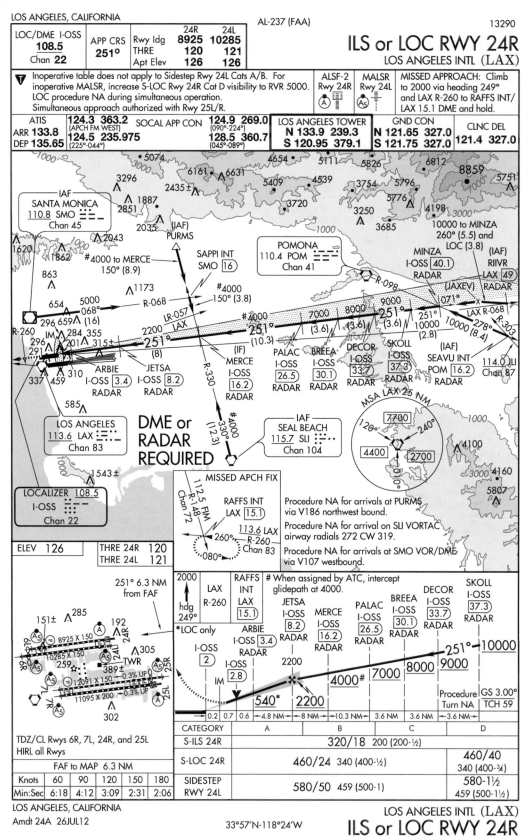

FIGURE 221.—ILS or LOC RWY 24R (LAX).

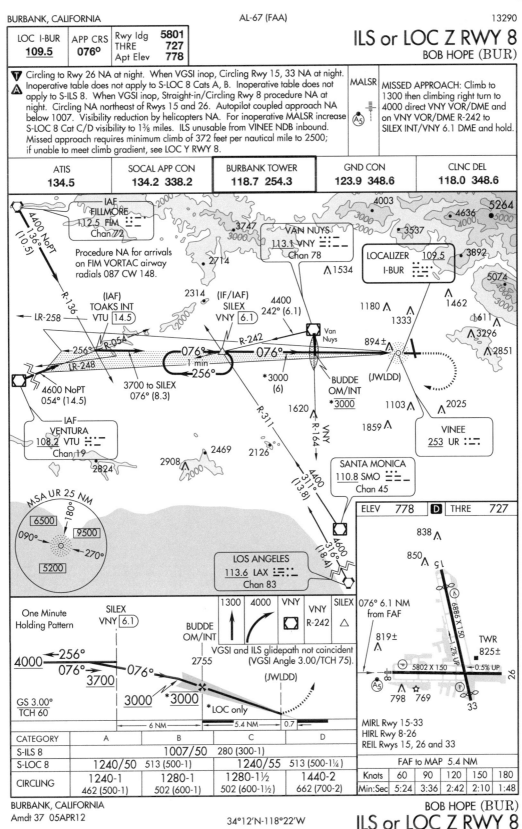

BURBANK, CALIFORNIA   AL-67 (FAA)   13290

LOC I-BUR	APP CRS	Rwy Idg	5801
109.5	076°	THRE	727
		Apt Elev	778

ILS or LOC Z RWY 8
BOB HOPE (BUR)

▼ Circling to Rwy 26 NA at night. When VGSI inop, Circling Rwy 15, 33 NA at night.
⚠ Inoperative table does not apply to S-LOC 8 Cats A, B. Inoperative table does not
apply to S-ILS 8. When VGSI inop, Straight-in/Circling Rwy 8 procedure NA at
night. Circling NA northeast of Rwys 15 and 26. Autopilot coupled approach NA
below 1007. Visibility reduction by helicopters NA. For inoperative MALSR increase
S-LOC 8 Cat C/D visibility to 1⅜ miles. ILS unusable from VINEE NDB inbound.
Missed approach requires minimum climb of 372 feet per nautical mile to 2500;
if unable to meet climb gradient, see LOC Y RWY 8.

MALSR

MISSED APPROACH: Climb to
1300 then climbing right turn to
4000 direct VNY VOR/DME and
on VNY VOR/DME R-242 to
SILEX INT/VNY 6.1 DME and hold.

ATIS	SOCAL APP CON	BURBANK TOWER	GND CON	CLNC DEL
134.5	134.2 338.2	118.7 254.3	123.9 348.6	118.0 348.6

BURBANK, CALIFORNIA
Amdt 37 05APR12

34°12'N-118°22'W

BOB HOPE (BUR)
ILS or LOC Z RWY 8

FIGURE 222.—ILS or LOC Z RWY 8 (BUR).

Appendix 2

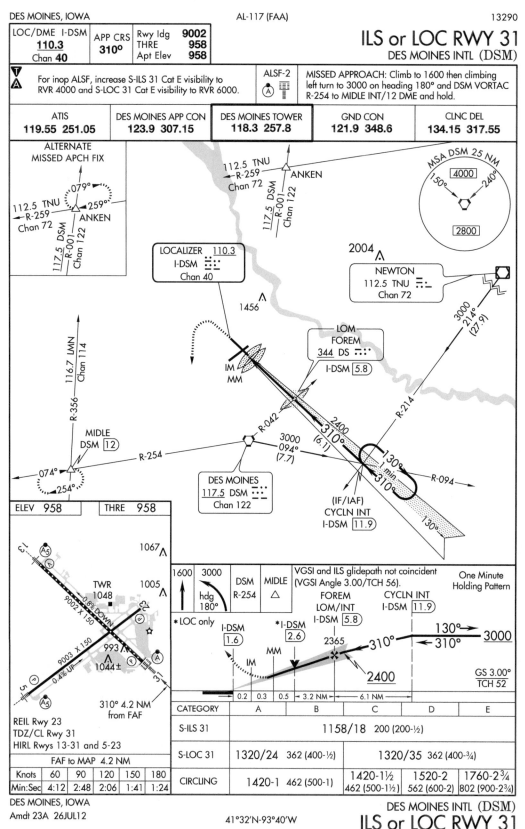

LOC/DME I-DSM **110.3** Chan 40	APP CRS **310°**	Rwy Idg **9002** THRE **958** Apt Elev **958**

ILS or LOC RWY 31
DES MOINES INTL (DSM)

For inop ALSF, increase S-ILS 31 Cat E visibility to RVR 4000 and S-LOC 31 Cat E visibility to RVR 6000.

ALSF-2

MISSED APPROACH: Climb to 1600 then climbing left turn to 3000 on heading 180° and DSM VORTAC R-254 to MIDLE INT/12 DME and hold.

ATIS	DES MOINES APP CON	DES MOINES TOWER	GND CON	CLNC DEL
119.55 251.05	123.9 307.15	118.3 257.8	121.9 348.6	134.15 317.55

ALTERNATE MISSED APCH FIX

112.5 TNU R-259 Chan 72   079°   259°   ANKEN

117.5 DSM R-001 Chan 122

112.5 TNU R-259 Chan 72   ANKEN

117.5 DSM R-001 Chan 122

MSA DSM 25 NM
150° 240°
4000
2800

LOCALIZER 110.3
I-DSM
Chan 40

2004

NEWTON
112.5 TNU
Chan 72

1456

R-356 116.7 LMN Chan 114

IM MM

LOM FOREM
344 DS
I-DSM 5.8

3000 214° (27.9)

R-214

R-042

2400 310° (6.1)

R-254

MIDLE DSM 12

074° 254°

DES MOINES
117.5 DSM
Chan 122

3000 094° (7.7)

130° 1 min 310°

R-094

(IF/IAF)
CYCLN INT
I-DSM 11.9

130°

ELEV 958	THRE 958

1067

TWR 1048

1005

9002 X 150   0.8% DOWN

9003 X 150

993

1044±

0.4% UP

310° 4.2 NM from FAF

REIL Rwy 23
TDZ/CL Rwy 31
HIRL Rwys 13-31 and 5-23

| 1600 | 3000 | DSM R-254 | MIDLE △ | VGSI and ILS glidepath not coincident (VGSI Angle 3.00/TCH 56). | One Minute Holding Pattern |

hdg 180°

*LOC only

FOREM LOM/INT I-DSM 5.8

CYCLN INT I-DSM 11.9

I-DSM 1.6   *I-DSM 2.6

2365

130° 310°   310° 3000

IM   MM

2400

GS 3.00° / TCH 52

| | 0.2 | 0.3 | 0.5 | 3.2 NM | 6.1 NM | |

CATEGORY	A	B	C	D	E
S-ILS 31			1158/18 200 (200-½)		
S-LOC 31	1320/24 362 (400-½)		1320/35 362 (400-¾)		
CIRCLING	1420-1 462 (500-1)		1420-1½ 462 (500-1½)	1520-2 562 (600-2)	1760-2¾ 802 (900-2¾)

FAF to MAP 4.2 NM					
Knots	60	90	120	150	180
Min:Sec	4:12	2:48	2:06	1:41	1:24

DES MOINES, IOWA
Amdt 23A 26JUL12

41°32'N-93°40'W

DES MOINES INTL (DSM)
ILS or LOC RWY 31

FIGURE 223.—ILS or LOC RWY 31 (DSM).

190

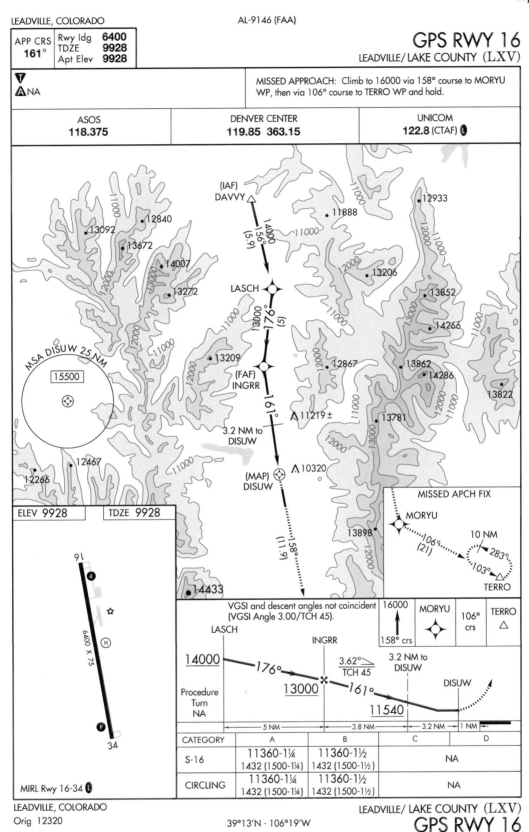

LEADVILLE, COLORADO
AL-9146 (FAA)

GPS RWY 16
LEADVILLE/ LAKE COUNTY (LXV)

APP CRS 161°	Rwy ldg 6400
	TDZE 9928
	Apt Elev 9928

MISSED APPROACH: Climb to 16000 via 158° course to MORYU WP, then via 106° course to TERRO WP and hold.

| ASOS 118.375 | DENVER CENTER 119.85 363.15 | UNICOM 122.8 (CTAF) |

FIGURE 224.—GPS RWY 16 (LXV).

LEADVILLE, COLORADO
Orig 12320

39°13'N - 106°19'W

LEADVILLE/ LAKE COUNTY (LXV)
GPS RWY 16

191

Appendix 2

L8

TAKEOFF MINIMUMS AND (OBSTACLE) DEPARTURE PROCEDURES

13262

KREMMLING, CO
MC ELROY AIRFIELD (20V)
TAKEOFF MINIMUMS: **Rwy 9,** 2600-2 or std. with a min. climb of 370' per NM to 12700. **Rwy 27,** 3200-2 or std. with a min. climb of 500' per NM to 12700.
DEPARTURE PROCEDURE: **Rwy 9,** climb runway heading to 10000, then climbing right turn. **Rwy 27,** climb runway heading to 10900, then climbing left turn. **All aircraft** proceed direct RLG VOR/DME. Continue climb to 13,000 in RLG holding pattern (hold SW, left turns, 051° inbound).

LA JUNTA, CO
LA JUNTA MUNI (LHX)
AMDT 3 03191 (FAA)
DEPARTURE PROCEDURE: **Rwy 8,** climb via heading 080°. **Rwy 12,** climb via heading 120°. **Rwy 26,** turn left heading 160°. **Rwy 30,** turn left heading 140°. **All aircraft,** intercept LAA R-238 (V210) to LAA VOR/DME. When at or above 8000 proceed on course.

LAMAR, CO
LAMAR MUNI (LAA)
DEPARTURE PROCEDURE: **Rwys 8,36,** turn left. **Rwy 18,** turn left/right. **Rwy 26,** turn right. Direct LAA VOR/DME. Aircraft departing LAA R-048 CW R-118 climb on course. All others continue climbing in LAA holding pattern (N, right turns, 169° inbound) to 6000 before proceeding on course.

LAS CRUCES, NM
LAS CRUCES INTL (LRU)
AMDT 1 96340 (FAA)
DEPARTURE PROCEDURE: **Rwys 4, 8,** climbing right turn. **Rwy 12,** CAT A,B, climb runway heading CAT C,D, NA. **Rwys 22, 26,** climbing left turn. **Rwy 30,** climbing runway heading to 5100 then climbing left turn.
All aircraft climb direct HAWKE LOM. Continue climb in HAWKE holding pattern (SE, left turns, 304° inbound) to cross HAWKE LOM at or above 10000 before proceeding on course.

LAS VEGAS, NM
LAS VEGAS MUNI (LVS)
AMDT 1 06103 (FAA)
DEPARTURE PROCEDURE: **Rwys 2, 14** turn left/right. **Rwy 20,** turn left (except via FTI R-215). **Rwy 32,** turn right.
Departures via FTI VORTAC R-001 CW R-215 climb on course. Departures via FTI VORTAC R-216 CW R-360 proceed direct FTI VORTAC. Climb in FTI VORTAC holding pattern (hold north, left turn, 192° inbound) to cross FTI at airway MEA/MCA. (NOTE: climb in hold not authorized for turbojet aircraft).

LEADVILLE, CO
LAKE COUNTY (LXV)
AMDT 2 08101 (FAA)
DEPARTURE PROCEDURE: **Rwy 16,** use LOZUL (RNAV) DEPARTURE. **Rwy 34,** use DAVVY (RNAV) DEPARTURE.

LONGMONT, CO
VANCE BRAND (LMO)
AMDT 1 12040 (FAA)
DEPARTURE PROCEDURE: **Rwy 11,** climbing left turn to intercept GLL VOR/DME R-221 to 7000 ... **Rwy 29,** climbing right turn to intercept GLL VOR/DME R-221 to 7000 ...
... All aircraft proceed on GLL R-221 to GLL VOR/DME. Cross GLL VOR/DME at or above MEA/MCA for route of flight.
NOTE: **Rwy 11,** trees beginning 130' from DER, 191' right of centerline, up to 80' AGL/5119' MSL. Vehicles on roadway, 449' from DER, 395' left and right of centerline, 17' AGL/5046' MSL. Trees beginning 1383' from DER, 434' left of centerline, up to 80' AGL/5109' MSL. **Rwy 29,** trees beginning 4105' from DER, 220' left of centerline, up to 80' AGL/5189' MSL.

LOS ALAMOS, NM
LOS ALAMOS (LAM)
AMDT 1 12152 (FAA)
TAKEOFF MINIMUMS: **Rwy 27,** NA-obstacles and airport restriction.
DEPARTURE PROCEDURE: **Rwy 9,** climb heading 092° to intercept SAF R-354. Northbound climbing to 11000 on V83. Southbound climbing to 9000 on V83.
NOTE: **Rwy 9,** terrain and trees beginning 101' from DER, 178' left and right of centerline, up to 60' AGL/7139' MSL.

LOVINGTON, NM
LEA COUNTY-ZIP FRANKLIN MEMORIAL (E06)
AMDT 1 99364 (FAA)
DEPARTURE PROCEDURE: **Rwy 3,** climb runway heading to 4700 before turning on course.
NOTE: **Rwy 12,** 35' AGL power line 1250' from DER 150' right of centerline. **Rwy 21,** 40' AGL tower 936' from DER 273' right of centerline. **Rwy 30,** 50' AGL windmill 1800' from DER 50' right of centerline.

MEEKER, CO
MEEKER (EEO)
AMDT 1 08157 (FAA)
TAKEOFF MINIMUMS: **Rwys 3, 21,** 4100-3 for climb in visual conditions.
DEPARTURE PROCEDURE: **Rwys 3, 21,** for climb in visual conditions: cross Meeker Airport at or above 10500 before proceeding on course.
NOTE: **Rwy 21,** multiple trees beginning 843' from DER, 20' left of centerline, up to 100' AGL/7190' MSL. Multiple trees beginning 227' from DER, 187' right of centerline, up to 100' AGL/6862' MSL.

MONTE VISTA, CO
MONTE VISTA MUNI (MVI)
AMDT 3 01025 (FAA)
DEPARTURE PROCEDURE: **Rwy 2,** climbing right turn. **Rwy 20,** climbing left turn. **All aircraft,** climb direct ALS VORTAC, continue climb in ALS holding pattern (SE, right turns, 301° inbound) to cross ALS VORTAC at or above 11000, except V210 westbound 11200 and J102 northeast bound 13700, before proceeding enroute.

13262

 TAKEOFF MINIMUMS AND (OBSTACLE) DEPARTURE PROCEDURES

FIGURE 225.—Takeoff Minimums and (Obstacle) Departure Procedures.

LAMAR MUNI (LAA)　3 SW　UTC–7(–6DT)　N38°04.18′ W102°41.31′　　　　WICHITA
　3706　B　S4　**FUEL** 100LL, JET A　OX 1, 3　NOTAM FILE LAA　　　　H–5A, L–10G
　RWY 18–36: H6304X100 (CONC–GRVD)　S–45, D–55, 2D–100　MIRL　　　　IAP
　　0.4% up S
　　RWY 18: REIL. VASI(V4L)—GA 3.0° TCH 45′. Road.
　　RWY 36: REIL. PAPI(P4L)—GA 3.0° TCH 45′. Hill.
　RWY 08–26: H5001X60 (ASPH–PFC)　S–35, D–50, 2D–95　MIRL
　　RWY 08: PAPI(P2L)—GA 3.0° TCH 30′. Road.
　　RWY 26: REIL. PAPI(P2L)—GA 3.0° TCH 31′. Fence.
　AIRPORT REMARKS: Attended 1500–0100Z‡. For svc after hrs phone
　　719–336–7701. Be alert, intensive USAF student training invof
　　Colorado Springs and Pueblo Colorado. Rwy 18–36 now has distance
　　remaining signs. Twr 500′ AGL 4.5 mile SE unlighted. ACTIVATE MIRL
　　Rwy 08–26 and Rwy 18–36—CTAF. NOTE: See Special
　　Notices—Aerobatic Operations in Colorado. USAF 306 FTG Flight
　　Training Areas, Vicinity of Colorado Springs and Pueblo Colorado.
　WEATHER DATA SOURCES: ASOS 135.625 (719) 336–3854.
　COMMUNICATIONS: CTAF/UNICOM 122.8
　　DENVER CENTER APP/DEP CON 133.4
　RADIO AIDS TO NAVIGATION: NOTAM FILE LAA.
　　(H) VORW/DME 116.9　LAA　Chan 116　N38°11.83′
　　W102°41.25′　168° 7.6 NM to fld. 3944/12E.

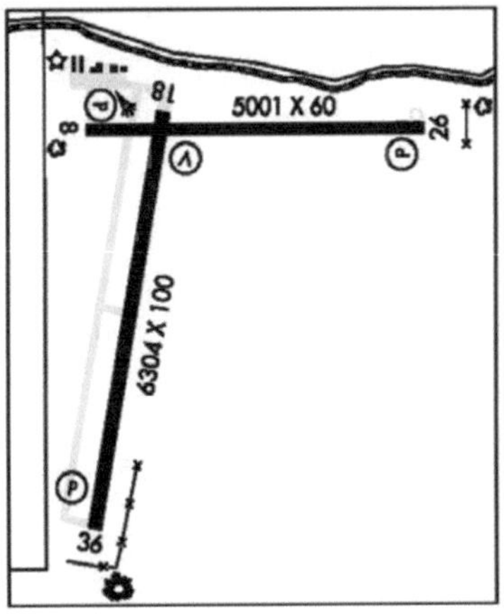

LAS ANIMAS

CITY OF LAS ANIMAS – BENT CO (7V9)　1 S　UTC–7(–6DT)　N38°03.24′ W103°14.31′　　WICHITA
　3915　S4　NOTAM FILE DEN　　　　L–10F
　RWY 08–26: H3870X40 (ASPH)　S–5　HIRL　0.4% up W
　　RWY 08: REIL. Fence.
　　RWY 26: REIL. Road.
　AIRPORT REMARKS: Attended Mon–Sat 1500–0000Z‡. Be alert, intensive USAF student training invof Colorado Springs and
　　Pueblo Colorado. Rwy 26 has +30′ poles 105′ from thld 210′ left of extd rwy centerline, +15′ tank 321′ from rwy
　　end 270′ right of centerline. Thld lgts NSTD; three lgts each end. Thld lgts OTS indef. Rwy 08 thld lgts 23′ from thld.
　　Rwy 26 thld lgts 12′ from thld. Rwy 08 numbers located 216′ from pavement end, Rwy 08–26 numbers smaller than
　　standard, no centerline markings. ACTIVATE HIRL Rwy 08–26—CTAF. Med ints 5 clicks, high ints 7 clicks. See Special
　　Notices—USAF 306 FTG Flight Training Areas, Vicinity of Colorado Springs and Pueblo Colorado.
　COMMUNICATIONS: CTAF 122.9
　RADIO AIDS TO NAVIGATION: NOTAM FILE LAA.
　　LAMAR (H) VORW/DME 116.9　LAA　Chan 116　N38°11.83′ W102°41.25′　240° 27.5 NM to fld. 3944/12E.

LEACH (See CENTER on page 220)

LEADVILLE

LAKE CO (LXV)　2 SW　UTC–7(–6DT)　N39°13.17′ W106°18.99′　　　　DENVER
　9934　B　**FUEL** 100LL, JET A　NOTAM FILE LXV　　　　H–3F, 5A, L–9E
　RWY 16–34: H6400X75 (ASPH)　S–20, D–20　MIRL　　　　IAP
　　RWY 16: PAPI(P2L)—GA 3.0° TCH 45′. Rgt tfc.
　　RWY 34: PAPI(P2L)—GA 3.0° TCH 45′.
　AIRPORT REMARKS: Attended May–Oct 1430–2330Z‡, Nov–Apr
　　1500–2330Z‡. For svc after hrs call sheriff dispatch 719–486–1249.
　　PPR for svc after hrs call 719–293–5110. Rwy 34 has +50′ power
　　lines 750′ from right of thld. Twy C and old ramp have potholes and
　　loose aggregate. All twys and new ramp area marked with blue and
　　white reflectors. ACTIVATE MIRL Rwy 16–34 and PAPI Rwy 16 and
　　Rwy 34—CTAF.
　WEATHER DATA SOURCES: ASOS 118.375 (719) 486–2735.
　COMMUNICATIONS: CTAF/UNICOM 122.8
　　DENVER CENTER APP/DEP CON 119.85
　RADIO AIDS TO NAVIGATION: NOTAM FILE DEN.
　　RED TABLE (H) VORW/DME 113.0　DBL　Chan 77　N39°26.36′
　　W106°53.68′　104° 30.0 NM to fld. 11800/12E.

　HELIPAD H1: H150X100 (ASPH–CONC)
　HELIPORT REMARKS: Rwy H1 has 6–8 inch lip all around edges, concrete has
　　longitudinal and corner cracking. Rwy H1 has 20′ to 30′ trees 130′ east of pad.

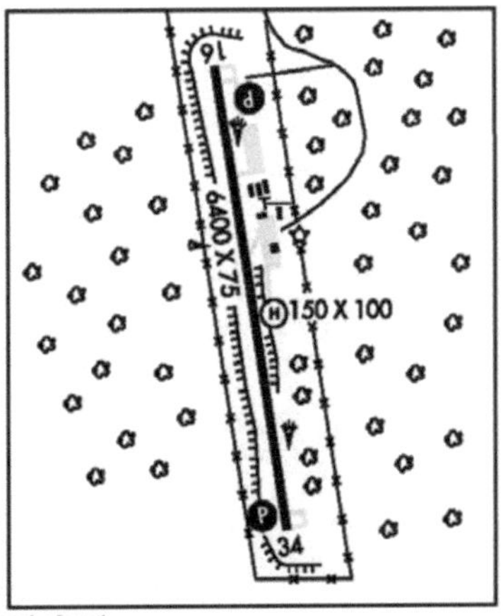

FIGURE 226.—Excerpt from Chart Supplement.

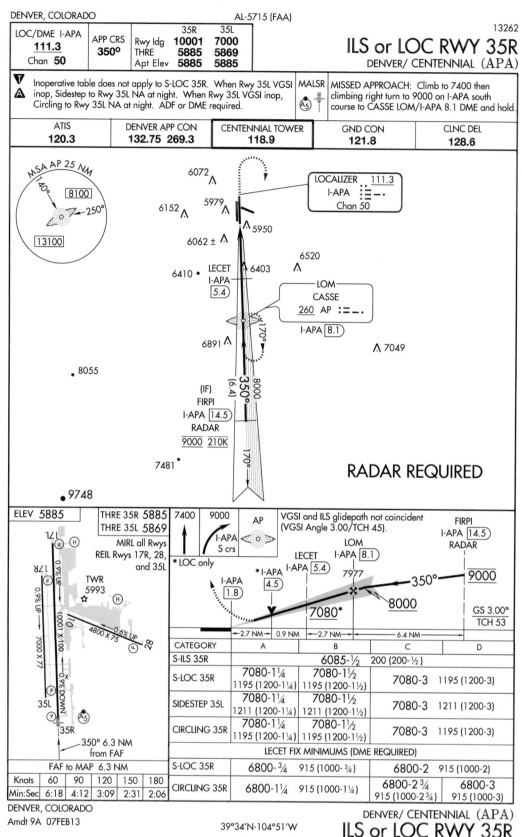

FIGURE 227.—ILS or LOC RWY 35R (APA).

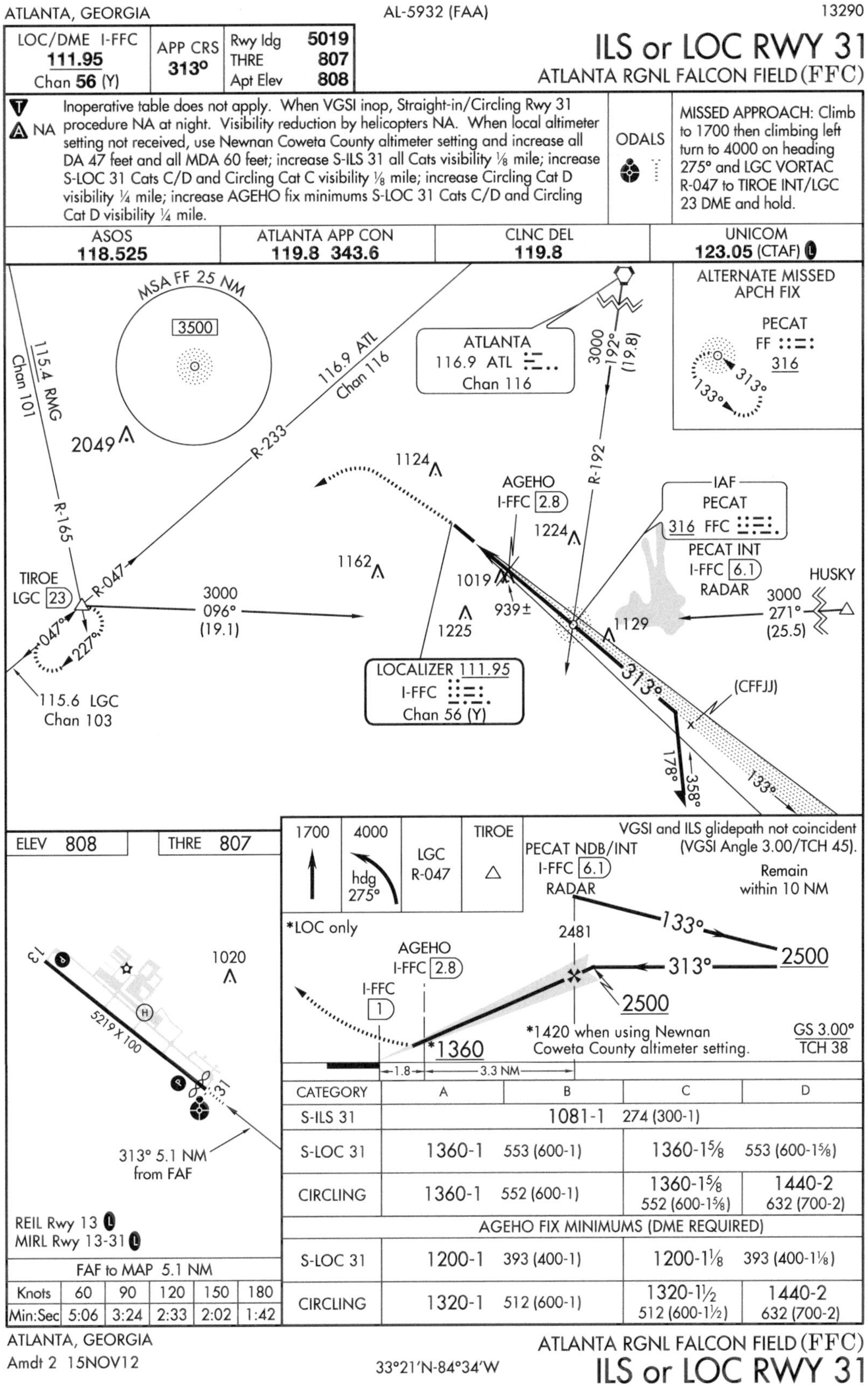

ATLANTA, GEORGIA   AL-5932 (FAA)   13290

LOC/DME I-FFC 111.95 Chan 56 (Y)	APP CRS 313°	Rwy Idg 5019 THRE 807 Apt Elev 808	ILS or LOC RWY 31 ATLANTA RGNL FALCON FIELD (FFC)

Inoperative table does not apply. When VGSI inop, Straight-in/Circling Rwy 31 procedure NA at night. Visibility reduction by helicopters NA. When local altimeter setting not received, use Newnan Coweta County altimeter setting and increase all DA 47 feet and all MDA 60 feet; increase S-ILS 31 all Cats visibility ⅛ mile; increase S-LOC 31 Cats C/D and Circling Cat C visibility ⅛ mile; increase Circling Cat D visibility ¼ mile; increase AGEHO fix minimums S-LOC 31 Cats C/D and Circling Cat D visibility ¼ mile.

⚠ NA

ODALS

MISSED APPROACH: Climb to 1700 then climbing left turn to 4000 on heading 275° and LGC VORTAC R-047 to TIROE INT/LGC 23 DME and hold.

ASOS 118.525	ATLANTA APP CON 119.8 343.6	CLNC DEL 119.8	UNICOM 123.05 (CTAF) Ⓛ

MSA FF 25 NM

3500

ALTERNATE MISSED APCH FIX

PECAT
FF ::=:
316

115.4 RMG Chan 101

116.9 ATL Chan 116

ATLANTA
116.9 ATL :.. ..
Chan 116

3000 192° (119.8)
R-192

133° 313°

R-233

2049 ⋀

1124 ⋀

AGEHO
I-FFC [2.8]

1224 ⋀

R-165

1162 ⋀

1019 ⋋

IAF
PECAT
316 FFC ::=:.
PECAT INT
I-FFC [6.1]
RADAR

HUSKY
3000
271°
(25.5)

TIROE
LGC [23]

R-047

3000
096°
(19.1)

939±

A
1225

1129

313°

(CFFJJ)
×

115.6 LGC
Chan 103

LOCALIZER 111.95
I-FFC ::=:
Chan 56 (Y)

178° 358° 133°

ELEV 808	THRE 807

1700	4000	TIROE	

hdg 275°

LGC R-047

△

PECAT NDB/INT
I-FFC [6.1]
RADAR

VGSI and ILS glidepath not coincident (VGSI Angle 3.00/TCH 45).

Remain within 10 NM

*LOC only

AGEHO
I-FFC [2.8]

I-FFC
[1]

*1360

2481

133°
313°
2500
2500

*1420 when using Newnan Coweta County altimeter setting.

GS 3.00°
TCH 38

←1.8→ ←3.3 NM→

1020 ⋀

5219 X 100

313° 5.1 NM
from FAF

REIL Rwy 13 Ⓛ
MIRL Rwy 13-31 Ⓛ

CATEGORY	A	B	C	D
S-ILS 31		1081-1 274 (300-1)		
S-LOC 31	1360-1 553 (600-1)		1360-1⅝ 553 (600-1⅝)	
CIRCLING	1360-1 552 (600-1)		1360-1⅝ 552 (600-1⅝)	1440-2 632 (700-2)
AGEHO FIX MINIMUMS (DME REQUIRED)				
S-LOC 31	1200-1 393 (400-1)		1200-1⅛ 393 (400-1⅛)	
CIRCLING	1320-1 512 (600-1)		1320-1½ 512 (600-1½)	1440-2 632 (700-2)

FAF to MAP 5.1 NM					
Knots	60	90	120	150	180
Min:Sec	5:06	3:24	2:33	2:02	1:42

ATLANTA, GEORGIA
Amdt 2 15NOV12

33°21'N-84°34'W

ATLANTA RGNL FALCON FIELD (FFC)
ILS or LOC RWY 31

FIGURE 228.—ILS or LOC RWY 31 (FFC).

ATLANTA, GEORGIA | AL-5932 (FAA) | 12320

RNAV (GPS) RWY 13
ATLANTA RGNL FALCON FIELD (FFC)

WAAS CH **61006** **W13A**	APP CRS **133°**	Rwy Idg **5219** THRE **797** Apt Elev **808**

▽△ For uncompensated Baro-VNAV systems, LNAV/VNAV NA below -9°C (16°F) or above 54°C (130°F). DME/DME RNP-0.3 NA. When local altimeter setting not received, use Newnan Coweta County altimeter setting and increase all DA 47 feet and all MDA 60 feet; increase LNAV/VNAV all Cats, LNAV Cats C/D, and Circling Cat D visibility ¼ mile; increase Circling Cat C visibility ⅛ mile. Baro-VNAV and VDP NA when using Newnan Coweta County altimeter setting.

MISSED APPROACH: Climb to 3000 direct INOGE and hold.

ASOS **118.525**	ATLANTA APP CON **119.8** **343.6**	CLNC DEL **119.8**	UNICOM **123.05** (CTAF) ◐

ATLANTA, GEORGIA
Amdt 2 15NOV12

33°21'N-84°34'W

VGSI and RNAV glidepath not coincident. (VGSI Angle 3.00/TCH 31).

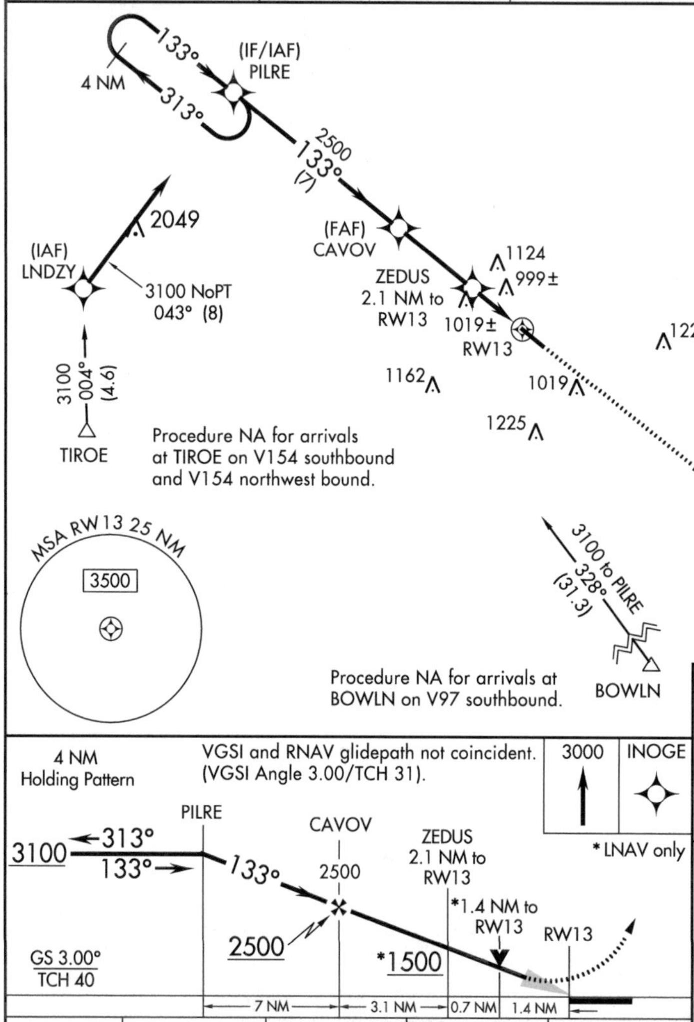

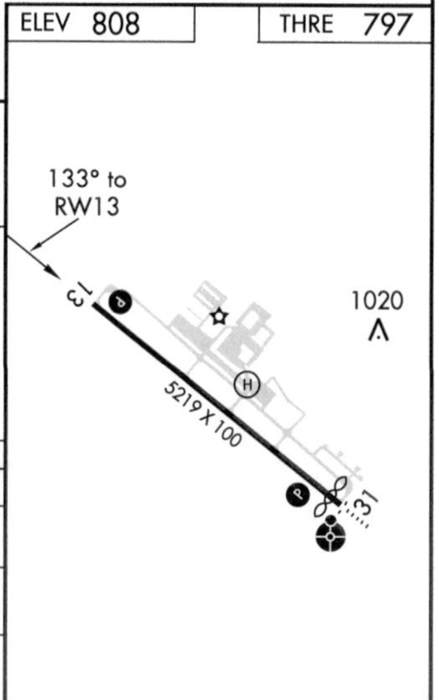

CATEGORY	A	B	C	D
LPV DA		997-¾ 200 (200-¾)		
LNAV/VNAV DA		1311-1¾ 514 (600-1¾)		
LNAV MDA	1280-1 483 (500-1)		1280-1⅜ 483 (500-1⅜)	
CIRCLING	1320-1 512 (600-1)		1320-1½ 512 (600-1½)	1440-2 632 (700-2)

REIL Rwy 13 ◐
MIRL Rwy 13-31 ◐

ATLANTA RGNL FALCON FIELD (FFC)
RNAV (GPS) RWY 13

FIGURE 229.—RNAV (GPS) RWY 13 (FFC).

BALDWIN, MICHIGAN AL-6787 (FAA)

VOR/DME HIC 117.6 Chan 123	APP CRS 345°	Rwy ldg TDZE Apt Elev	N/A N/A 828

VOR/DME or GPS-A
BALDWIN MUNI (7D3)

▼   NA
Use Manistee altimeter setting.
Procedure not authorized at night.

MISSED APPROACH: Climb to 2600, then left turn via the HIC VOR/DME R-345 to HOPPR/14 DME and hold.

MINNEAPOLIS CENTER 120.85 322.35	CTAF 122.9

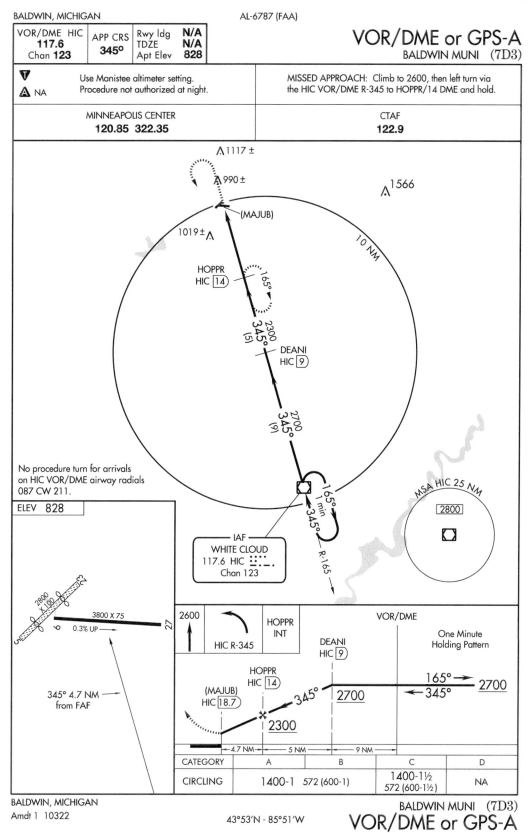

ELEV 828

No procedure turn for arrivals on HIC VOR/DME airway radials 087 CW 211.

345° 4.7 NM from FAF

MSA HIC 25 NM   2800

IAF
WHITE CLOUD
117.6 HIC ••••─•
Chan 123

CATEGORY	A	B	C	D
CIRCLING	1400-1 572 (600-1)		1400-1½ 572 (600-1½)	NA

BALDWIN, MICHIGAN
Amdt 1 10322

43°53'N - 85°51'W

BALDWIN MUNI (7D3)
VOR/DME or GPS-A

FIGURE 230.—VOR/DME or GPS-A (7D3).

130   MICHIGAN

BALDWIN MUNI (7D3)   2 S   UTC–5(–4DT)   N43°52.53´ W85°50.53´   **CHICAGO**
   828   TPA—1828(1000)   NOTAM FILE LAN   **L–28I**
   RWY 09–27: H3800X75 (ASPH)   S–10   0.3% up E   **IAP**
     RWY 09: Trees.
     RWY 27: Trees.
   RWY 05–23: 2800X100 (TURF)
     RWY 05: Thld dsplcd 800´. Trees.
     RWY 23: Thld dsplcd 800´. Trees.
   AIRPORT REMARKS: Unattended. Deer on and invof arpt. Arpt CLOSED Nov
     thru Apr; no snow removal. Arpt manager cell 231–250–2551. Rwy
     09–27 sfc considerable pavement cracking with vegetation growing
     through cracks. Rwy 05–23 and dsplcd thlds marked with 3´ yellow
     cones.
   COMMUNICATIONS: CTAF 122.9
   Ⓡ **MINNEAPOLIS CENTER APP/DEP CON** 120.85
   RADIO AIDS TO NAVIGATION: NOTAM FILE LAN.
     WHITE CLOUD (L) VOR/DME 117.6   HIC   Chan 123   N43°34.49´
       W85°42.97´   344° 18.9 NM to fld. 920/1W.
     VOR/DME unusable:
       020°–090° byd 30 NM blo 3,000´
     DME portion unusable:
       270°–290° byd 35 NM blo 3,000´

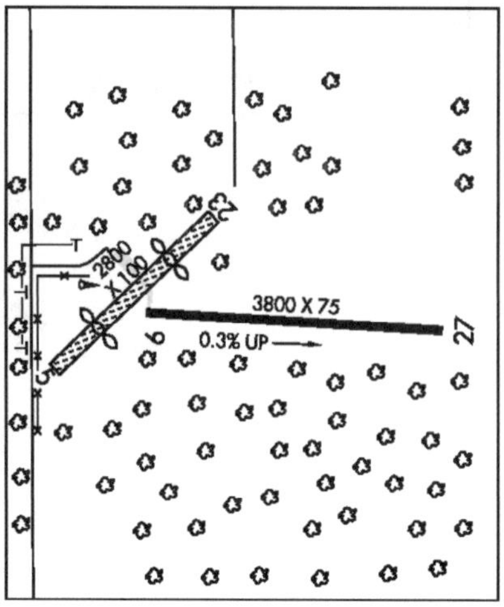

BANGU   N45°00.88´ W84°48.49´   NOTAM FILE GLR.   **LAKE HURON**
   NDB (LOM) 375   GL   097° 4.5 NM to Gaylord Rgnl. Unmonitored.

BANNISTER

SHADY LAWN FLD (4M4)   2 E   UTC–5(–4DT)   N43°07.72´ W84°22.88´   **CHICAGO**
   680   TPA—1680(1000)   NOTAM FILE LAN
   RWY 09–27: 1850X50 (TURF)   LIRL
     RWY 09: Bldg.
     RWY 27: Trees.
   AIRPORT REMARKS: Attended irregularly. Ultralight and AG activity on and invof arpt. Deer and birds on and invof arpt. Crops
     adjacent to rwy during summer months. NSTD LIRL color and configuration, by prior arrangement. Rwy 09 and Rwy 27
     marked by 3´ yellow cones.
   COMMUNICATIONS: CTAF 122.9

BARAGA (2P4)   4 W   UTC–5(–4DT)   N46°47.10´ W88°34.67´   **GREEN BAY**
   845   TPA—1845(1000)   NOTAM FILE GRB
   RWY 09–27: 2200X100 (TURF)
     RWY 09: Trees.
     RWY 27: Trees.
   AIRPORT REMARKS: Unattended. Arpt CLOSED Nov–Apr except to ski equipped acft. 25´ p–line 850´ from thld Rwy 27. Deer
     and birds on and invof arpt.
   COMMUNICATIONS: CTAF 122.9

BATH

UNIVERSITY AIRPARK (41G)   2 NW   UTC–5(–4DT)   N42°50.42´ W84°28.75´   **DETROIT**
   856   B   S2   NOTAM FILE LAN
   RWY 08–26: 1988X100 (TURF)   LIRL
     RWY 08: Trees.
     RWY 26: Tree.
   AIRPORT REMARKS: Attended irregularly. Rwy 08–26 occasionally soft/wet areas E end during spring thaw and after heavy rain.
     ACTIVATE LIRL Rwy 08–26 and NSTD rotating bcn—122.85. NSTD flashing strobe and alternating white/red bcn. Rwy
     08–26 marked with 3´ yellow cones.
   COMMUNICATIONS: CTAF 122.9

BATOL   N42°21.72´ W85°11.07´   NOTAM FILE BTL.   **CHICAGO**
   NDB (MHW/LOM) 272   BT   225° 4.4 NM to W K Kellogg.   **L–28I**

FIGURE 231.—Excerpt from Chart Supplement.

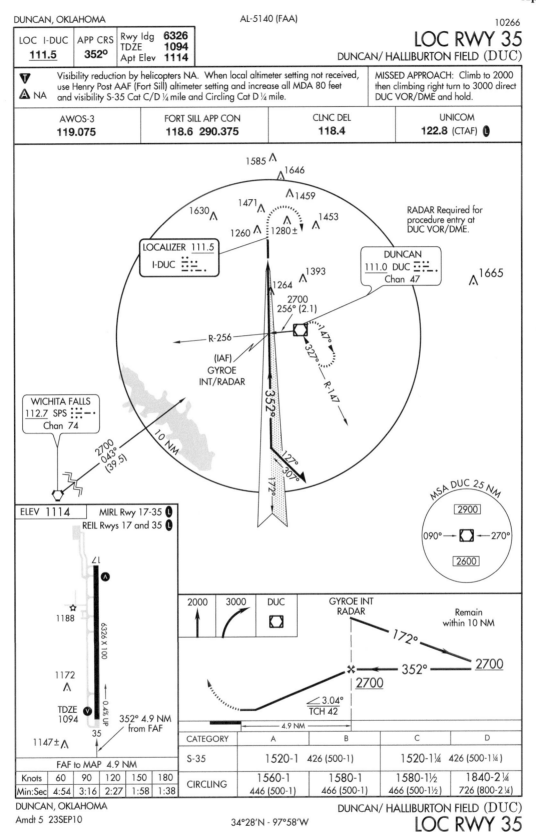

DUNCAN, OKLAHOMA
AL-5140 (FAA)
10266

LOC I-DUC	APP CRS	Rwy Idg	6326
111.5	**352°**	TDZE	**1094**
		Apt Elev	**1114**

LOC RWY 35
DUNCAN/ HALLIBURTON FIELD (DUC)

Visibility reduction by helicopters NA. When local altimeter setting not received, use Henry Post AAF (Fort Sill) altimeter setting and increase all MDA 80 feet and visibility S-35 Cat C/D ¼ mile and Circling Cat D ¼ mile.

⚠ NA

MISSED APPROACH: Climb to 2000 then climbing right turn to 3000 direct DUC VOR/DME and hold.

AWOS-3	FORT SILL APP CON	CLNC DEL	UNICOM
119.075	**118.6 290.375**	**118.4**	**122.8** (CTAF)

RADAR Required for procedure entry at DUC VOR/DME.

LOCALIZER 111.5
I-DUC

DUNCAN
111.0 DUC
Chan 47

2700
256° (2.1)

R-256

(IAF)
GYROE
INT/RADAR

R-147

WICHITA FALLS
112.7 SPS
Chan 74

2700
043°
(39.5)

10 NM

352°

127°
307°

172°

MSA DUC 25 NM

| 2900 |
| 090° — 270° |
| 2600 |

ELEV 1114

MIRL Rwy 17-35
REIL Rwys 17 and 35

1188

6326 X 100

1172

TDZE
1094

352° 4.9 NM
from FAF

1147±

FAF to MAP 4.9 NM

Knots	60	90	120	150	180
Min:Sec	4:54	3:16	2:27	1:58	1:38

2000 3000 DUC

GYROE INT
RADAR

Remain within 10 NM

172°

2700

352°

2700

∠3.04°
TCH 42

4.9 NM

CATEGORY	A	B	C	D
S-35	1520-1 426 (500-1)		1520-1¼ 426 (500-1¼)	
CIRCLING	1560-1 446 (500-1)	1580-1 466 (500-1)	1580-1½ 466 (500-1½)	1840-2¼ 726 (800-2¼)

DUNCAN, OKLAHOMA
Amdt 5 23SEP10

34°28'N - 97°58'W

DUNCAN/ HALLIBURTON FIELD (DUC)
LOC RWY 35

FIGURE 232.—LOC RWY 35 (DUC).

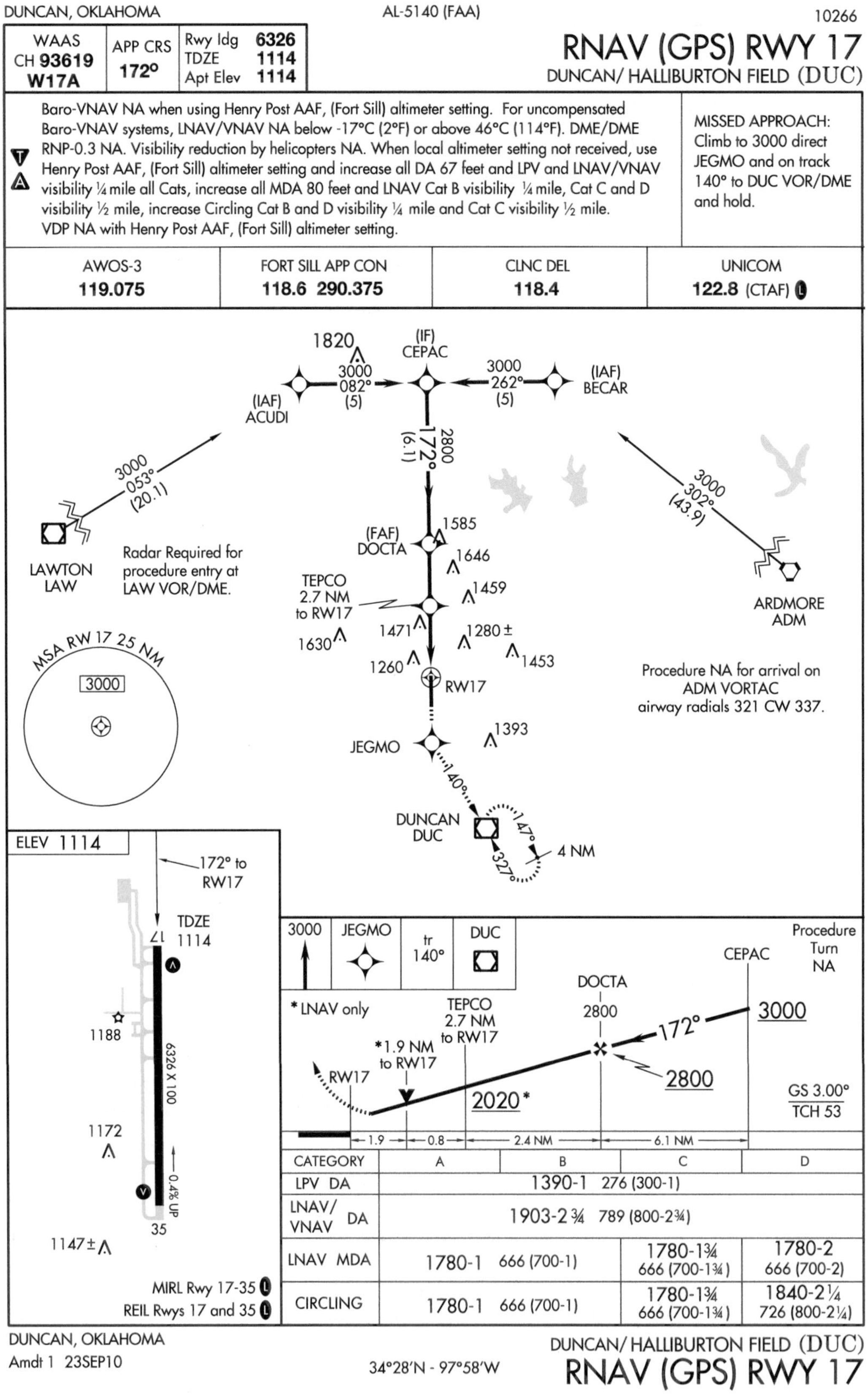

DUNCAN, OKLAHOMA

AL-5140 (FAA)

10266

WAAS CH **93619** **W17A**	APP CRS **172°**	Rwy ldg **6326** TDZE **1114** Apt Elev **1114**

RNAV (GPS) RWY 17
DUNCAN/ HALLIBURTON FIELD (DUC)

▽ ⚠ Baro-VNAV NA when using Henry Post AAF, (Fort Sill) altimeter setting. For uncompensated Baro-VNAV systems, LNAV/VNAV NA below -17°C (2°F) or above 46°C (114°F). DME/DME RNP-0.3 NA. Visibility reduction by helicopters NA. When local altimeter setting not received, use Henry Post AAF, (Fort Sill) altimeter setting and increase all DA 67 feet and LPV and LNAV/VNAV visibility ¼ mile all Cats, increase all MDA 80 feet and LNAV Cat B visibility ¼ mile, Cat C and D visibility ½ mile, increase Circling Cat B and D visibility ¼ mile and Cat C visibility ½ mile. VDP NA with Henry Post AAF, (Fort Sill) altimeter setting.

MISSED APPROACH: Climb to 3000 direct JEGMO and on track 140° to DUC VOR/DME and hold.

AWOS-3 **119.075**	FORT SILL APP CON **118.6 290.375**	CLNC DEL **118.4**	UNICOM **122.8** (CTAF) ◐

MSA RWY 17 25 NM

3000

Radar Required for procedure entry at LAW VOR/DME.

LAWTON LAW

3000 053° (20.1)

(IAF) ACUDI

1820 ⋀

3000 082° (5)

(IF) CEPAC

3000 262° (5)

(IAF) BECAR

172° (6.1) 2800

(FAF) DOCTA 1585

TEPCO 2.7 NM to RW17

1646 ⋀

1459 ⋀

1630 ⋀ 1471 ⋀

1280 ± ⋀

1453 ⋀

1260 ⋀ ⊕ RW17

1393 ⋀

JEGMO

DUNCAN DUC

140°

147°

327°

4 NM

3000 302° (43.9)

ARDMORE ADM

Procedure NA for arrival on ADM VORTAC airway radials 321 CW 337.

ELEV 1114

172° to RW17

TDZE 1114

1188 ☆

6326 X 100

1172 ⋀

1147 ± ⋀

35

0.4% UP

MIRL Rwy 17-35 ◐
REIL Rwys 17 and 35 ◐

3000	JEGMO	tr 140°	DUC			Procedure Turn NA

CEPAC

DOCTA 2800

172°

3000

2800

GS 3.00° TCH 53

*LNAV only

TEPCO 2.7 NM to RW17

*1.9 NM to RW17

RW17

2020*

|← 1.9 →|← 0.8 →|← 2.4 NM →|← 6.1 NM →|

CATEGORY	A	B	C	D
LPV DA	1390-1	276 (300-1)		
LNAV/ VNAV DA	1903-2¾	789 (800-2¾)		
LNAV MDA	1780-1	666 (700-1)	1780-1¾ 666 (700-1¾)	1780-2 666 (700-2)
CIRCLING	1780-1	666 (700-1)	1780-1¾ 666 (700-1¾)	1840-2¼ 726 (800-2¼)

DUNCAN, OKLAHOMA
Amdt 1 23SEP10

34°28'N - 97°58'W

DUNCAN/ HALLIBURTON FIELD (DUC)
RNAV (GPS) RWY 17

FIGURE 233.—RNAV (GPS) RWY 17 (DUC).

LINCOLN, NEBRASKA   AL-232 (FAA)   13066

LOC I-OCZ	APP CRS	Rwy Idg	12901
111.1	174°	THRE	1195
		Apt Elev	1219

ILS or LOC RWY 18
LINCOLN (LNK)

▽ *RVR 1800 authorized with the use of FD or AP or HUD to DA. When local altimeter setting
△ not received use Beatrice altimeter setting and increase all DA 91 feet and all MDA 100 feet,
increase S-LOC 18 Cat C/D/E visibility to 1½, Circling Cat C visibility to 2 and Cat D visibility
to 2¼; increase ROROC fix minimums S-LOC 18 Cat C/D/E visibility to 1⅜ Circling Cat C
visibility to 1¾ and Cat D visibility to 2¼. For inoperative MALSR, increase S-ILS 18 Cat E
visibility to RVR 4000, S-LOC 18 Cat E visibility to 1¾, and ROROC fix minimums S-LOC 18
Cat E visibility to 1½. For inoperative MALSR when using Beatrice altimeter setting, increase
S-ILS 18 all Cats visibility to RVR 4500, S-LOC 18 Cat E visibility to 2, and ROROC fix
minimums S-LOC 18 Cat C/D/E visibility to 1¾.

MALSR
(A5)

MISSED APPROACH:
Climb to 1700 then
climbing right turn to
3000 direct LNK
VORTAC and hold.

| ATIS | LINCOLN APP CON | LINCOLN TOWER★ | GND CON | CLNC DEL | UNICOM |
| 118.05 290.9 | 124.0 270.3 | 118.5 (CTAF) 253.5 | 121.9 275.8 | 120.7 225.4 | 122.95 |

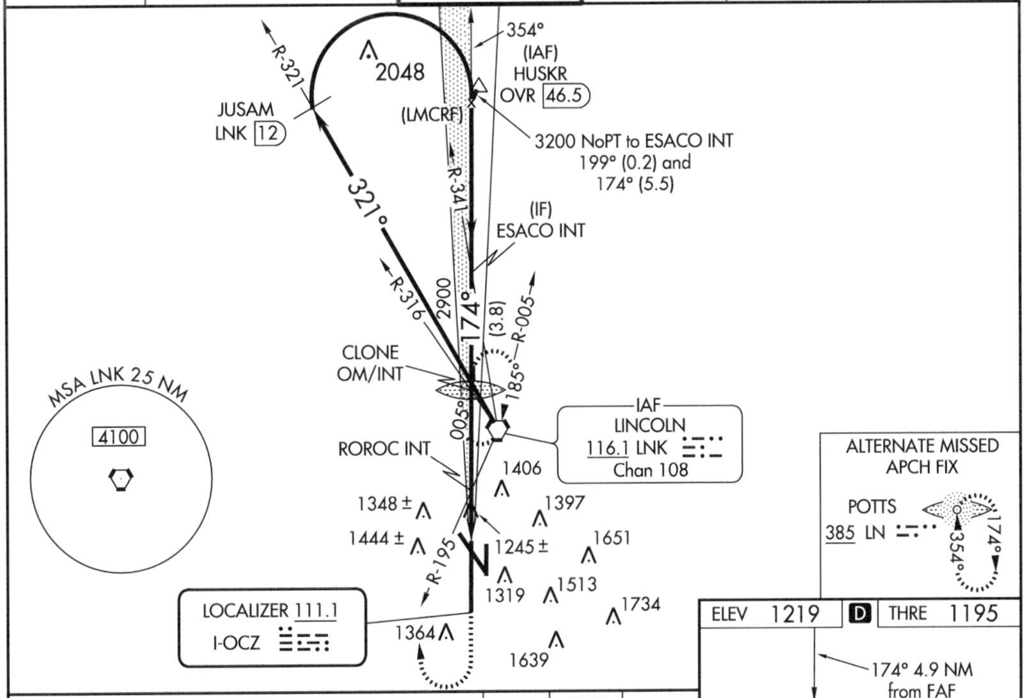

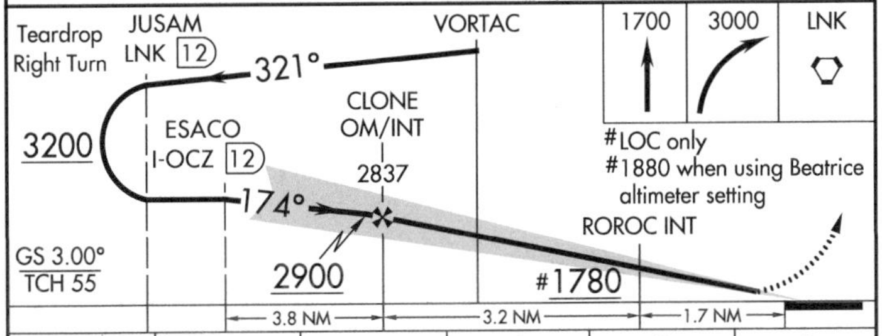

CATEGORY	A	B	C	D	E
S-ILS 18		*1395/24 200 (200-½)			
S-LOC 18	1780/24 585 (600-½)		1780-1¼ 585 (600-1¼)		
CIRCLING	1780-1 561 (600-1)		1780-1¾ 561 (600-1¾)	1820-2 601 (700-2)	2040-3 821 (900-3)
ROROC FIX MINIMUMS (DUAL VOR RECEIVERS REQUIRED)					
S-LOC 18	1720/24 525 (600-½)		1720/55 525 (600-1¼)		
CIRCLING	1720-1 501 (600-1)	1760-1 541 (600-1)	1760-1½ 541 (600-1½)	1820-2 601 (700-2)	2040-3 821 (900-3)

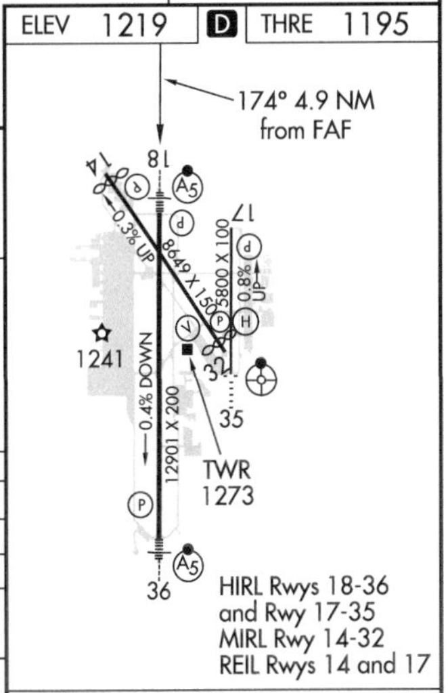

FAF to MAP 4.9 NM					
Knots	60	90	120	150	180
Min:Sec	4:54	3:16	2:27	1:58	1:38

LINCOLN, NEBRASKA
Amdt 7 05APR12   40°51'N-96°46'W

LINCOLN (LNK)
ILS or LOC RWY 18

FIGURE 234.—ILS or LOC RWY 18 (LNK).

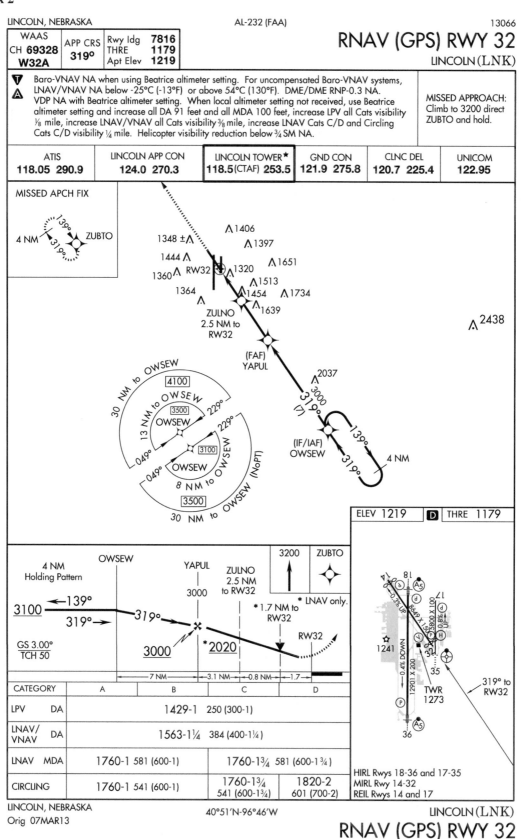

LINCOLN, NEBRASKA | AL-232 (FAA) | 13066

WAAS CH **69328** W32A	APP CRS **319°**	Rwy ldg **7816** THRE **1179** Apt Elev **1219**

RNAV (GPS) RWY 32
LINCOLN (LNK)

▼ Baro-VNAV NA when using Beatrice altimeter setting. For uncompensated Baro-VNAV systems, LNAV/VNAV NA below -25°C (-13°F) or above 54°C (130°F). DME/DME RNP-0.3 NA.
△ VDP NA with Beatrice altimeter setting. When local altimeter setting not received, use Beatrice altimeter setting and increase all DA 91 feet and all MDA 100 feet, increase LPV all Cats visibility ⅛ mile, increase LNAV/VNAV all Cats visibility ⅜ mile, increase LNAV Cats C/D and Circling Cats C/D visibility ¼ mile. Helicopter visibility reduction below ¾ SM NA.

MISSED APPROACH: Climb to 3200 direct ZUBTO and hold.

ATIS **118.05 290.9**	LINCOLN APP CON **124.0 270.3**	LINCOLN TOWER★ **118.5**(CTAF) **253.5**	GND CON **121.9 275.8**	CLNC DEL **120.7 225.4**	UNICOM **122.95**

CATEGORY	A	B	C	D
LPV DA	1429-1 250 (300-1)			
LNAV/ VNAV DA	1563-1¼ 384 (400-1¼)			
LNAV MDA	1760-1 581 (600-1)		1760-1¾ 581 (600-1¾)	
CIRCLING	1760-1 541 (600-1)		1760-1¾ 541 (600-1¾)	1820-2 601 (700-2)

ELEV 1219 [D] THRE 1179

HIRL Rwys 18-36 and 17-35
MIRL Rwy 14-32
REIL Rwys 14 and 17

LINCOLN, NEBRASKA
Orig 07MAR13

40°51'N-96°46'W

LINCOLN (LNK)
RNAV (GPS) RWY 32

FIGURE 235.—RNAV (GPS) RWY 32 (LNK).

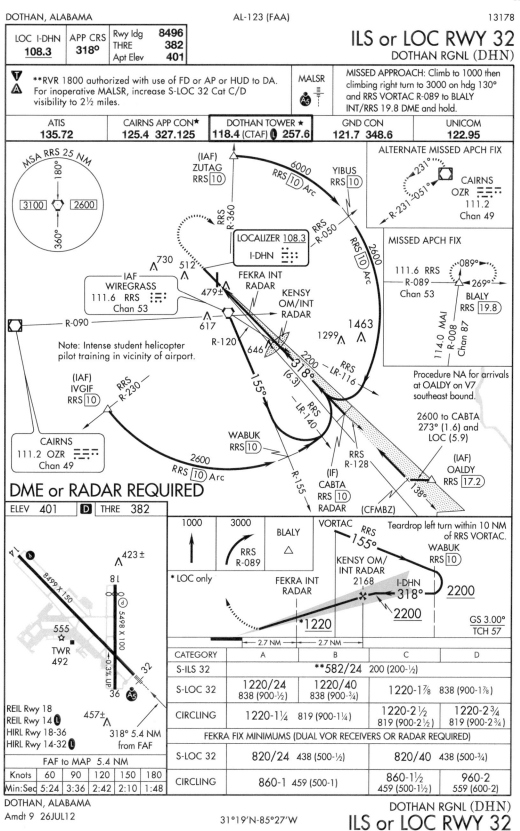

FIGURE 236.—ILS or RWY 32 (DHN).

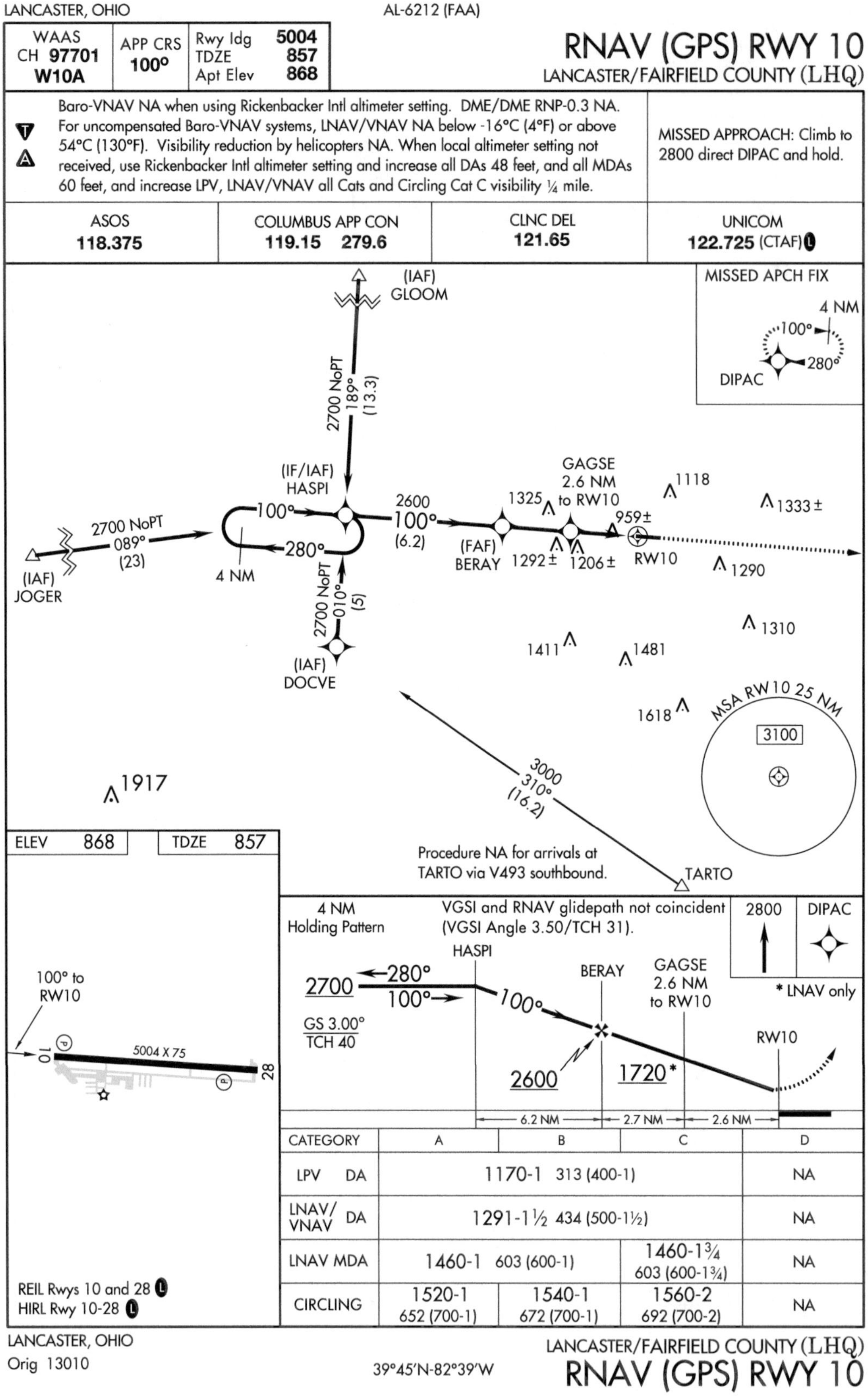

LANCASTER, OHIO

AL-6212 (FAA)

WAAS CH **97701** **W10A**	APP CRS **100°**	Rwy ldg **5004** TDZE **857** Apt Elev **868**

RNAV (GPS) RWY 10
LANCASTER/FAIRFIELD COUNTY (LHQ)

▼
Ⓐ Baro-VNAV NA when using Rickenbacker Intl altimeter setting. DME/DME RNP-0.3 NA. For uncompensated Baro-VNAV systems, LNAV/VNAV NA below -16°C (4°F) or above 54°C (130°F). Visibility reduction by helicopters NA. When local altimeter setting not received, use Rickenbacker Intl altimeter setting and increase all DAs 48 feet, and all MDAs 60 feet, and increase LPV, LNAV/VNAV all Cats and Circling Cat C visibility ¼ mile.

MISSED APPROACH: Climb to 2800 direct DIPAC and hold.

ASOS **118.375**	COLUMBUS APP CON **119.15 279.6**	CLNC DEL **121.65**	UNICOM **122.725** (CTAF)Ⓛ

ELEV 868 | TDZE 857

REIL Rwys 10 and 28 Ⓛ
HIRL Rwy 10-28 Ⓛ

Procedure NA for arrivals at TARTO via V493 southbound.

CATEGORY	A	B	C	D
LPV DA	1170-1 313 (400-1)			NA
LNAV/VNAV DA	1291-1½ 434 (500-1½)			NA
LNAV MDA	1460-1 603 (600-1)		1460-1¾ 603 (600-1¾)	NA
CIRCLING	1520-1 652 (700-1)	1540-1 672 (700-1)	1560-2 692 (700-2)	NA

LANCASTER, OHIO
Orig 13010

39°45'N-82°39'W

LANCASTER/FAIRFIELD COUNTY (LHQ)
RNAV (GPS) RWY 10

FIGURE 237.—RNAV (GPS) RWY 10 (LHQ).

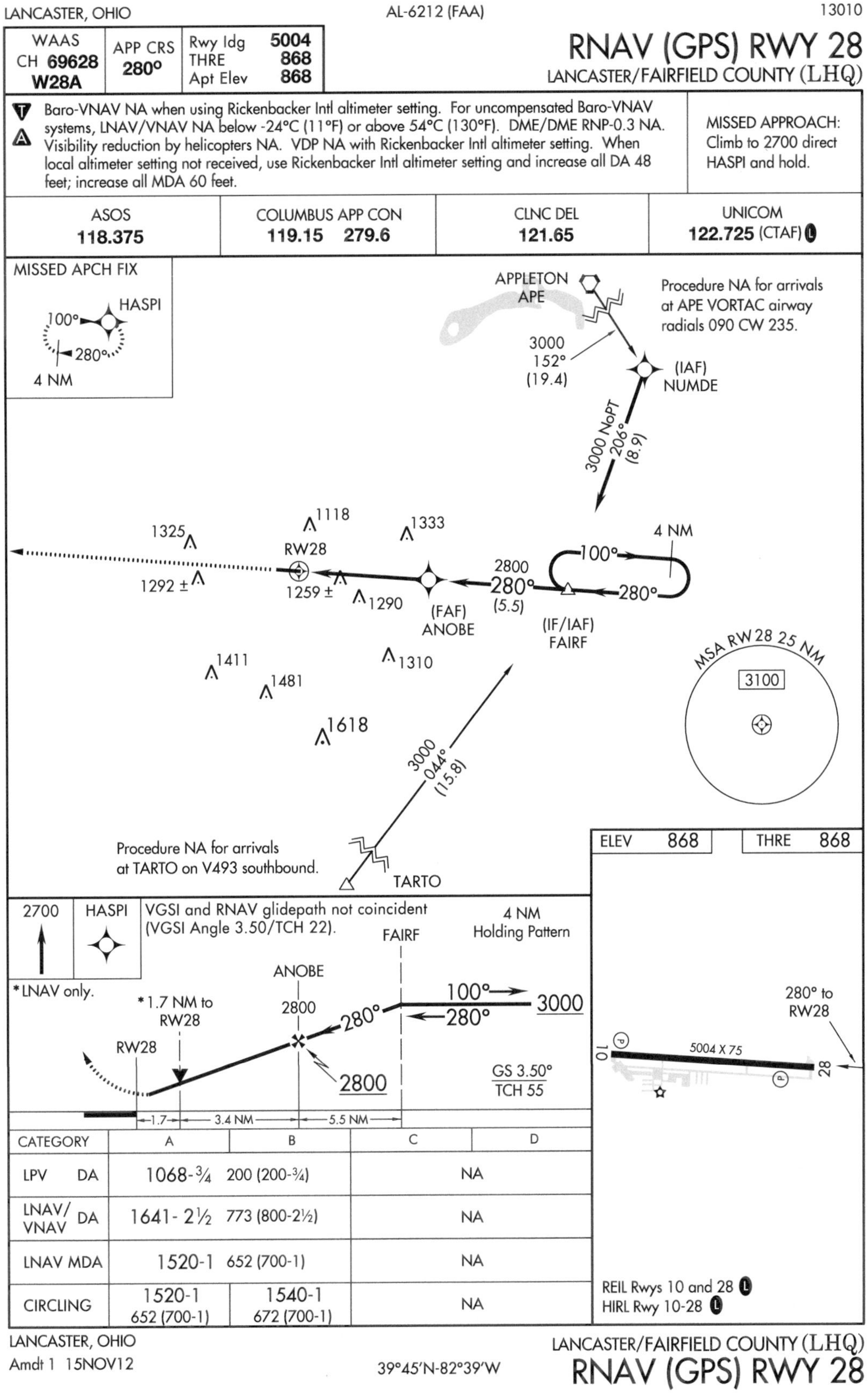

LANCASTER, OHIO   AL-6212 (FAA)   13010

WAAS CH 69628 W28A	APP CRS 280°	Rwy Idg 5004 THRE 868 Apt Elev 868

RNAV (GPS) RWY 28
LANCASTER/FAIRFIELD COUNTY (LHQ)

▼ Baro-VNAV NA when using Rickenbacker Intl altimeter setting. For uncompensated Baro-VNAV systems, LNAV/VNAV NA below -24°C (11°F) or above 54°C (130°F). DME/DME RNP-0.3 NA.
⚠ Visibility reduction by helicopters NA. VDP NA with Rickenbacker Intl altimeter setting. When local altimeter setting not received, use Rickenbacker Intl altimeter setting and increase all DA 48 feet; increase all MDA 60 feet.

MISSED APPROACH: Climb to 2700 direct HASPI and hold.

ASOS 118.375	COLUMBUS APP CON 119.15 279.6	CLNC DEL 121.65	UNICOM 122.725 (CTAF) Ⓛ

MISSED APCH FIX

APPLETON APE

Procedure NA for arrivals at APE VORTAC airway radials 090 CW 235.

3000 152° (19.4)

(IAF) NUMDE

3000 NoPT 206° (8.9)

4 NM

100°

RW28

1325
1292 ±
1259 ±
1290
1118
1333
1310
1411
1481
1618

2800 280° (5.5)

280°
100°
4 NM
280°

(FAF) ANOBE

(IF/IAF) FAIRF

MSA RW28 25 NM
3100

3000 044° (15.8)

Procedure NA for arrivals at TARTO on V493 southbound.

TARTO

ELEV 868	THRE 868

2700 HASPI VGSI and RNAV glidepath not coincident (VGSI Angle 3.50/TCH 22).

4 NM Holding Pattern

FAIRF

*LNAV only.

ANOBE

*1.7 NM to RW28

2800
280°
100°
3000

RW28

280°

2800

GS 3.50° / TCH 55

1.7   3.4 NM   5.5 NM

5004 X 75

280° to RW28

REIL Rwys 10 and 28 Ⓛ
HIRL Rwy 10-28 Ⓛ

CATEGORY	A	B	C	D
LPV DA	1068-¾	200 (200-¾)	NA	
LNAV/VNAV DA	1641-2½	773 (800-2½)	NA	
LNAV MDA	1520-1	652 (700-1)	NA	
CIRCLING	1520-1 652 (700-1)	1540-1 672 (700-1)	NA	

LANCASTER, OHIO
Amdt 1 15NOV12

39°45'N-82°39'W

LANCASTER/FAIRFIELD COUNTY (LHQ)
RNAV (GPS) RWY 28

FIGURE 238.—RNAV (GPS) RWY 28 (LHQ).

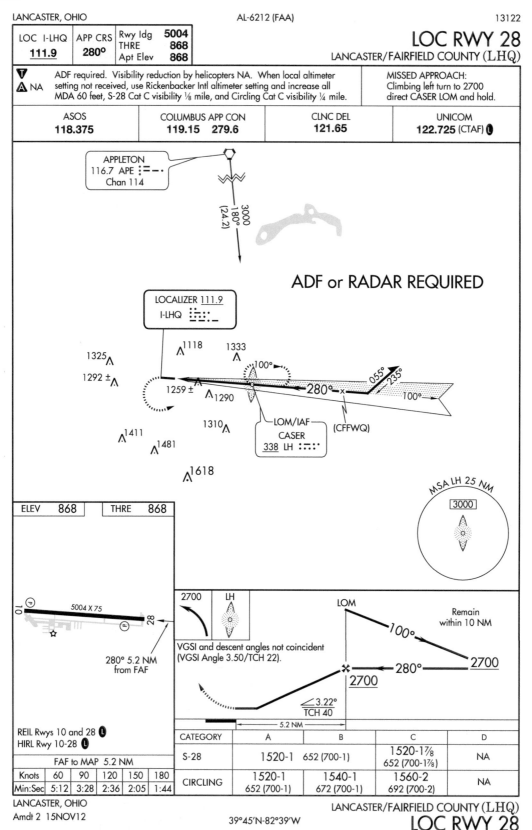

LANCASTER, OHIO

AL-6212 (FAA)

13122

LOC I-LHQ	APP CRS	Rwy Idg	5004
111.9	**280°**	THRE	868
		Apt Elev	868

LOC RWY 28
LANCASTER/FAIRFIELD COUNTY (LHQ)

ADF required. Visibility reduction by helicopters NA. When local altimeter setting not received, use Rickenbacker Intl altimeter setting and increase all MDA 60 feet, S-28 Cat C visibility ⅛ mile, and Circling Cat C visibility ¼ mile.

▼ ⚠ NA

MISSED APPROACH: Climbing left turn to 2700 direct CASER LOM and hold.

ASOS	COLUMBUS APP CON	CLNC DEL	UNICOM
118.375	**119.15 279.6**	**121.65**	**122.725** (CTAF)

APPLETON
116.7 APE
Chan 114

ADF or RADAR REQUIRED

LOCALIZER 111.9
I-LHQ

3000
180°
(24.2)

280°

100°

055° 235°

100°

1325 1118 1333 1100°
1292 ± 1259 ± 1290
1310 1411 1481
1618

LOM/IAF
CASER
338 LH

(CFFWQ)

MSA LH 25 NM
3000

ELEV	868	THRE	868

10
5004 X 75
28

280° 5.2 NM
from FAF

2700   LH

VGSI and descent angles not coincident
(VGSI Angle 3.50/TCH 22).

LOM

100°

Remain within 10 NM

2700

280°

2700

2700

3.22°
TCH 40

5.2 NM

REIL Rwys 10 and 28
HIRL Rwy 10-28

CATEGORY	A	B	C	D
S-28	1520-1 652 (700-1)		1520-1⅞ 652 (700-1⅞)	NA
CIRCLING	1520-1 652 (700-1)	1540-1 672 (700-1)	1560-2 692 (700-2)	NA

FAF to MAP 5.2 NM

Knots	60	90	120	150	180
Min:Sec	5:12	3:28	2:36	2:05	1:44

LANCASTER, OHIO
Amdt 2 15NOV12

39°45'N-82°39'W

LANCASTER/FAIRFIELD COUNTY (LHQ)
LOC RWY 28

FIGURE 239.—LOC RWY 28 (LHQ).

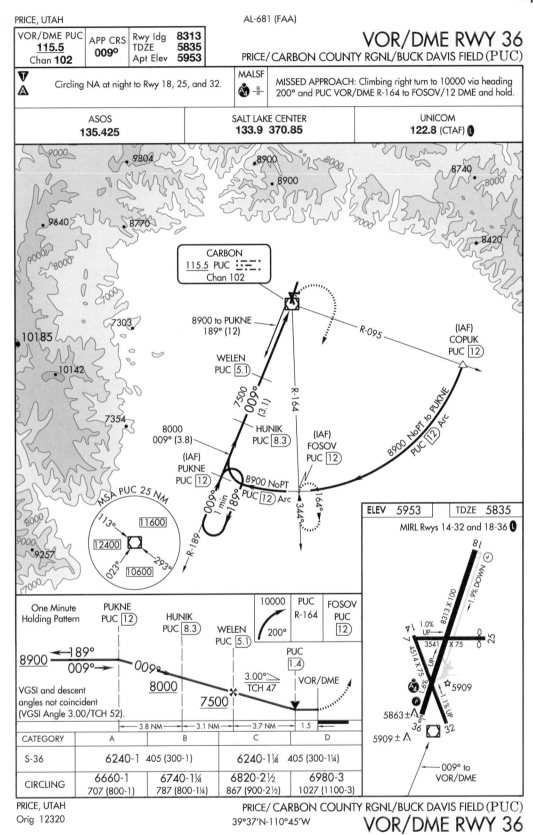

FIGURE 240.—VOR/DME RWY 36 (PUC).

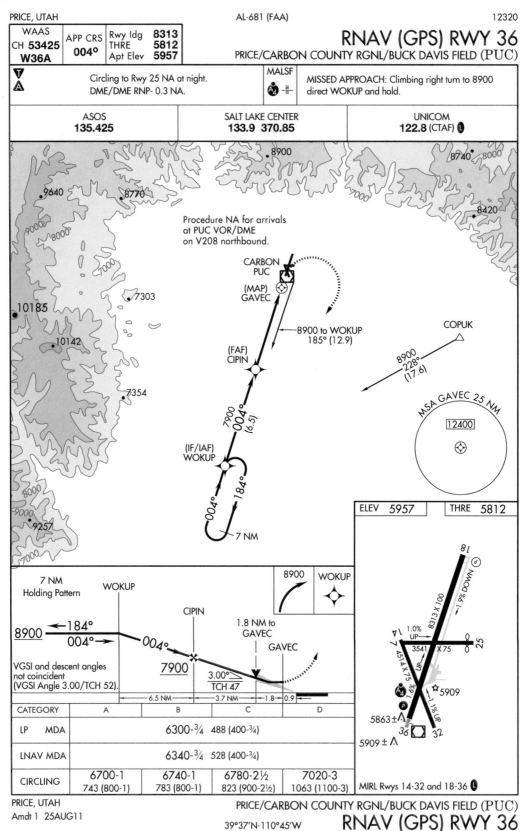

PRICE, UTAH   AL-681 (FAA)   12320

WAAS CH 53425 W36A	APP CRS 004°	Rwy Idg 8313 THRE 5812 Apt Elev 5957

RNAV (GPS) RWY 36
PRICE/CARBON COUNTY RGNL/BUCK DAVIS FIELD (PUC)

Circling to Rwy 25 NA at night.
DME/DME RNP- 0.3 NA.

MALSF

MISSED APPROACH: Climbing right turn to 8900 direct WOKUP and hold.

ASOS 135.425	SALT LAKE CENTER 133.9 370.85	UNICOM 122.8 (CTAF)

Procedure NA for arrivals at PUC VOR/DME on V208 northbound.

CARBON PUC

(MAP) GAVEC

8900 to WOKUP 185° (12.9)

COPUK

8900 228° (17.6)

(FAF) CIPIN

MSA GAVEC 25 NM

12400

7900 004° (6.5)

(IF/IAF) WOKUP

004°   184°

7 NM

ELEV 5957	THRE 5812

7 NM Holding Pattern

WOKUP   184°   8900   004°

8900   WOKUP

CIPIN   004°

1.8 NM to GAVEC

GAVEC

VGSI and descent angles not coincident (VGSI Angle 3.00/TCH 52).

7900

3.00° TCH 47

6.5 NM   3.7 NM   1.8   0.9

CATEGORY	A	B	C	D
LP MDA	6300-¾ 488 (400-¾)			
LNAV MDA	6340-¾ 528 (400-¾)			
CIRCLING	6700-1 743 (800-1)	6740-1 783 (800-1)	6780-2½ 823 (900-2½)	7020-3 1063 (1100-3)

MIRL Rwys 14-32 and 18-36

PRICE, UTAH
Amdt 1 25AUG11

PRICE/CARBON COUNTY RGNL/BUCK DAVIS FIELD (PUC)

39°37'N-110°45'W

RNAV (GPS) RWY 36

FIGURE 241.—RNAV (GPS) RWY 36 (PUC).

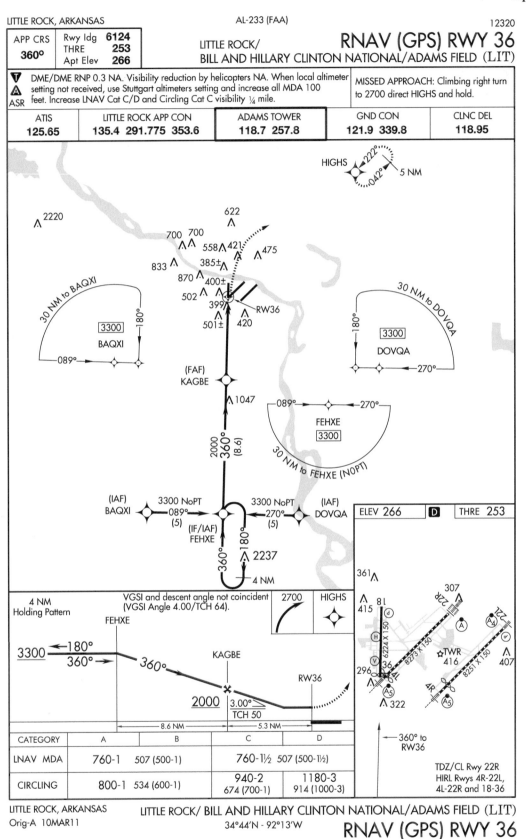

FIGURE 242.—RNAV RWY 36 (LIT).

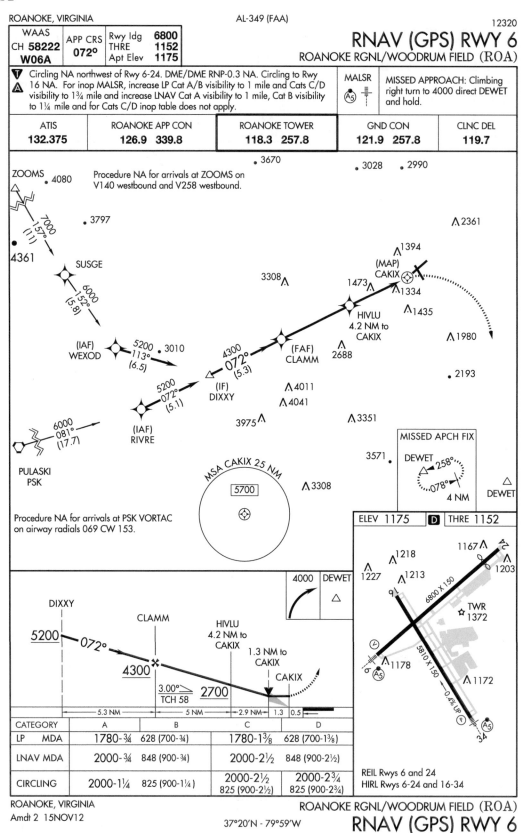

FIGURE 243.—RNAV (GPS) RWY 6 (ROA).

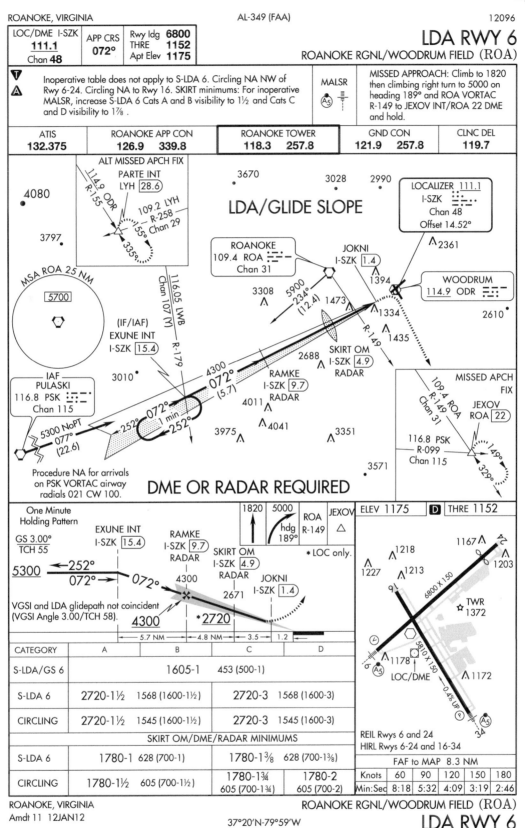

ROANOKE, VIRGINIA   AL-349 (FAA)   12096

LOC/DME I-SZK **111.1** Chan **48**	APP CRS **072°**	Rwy Idg **6800** THRE **1152** Apt Elev **1175**

LDA RWY 6
ROANOKE RGNL/WOODRUM FIELD (ROA)

Inoperative table does not apply to S-LDA 6. Circling NA NW of Rwy 6-24. Circling NA to Rwy 16. SKIRT minimums: For inoperative MALSR, increase S-LDA 6 Cats A and B visibility to 1½ and Cats C and D visibility to 1⅞ .

MALSR

MISSED APPROACH: Climb to 1820 then climbing right turn to 5000 on heading 189° and ROA VORTAC R-149 to JEXOV INT/ROA 22 DME and hold.

ATIS **132.375**	ROANOKE APP CON **126.9** **339.8**	ROANOKE TOWER **118.3** **257.8**	GND CON **121.9** **257.8**	CLNC DEL **119.7**

LDA/GLIDE SLOPE

DME OR RADAR REQUIRED

Procedure NA for arrivals on PSK VORTAC airway radials 021 CW 100.

One Minute Holding Pattern

GS 3.00° / TCH 55

VGSI and LDA glidepath not coincident (VGSI Angle 3.00/TCH 58).

* LOC only.

ELEV 1175   THRE 1152

CATEGORY	A	B	C	D
S-LDA/GS 6		1605-1	453 (500-1)	
S-LDA 6	2720-1½	1568 (1600-1½)	2720-3 1568 (1600-3)	
CIRCLING	2720-1½	1545 (1600-1½)	2720-3 1545 (1600-3)	
		SKIRT OM/DME/RADAR MINIMUMS		
S-LDA 6	1780-1 628 (700-1)		1780-1⅜ 628 (700-1⅜)	
CIRCLING	1780-1½ 605 (700-1½)		1780-1¾ 605 (700-1¾)	1780-2 605 (700-2)

REIL Rwys 6 and 24
HIRL Rwys 6-24 and 16-34

FAF to MAP 8.3 NM

Knots	60	90	120	150	180
Min:Sec	8:18	5:32	4:09	3:19	2:46

ROANOKE, VIRGINIA
Amdt 11   12JAN12

37°20'N-79°59'W

ROANOKE RGNL/WOODRUM FIELD (ROA)
LDA RWY 6

FIGURE 244.—LDA RWY 6 (ROA).

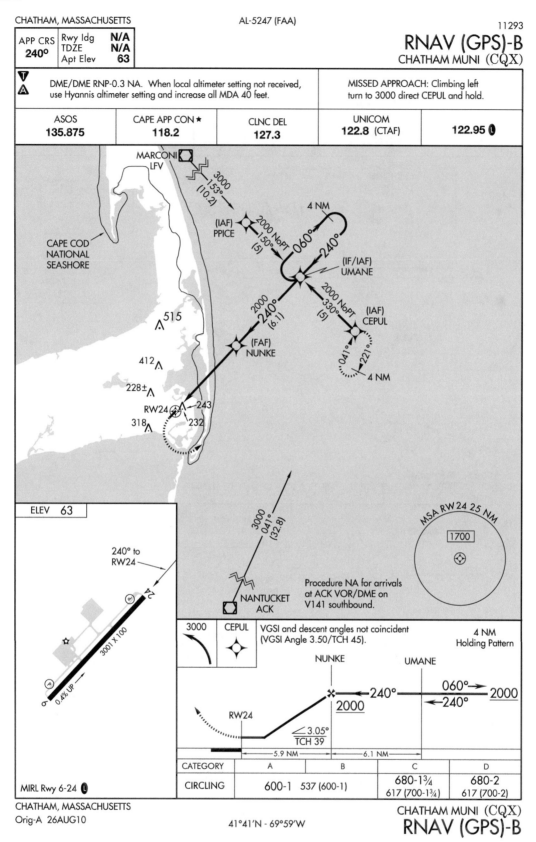

FIGURE 245.—RNAV (GPS)-B (CQX).

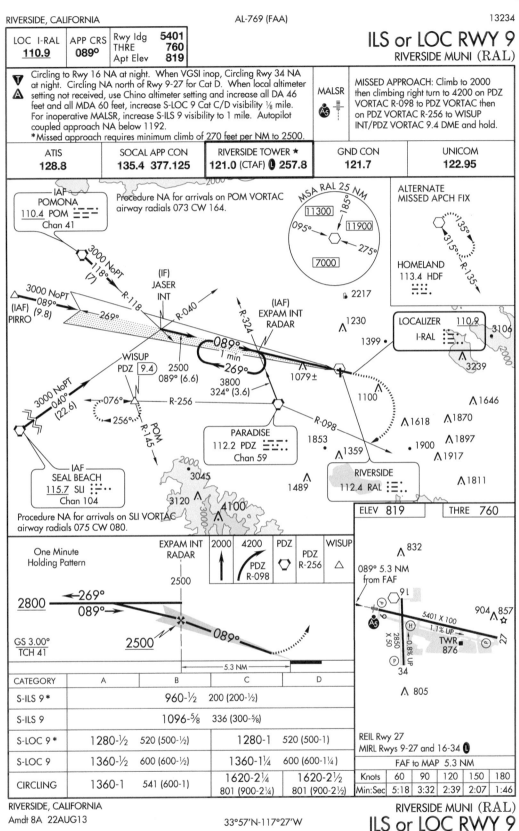

FIGURE 247.—ILS or RWY 9 (RAL).

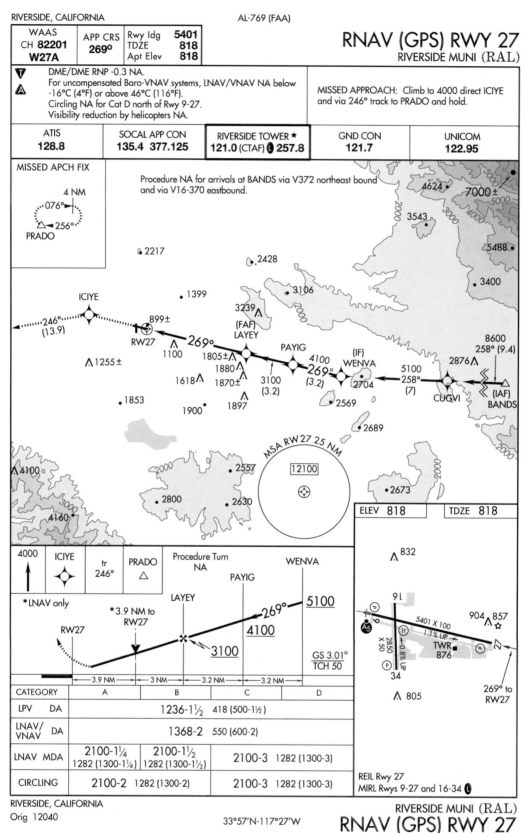

RIVERSIDE, CALIFORNIA   AL-769 (FAA)

WAAS CH 82201 W27A	APP CRS 269°	Rwy Idg 5401 TDZE 818 Apt Elev 818

RNAV (GPS) RWY 27
RIVERSIDE MUNI (RAL)

▽ DME/DME RNP -0.3 NA.
⚠ For uncompensated Baro-VNAV systems, LNAV/VNAV NA below
-16°C (4°F) or above 46°C (116°F).
Circling NA for Cat D north of Rwy 9-27.
Visibility reduction by helicopters NA.

MISSED APPROACH: Climb to 4000 direct ICIYE
and via 246° track to PRADO and hold.

ATIS 128.8	SOCAL APP CON 135.4 377.125	RIVERSIDE TOWER ★ 121.0 (CTAF) ◐ 257.8	GND CON 121.7	UNICOM 122.95

MISSED APCH FIX

4 NM
076°
256°
PRADO

Procedure NA for arrivals at BANDS via V372 northeast bound
and via V16-370 eastbound.

ELEV 818   TDZE 818

4000 ↑	ICIYE ◇	tr 246°	PRADO △	Procedure Turn NA		WENVA

*LNAV only

GS 3.01°
TCH 50

CATEGORY	A	B	C	D
LPV DA	1236-1½ 418 (500-1½)			
LNAV/ VNAV DA	1368-2 550 (600-2)			
LNAV MDA	2100-1¼ 1282 (1300-1¼)	2100-1½ 1282 (1300-1½)	2100-3 1282 (1300-3)	
CIRCLING	2100-2 1282 (1300-2)		2100-3 1282 (1300-3)	

REIL Rwy 27
MIRL Rwys 9-27 and 16-34 ◐

RIVERSIDE, CALIFORNIA
Orig 12040   33°57'N-117°27'W

RIVERSIDE MUNI (RAL)
RNAV (GPS) RWY 27

FIGURE 248.—RNAV (GPS) RWY 27 (RAL).

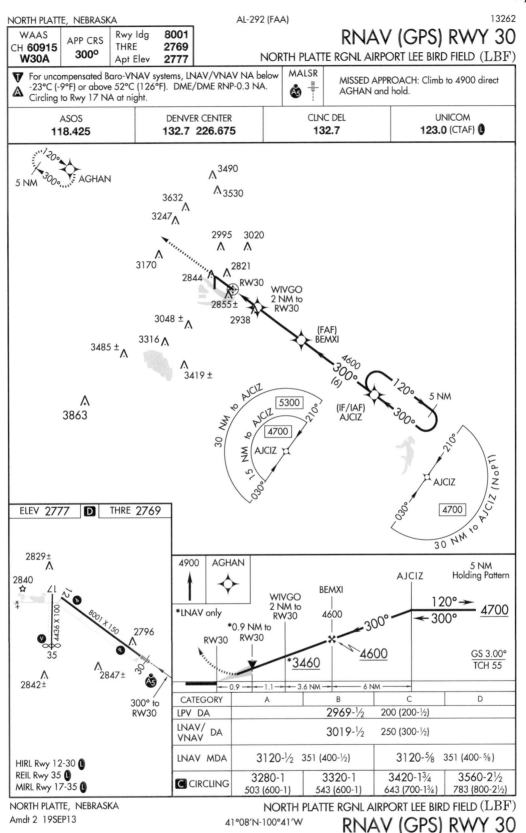

NORTH PLATTE, NEBRASKA   AL-292 (FAA)   13262

WAAS CH **60915** **W30A**	APP CRS **300°**	Rwy Idg **8001** THRE **2769** Apt Elev **2777**

RNAV (GPS) RWY 30
NORTH PLATTE RGNL AIRPORT LEE BIRD FIELD (LBF)

For uncompensated Baro-VNAV systems, LNAV/VNAV NA below -23°C (-9°F) or above 52°C (126°F). DME/DME RNP-0.3 NA. Circling to Rwy 17 NA at night.

MALSR

MISSED APPROACH: Climb to 4900 direct AGHAN and hold.

ASOS **118.425**	DENVER CENTER **132.7 226.675**	CLNC DEL **132.7**	UNICOM **123.0** (CTAF)

ELEV 2777   D   THRE 2769

HIRL Rwy 12-30
REIL Rwy 35
MIRL Rwy 17-35

CATEGORY	A	B	C	D
LPV DA	2969-½	200 (200-½)		
LNAV/VNAV DA	3019-½	250 (300-½)		
LNAV MDA	3120-½ 351 (400-½)		3120-⅝ 351 (400-⅝)	
C CIRCLING	3280-1 503 (600-1)	3320-1 543 (600-1)	3420-1¾ 643 (700-1¾)	3560-2½ 783 (800-2½)

NORTH PLATTE, NEBRASKA
Amdt 2 19SEP13

41°08'N-100°41'W

NORTH PLATTE RGNL AIRPORT LEE BIRD FIELD (LBF)
RNAV (GPS) RWY 30

FIGURE 249.—RNAV (GPS) RWY 30 (LBF).

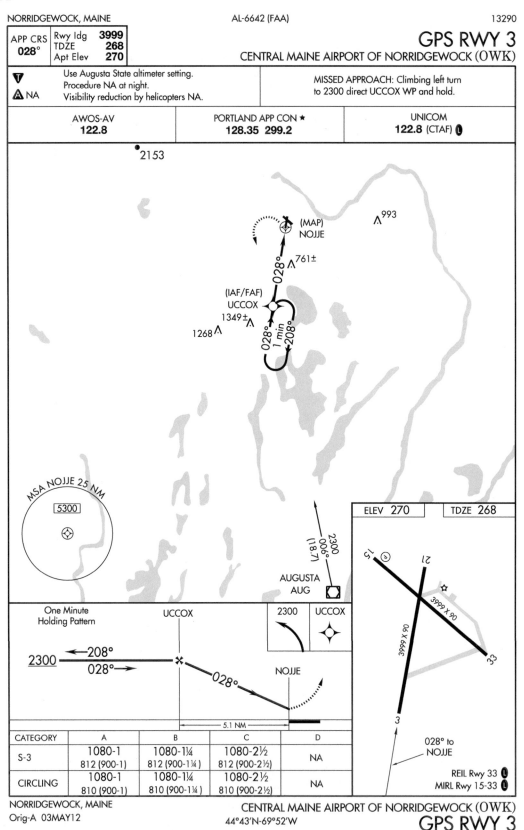

NORRIDGEWOCK, MAINE AL-6642 (FAA) 13290

APP CRS 028°	Rwy Idg	3999
	TDZE	268
	Apt Elev	270

GPS RWY 3
CENTRAL MAINE AIRPORT OF NORRIDGEWOCK (OWK)

▽ Use Augusta State altimeter setting.
▲ NA Procedure NA at night.
Visibility reduction by helicopters NA.

MISSED APPROACH: Climbing left turn to 2300 direct UCCOX WP and hold.

| AWOS-AV 122.8 | PORTLAND APP CON ★ 128.35 299.2 | UNICOM 122.8 (CTAF) ◓ |

• 2153

⋀ 993

(MAP) NOJJE

028° ⋀ 761±

(IAF/FAF) UCCOX

1349± ⋀

028° 1 min 208°

1268 ⋀

MSA NOJJE 25 NM
5300

2300 006° (18.7)

AUGUSTA AUG

| ELEV 270 | TDZE 268 |

One Minute Holding Pattern

UCCOX

2300 ←208°
028°→

2300 UCCOX

NOJJE

028°

←—— 5.1 NM ——→

3999 X 90
3999 X 90

028° to NOJJE

REIL Rwy 33 ◓
MIRL Rwy 15-33 ◓

CATEGORY	A	B	C	D
S-3	1080-1 812 (900-1)	1080-1¼ 812 (900-1¼)	1080-2½ 812 (900-2½)	NA
CIRCLING	1080-1 810 (900-1)	1080-1¼ 810 (900-1¼)	1080-2½ 810 (900-2½)	NA

NORRIDGEWOCK, MAINE
Orig-A 03MAY12

CENTRAL MAINE AIRPORT OF NORRIDGEWOCK (OWK)
44°43'N-69°52'W

GPS RWY 3

FIGURE 250.—GPS RWY 3 (OWK).

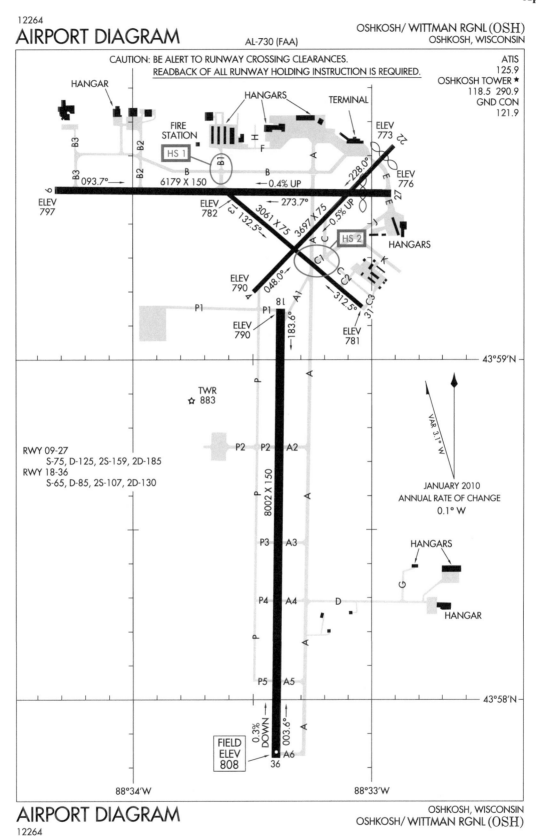

FIGURE 251.—Airport Diagram: Osh Kosh/Wittman Regional (OSH).

217

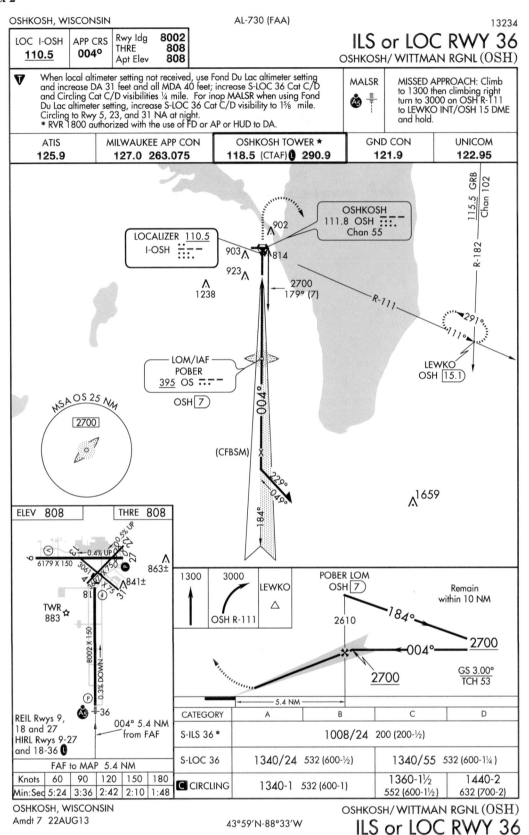

OSHKOSH, WISCONSIN

AL-730 (FAA)

13234

ILS or LOC RWY 36
OSHKOSH/ WITTMAN RGNL (OSH)

LOC I-OSH **110.5**	APP CRS **004°**	Rwy Idg **8002** THRE **808** Apt Elev **808**

When local altimeter setting not received, use Fond Du Lac altimeter setting and increase DA 31 feet and all MDA 40 feet; increase S-LOC 36 Cat C/D and Circling Cat C/D visibilities ¼ mile. For inop MALSR when using Fond Du Lac altimeter setting, increase S-LOC 36 Cat C/D visibility to 1⅝ mile. Circling to Rwy 5, 23, and 31 NA at night.
* RVR 1800 authorized with the use of FD or AP or HUD to DA.

MALSR

MISSED APPROACH: Climb to 1300 then climbing right turn to 3000 on OSH R-111 to LEWKO INT/OSH 15 DME and hold.

ATIS **125.9**	MILWAUKEE APP CON **127.0 263.075**	OSHKOSH TOWER ★ **118.5** (CTAF) **290.9**	GND CON **121.9**	UNICOM **122.95**

CATEGORY	A	B	C	D
S-ILS 36 *	1008/24 200 (200-½)			
S-LOC 36	1340/24 532 (600-½)		1340/55 532 (600-1¼)	
C CIRCLING	1340-1 532 (600-1)		1360-1½ 552 (600-1½)	1440-2 632 (700-2)

ELEV 808 | THRE 808

TWR 883

REIL Rwys 9, 18 and 27
HIRL Rwys 9-27 and 18-36

004° 5.4 NM from FAF

FAF to MAP 5.4 NM

Knots	60	90	120	150	180
Min:Sec	5:24	3:36	2:42	2:10	1:48

MSA OS 25 NM 2700

LOCALIZER 110.5 I-OSH

OSHKOSH 111.8 OSH Chan 55

LOM/IAF POBER 395 OS OSH 7

2700 179° (7)

LEWKO OSH 15.1

POBER LOM OSH 7
Remain within 10 NM
2610
184°
2700
004°
2700
GS 3.00° TCH 53
5.4 NM

1300 | 3000 OSH R-111 | LEWKO

OSHKOSH, WISCONSIN
Amdt 7 22AUG13

43°59'N-88°33'W

OSHKOSH/ WITTMAN RGNL (OSH)
ILS or LOC RWY 36

FIGURE 252.—ILS or LOC RWY 36 (OSH).

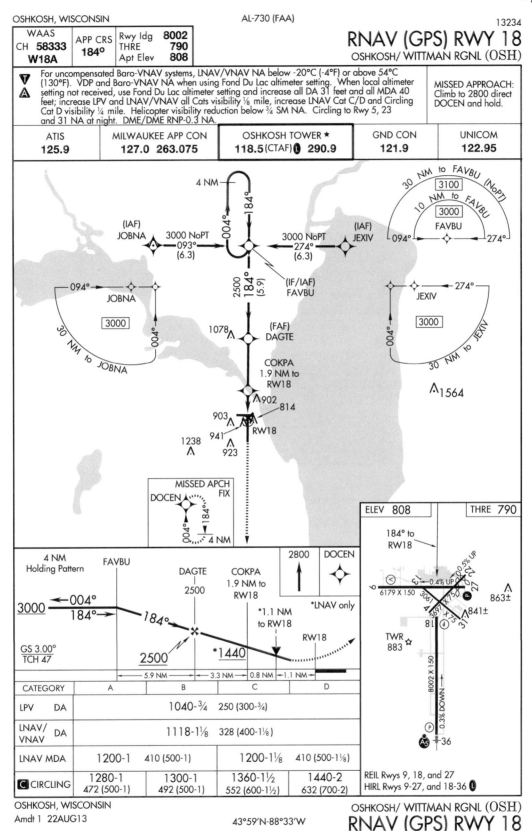

FIGURE 253.—RNAV (GPS) RWY 18 (OSH).

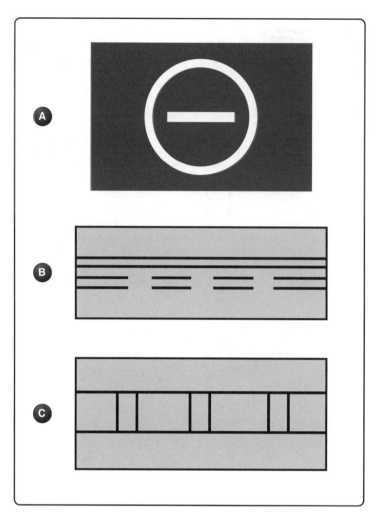

FIGURE 254.—Airport Sign.

FIGURE 255.—Two Signs.

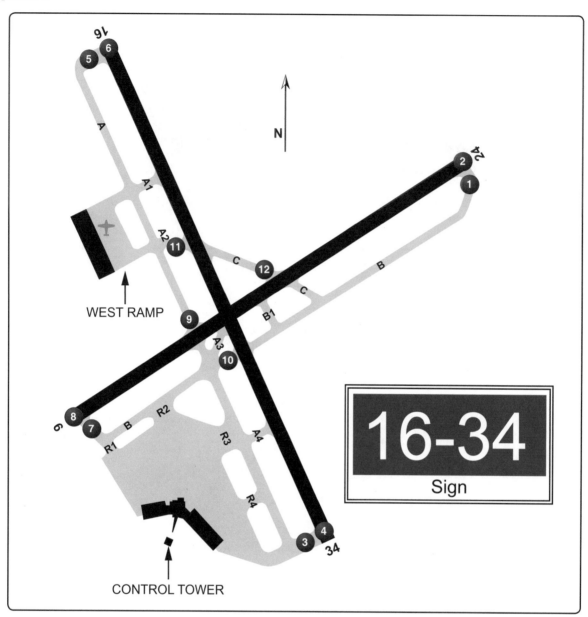

FIGURE 256.—Airport Diagram and Sign.

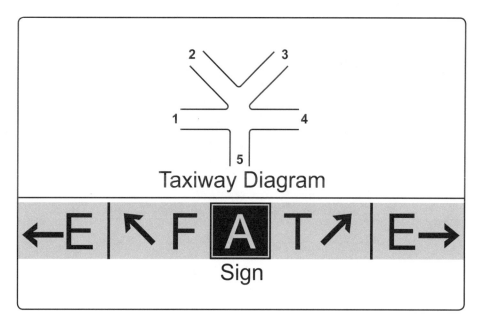

FIGURE 257.—Taxiway Diagram and Sign.

FIGURE 258.—Instrument Landing System (ILS) Critical Area Markings.

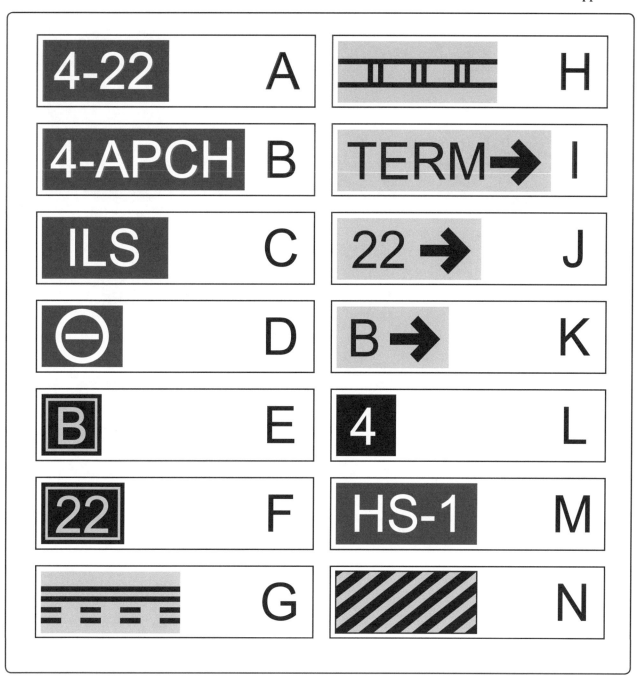

FIGURE 259.—Airport Signs.

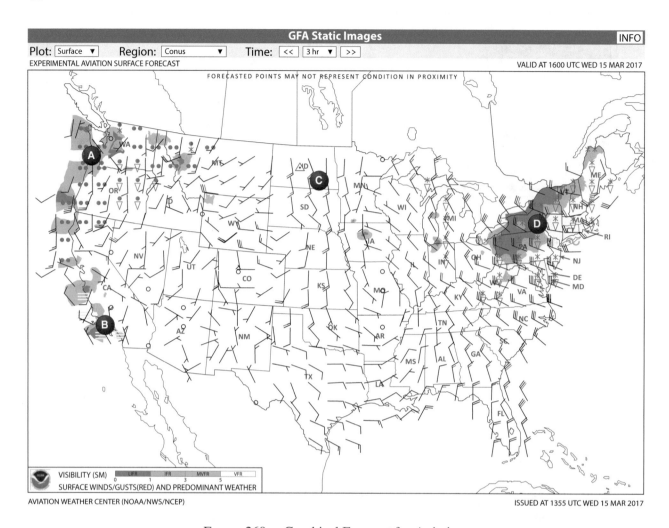

FIGURE 260.—Graphical Forecast for Aviation.

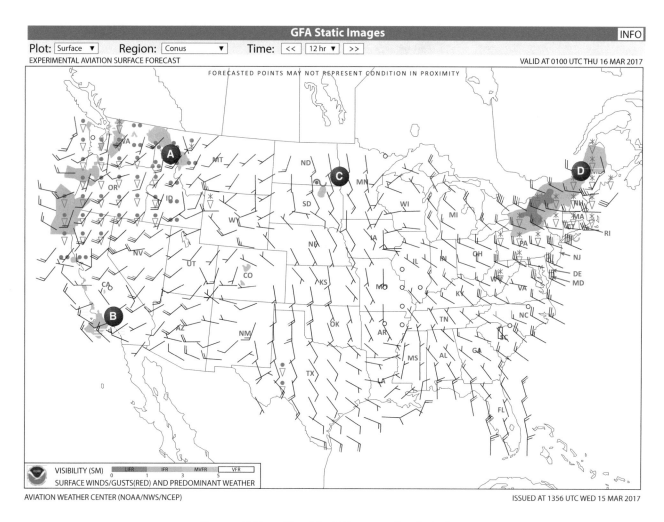

FIGURE 261.—Graphical Forecast for Aviation.

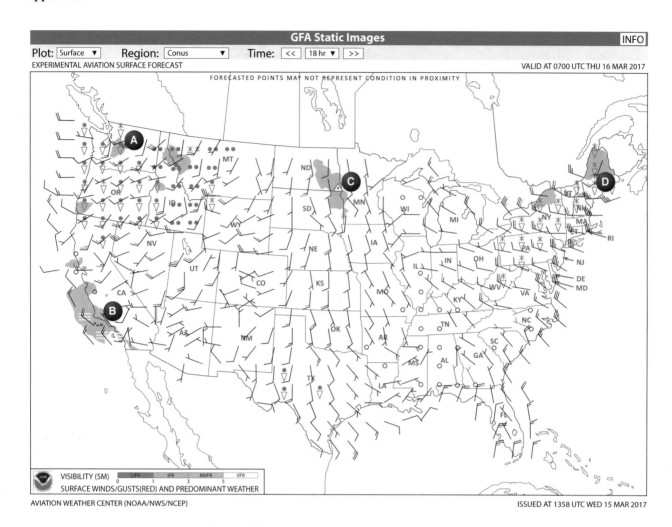

FIGURE 262.—Graphical Forecast for Aviation.

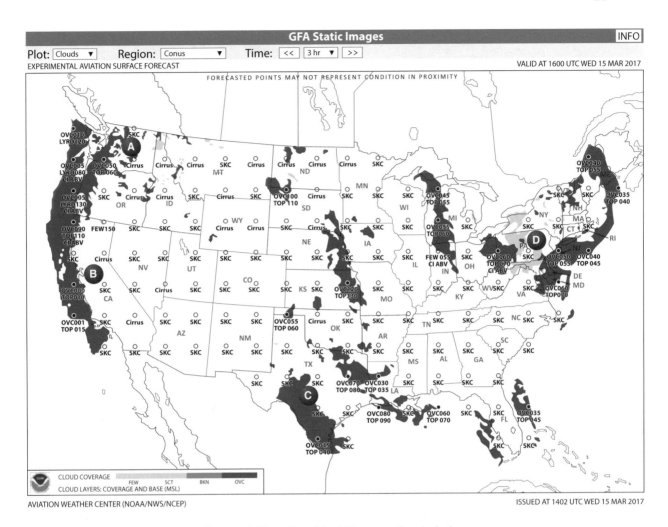

FIGURE 263.—Graphical Forecast for Aviation.

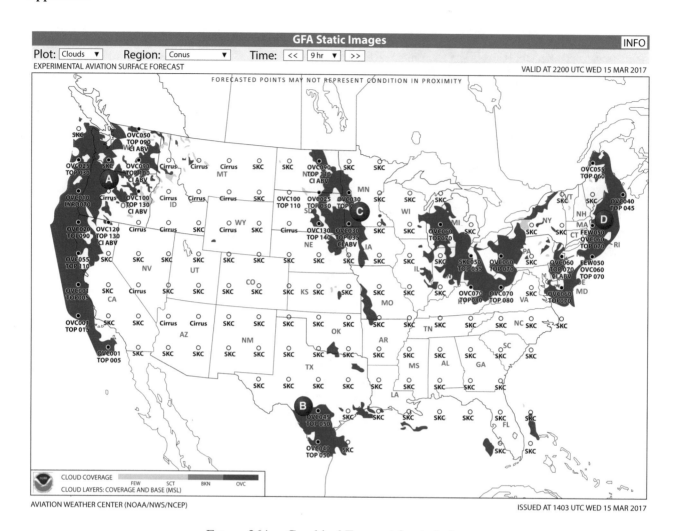

FIGURE 264.—Graphical Forecast for Aviation.

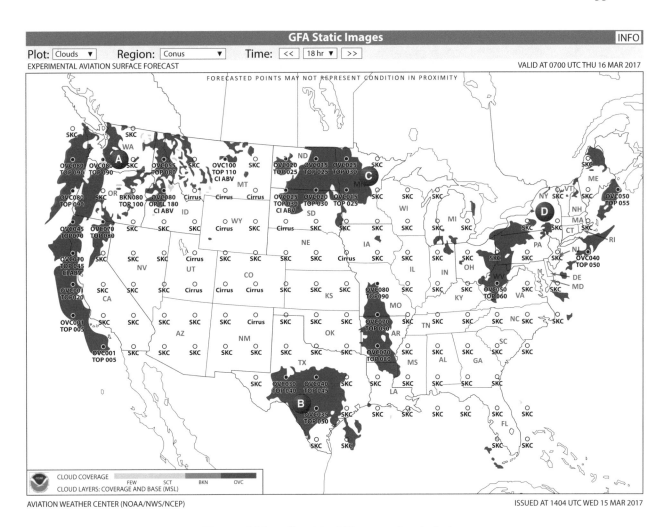

FIGURE 265.—Graphical Forecast for Aviation.

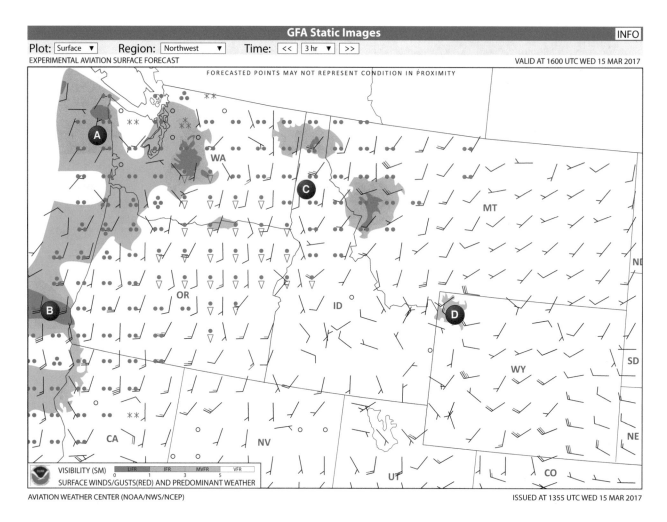

FIGURE 266.—Graphical Forecast for Aviation.

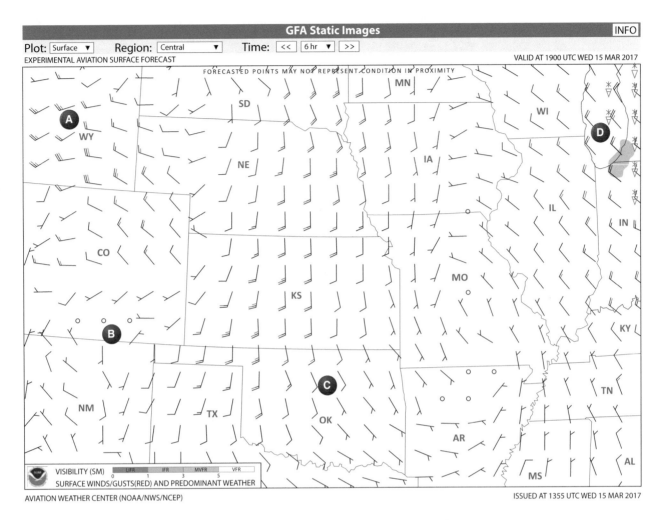

FIGURE 267.—Graphical Forecast for Aviation.

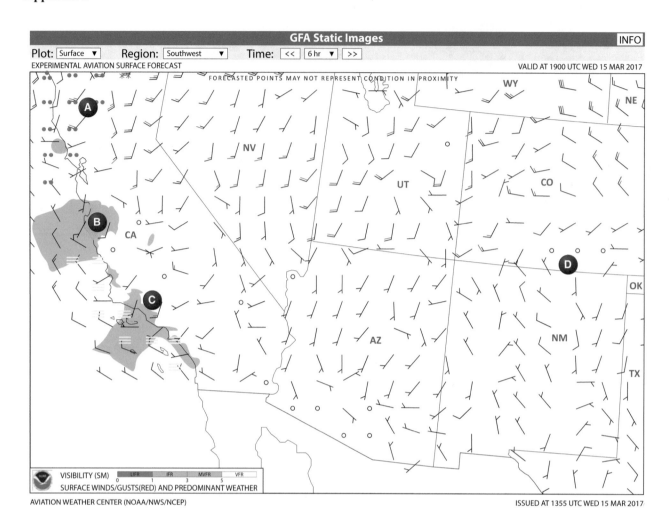

FIGURE 268.—Graphical Forecast for Aviation.

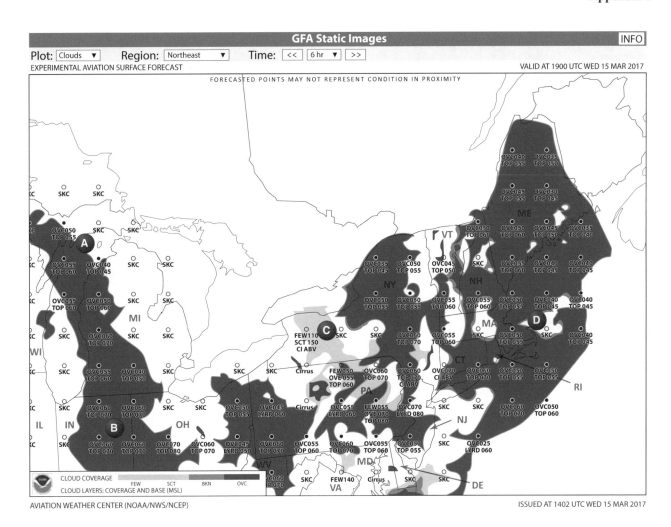

FIGURE 269.—Graphical Forecast for Aviation.

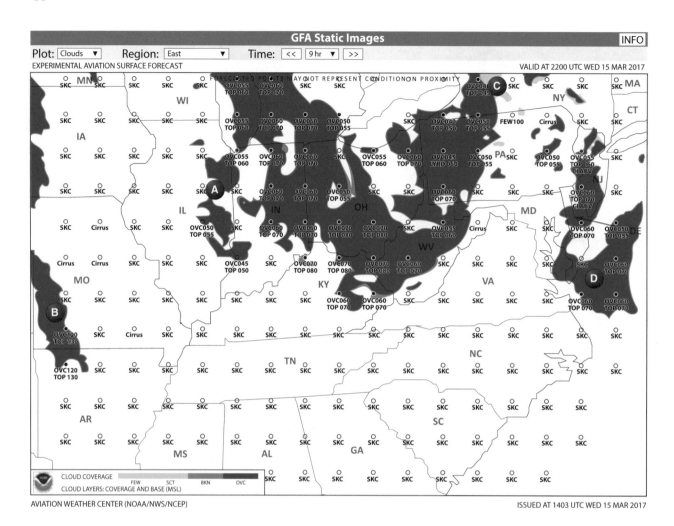

FIGURE 270.—Graphical Forecast for Aviation.

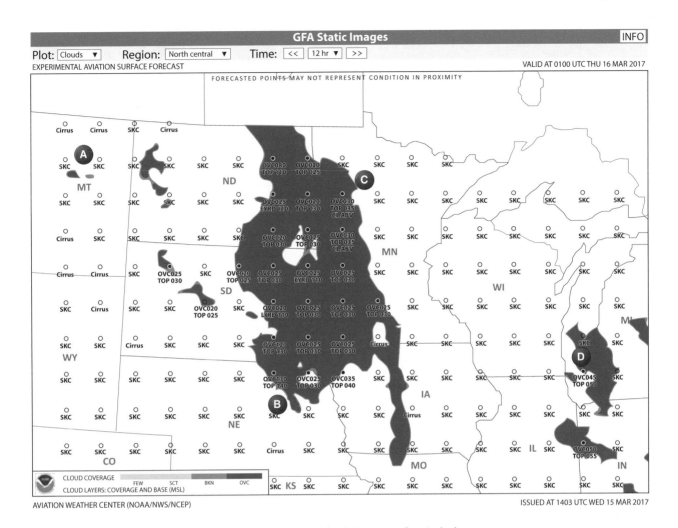

FIGURE 271.—Graphical Forecast for Aviation.